THINKING ABOUT
LITERATURE

TA-BRL-102

THINKING ABOUT LITERATURE

New Ideas for
High School Teachers

ROBERT McMAHON

Foreword by Carol Jago

Heinemann
Portsmouth, NH

Heinemann
A division of Reed Elsevier Inc.
361 Hanover Street
Portsmouth, NH 03801-3912
www.heinemann.com

Offices and agents throughout the world

Library of Congress Cataloging-in-Publication Data
McMahon, Robert, 1950–
    Thinking about literature : new ideas for high school teachers / Robert McMahon.
       p. cm.
Includes bibliographical references.
    ISBN 0-86709-512-1 (pbk.)
    1. Literature—Study and teaching (Secondary)—United States. I. Title.

    PN70 .M39 2002
    807' 1'273—dc21

                                            2002001577

Editor: Lisa Luedeke
Production: Lynne Reed
Cover design: Jenny Jensen Greenleaf
Cover photograph: digitalvision
Typesetter: Argosy
Manufacturing: Steve Bernier

Printed in the United States of America on acid-free paper
06 05 04 03 02 RRD 1 2 3 4 5

For Kim,
without whom, not,
and for my mother and father,
first teachers.

Contents

Contents

Foreword

As a young teacher I was convinced that the school contrived to assign me the most rambunctious and noisome students in the whole school. I could see that down the hall a similar group of teenagers was patiently attending to the lesson at hand while my charges, though delightful, not only seemed loathe to follow my lead but also took considerable pleasure in leading the lesson anywhere but in the direction I had planned. It took me years to discover that the problem wasn't with the students or with the literature but with my methods of leading. The book you hold in your hands could have saved me many wrong turns. Robert McMahon offers readers a system of teaching English that achieves classroom "control" through content. That is, an approach to lesson planning so intellectually engaging that students are keen to follow.

Leading classroom discussions is one of the greatest challenges of an English teacher's job. With fond memories of lively conversations in Advanced Placement literature classes—the kind that are likely to have drawn young people to the profession in the first place—new teachers wonder what has gone wrong when kids respond with stony silence to questions like "What is the theme?" "So what do you think?" produces a few hands but seldom the spirited responses that lead to new understandings. It isn't that students have nothing to say. Most even have a pretty good idea of what a theme is. Yet teenagers know that if they sit back and wait, the teacher will answer her own questions. As we fill the empty space with teacher talk, the kids go peacefully to sleep, with their eyes wide open, of course.

Later we wonder if the book or poem was "over" students' heads. Would students speak up if they could relate more easily to the story or if the characters were more obviously like them? Yes and no. The problem with this solution, which I have tried (trust me, there is no antidote to student apathy that I haven't tried in my twenty-nine years in the classroom), is that simpler texts don't offer enough "meat" to sustain extended discussion. As Cassius explained to his friend, "The fault, dear Brutus is not in the stars / But in ourselves." The fault, dear colleagues, is not in the books, but in our approach.

For most students, literary texts are mysterious things only teachers have access to. They assume that insight into symbols and character is bestowed at graduation to English majors or revealed in secret code in teachers' manuals. Some—observing a hand-raising classmate—speculate that the ability to comprehend literature may be a part of an English teacher's, or future English teacher's, DNA structure. It seldom crosses students' minds that this might be an acquired skill.

It is much the same with other deeply held skills. Once you've learned to ski you forget all the details about shifting weight and placement of poles. Your muscles remember what they learned and overlearned and respond to the slope and snow. Very little conscious thought is involved. But, unless you are a natural athlete, you only reach this point of ease through painstaking instruction and practice. Because middle and high school students, for the most part, come to us able to read, we mistakenly assume that with a bit of additional effort they should be able to comprehend and respond to challenging literature. In fact most of the texts we assign in a literature class require a whole new set of reading skills.

Robert McMahon's basic questions offer an approach to instruction that helps students acquire these specialized reading skills. Over time, practice with the questions he provides helps build a kind of muscle memory for reading challenging texts. They can be used with any rich piece of literature, classic or contemporary, and point the way to powerful student interaction with texts. On the pages that follow, McMahon distinguishes between factual and interpretive, and interpretive and evaluative questions. In his experience, and mine as well, students jump too quickly from a determination of facts to evaluation without fully exploring the possibilities of interpretation.

In the story of "The Prodigal Son," for example, McMahon demonstrates how raising the question of a son's interpretation of "home" and "far country" compared with the father's interpretation of the terms invites students to explore their own attitudes within the context of the story. Such provocative questions send students back to the text in search of evidence for their views and, in turn, shed light on readers' own experiences. Instead of playing the dull game of guess-what-the-teacher-is-thinking, McMahon's students engage in authentic conversations about issues that matter. Isn't this why we teach literature?

I read the chapter here on *Oedipus the King* shortly after teaching the play. Putting down the manuscript I ran to email all my students to tell them that when classes resumed after winter break, we needed to talk more about the ill-fated man. I had never before seen how the oracle only foretold that Oedipus would kill his father and marry his mother, not that Oedipus would necessarily become aware of what he had done. Fate and free will can coexist! I was also keen to have students explore McMahon's question about whether Oedipus was better or worse off at the end of the play. Unfortunately, I didn't have students' addresses on my laptop computer. They probably would have thought I had lost my mind, anyway. One thing I am certain of is that I will do a better job teaching Sophocles next year for having read Robert McMahon's book.

Enough of me and my reading. It is time to begin your own.

Carol Jago
Ogeu les Bains

Preface
To My Readers

This book is meant to be of practical use to English teachers in the classroom. It suggests ways to teach students to think about literature by asking them questions, giving them imaginative exercises, and working with their responses. It does not pretend to be a "complete guide to teaching English"—the book ignores lecturing, grading, and course planning. It might well have been titled "Doing Things with Literary Works and Students."

All the chapters treat narrative and drama as sources of understanding about human beings, specifically about our motives: "Why does the prodigal son leave home?" "Why does Gatsby fall in love with Daisy?" These are but instances of questions that interest all of us, as are "Why did she do that?" and "Why do I feel this way about that event?" Chapter 1, "Asking Questions to Explore Motives for Acts," introduces a set of questions about motives and shows how to use them with Luke's parable of "The Prodigal Son" (Luke 15:11–32), which is treated as a story about a rebellious adolescent. Perhaps it is the best-known story in our culture, and being so short, even those unfamiliar with it can read the parable in a few minutes (see Appendix A). Because the same questions are used in every chapter, they are listed in "Summary of Basic Questions," which follows the Acknowledgments, for easy reference as you read the book.

The set of questions is derived from Kenneth Burke's literary criticism and theory. The power of these questions lies in their making explicit what skillful readers already do while reading. You ask these questions so habitually that you do not notice them, so experienced are you in finding the answers. But your students do not have your reading experience, and teaching them to ask questions gives them a way to begin thinking clearly and fully about a literary work. If you use the questions repeatedly over the course of a year, with different works and perhaps in different combinations, your students will soon learn to ask and answer them on their own. As a result, your students will soon possess a set of conceptual tools to help them understand anything they read more thoroughly.

Chapter 1 sets out the foundation for this book, and Chapters 2 through 5 cannot be understood without it. In my view, it would be best to read the chapters in sequence, while studying the work each chapter treats. (The story explored in Chapter 2, James Joyce's "Eveline," is reprinted in its entirety in Appendix B.) Every chapter in this book uses the set of basic questions in Chapter 1 to explore an often-taught literary work: James Joyce's "Eveline," Alice Walker's "Everyday Use," F. Scott Fitzgerald's *The Great Gatsby*, and Sophocles' *Oedipus the King*. The short stories are treated in some depth and detail; however, the novel and the drama are too long for thorough analysis. Nevertheless, the last two chapters explore the motives for one significant act in detail, review and analyze the structure of the whole work, and discuss teaching strategies.

As a group, it is my hope that these chapters will familiarize you with how to teach using the set of basic questions first employed in Chapter 1 and summarized on page xx. The chapters are also meant to stimulate your own capacity for asking and answering questions about literary works. Learning to ask good questions is not an easy task: I have been working at it for twenty years and am still learning. But if we wish to teach our students to think about what they read, we must teach them to ask questions about what they read. This means both encouraging them to inquire and showing them how. This book contains some general questions applicable to many different works. They will not show you how to finish your inquiry into a story or play, but they will get you started and take you a long way. In addition, you will find that your students are interested in understanding why people do what they do. With a little help from you, they will enjoy discussing the interpretive and evaluative questions set forth here. They will be doing more work in class, you will be doing less, and students will not even think of it as "work."

The analyses in these chapters may go rather beyond what you will want to do in class. One reason they are so extensive is to persuade teachers who are unsure about leading discussions to try this way of teaching. The chapters on the two short stories, *The Great Gatsby* and *Oedipus the King*, work to provide a solid foundation for teaching these works by asking questions and working with students' answers. Confidence is crucial to good teaching. If the once-uncertain teacher can enjoy a string of successful discussions, she will lead discussions about other works with more confidence.

In addition to full-length chapters, this book contains shorter pieces called "Provocations." Most of them present imaginative assignments for writing, or oral presentation, or both. I think that students should write far more than they do, but with this proviso: "Just because they write it doesn't mean you have to read it." As in Provocation #10, "Reading Journals," you can require your students to keep always-up-to-date portfolios, and you can collect them without prior notice and grade for completeness, penalizing them heavily for missing assignments.

But you can also employ a practice I call "Performance Day"—when students stand in front of the class to present their work. The other students must listen attentively and applaud politely at the end. Every student will appear in front of the class, sooner or later, and they need to form an appreciative audience for one another. Those who perform must *perform*, preparing themselves to read well, act well, recite well. You should find some way to make these performances part of the student's grade. Performing actively involves students in learning, contributes to their poise in front of audiences, and stimulates some otherwise unexceptional students to do some exceptional work.

Here is a principle, now well-understood, that underlies the imaginative exercises in the Provocations: Different students have different learning styles. A wide variety of assignments enables a wide variety of students to learn, to express their understandings, and to enjoy some success in a class. Highly verbal, linear thinkers write wonderful essays; nonlinear thinkers struggle with essays, but often do very well with writing poetry or illustrating a scene from a story. If you wish to survey a summary range of these exercises, you might read through Provocation #2, "Eighteen Exercises for 'Eveline' or Other Works."

The Provocations may be read in any order. Those concerning narrative and drama are arranged around Chapters 1 through 5; a group on teaching poetry comes at the end. I do not pretend to have created original exercises in these Provocations, having borrowed from other teachers whenever I could. One of Kenneth Burke's maxims for literary criticism—"Use all there is to use"—I long ago adapted for teaching: "Use everything you can put to use."

We English teachers often say that reading extends and deepens our experience, just as our experience illuminates what we read. Reading extends our experience by allowing us to enter into the thoughts and feelings and lives of other people. However complex and rich contemporary life may be, its very familiarity tends to blind us. But a literary work proves a distant mirror: Its unfamiliarity enables us to see ourselves and others and our world in a new way. We must draw on our experience to understand sympathetically what we read, and what we read enables us to understand our experience more deeply. In this sense, reading a work carefully is like making a close friend. The better we understand a friend, the better we understand ourselves. The more deeply we enter into the experience of a literary work, the greater its power to illuminate our experience of ourselves, others, and the world. This power of illumination is greatly increased when we can discuss our understandings and evaluations with others. This whole book springs from my belief in the illuminating power of careful reading and thoughtful discussion. They enable us to understand literary works, ourselves, and others more fully, a kind of friendship all the way around.

Acknowledgments

―――

―――

It is a pleasure for me to express my gratitude to the friends who have supported, encouraged, advised, and materially aided my work on this project. Many members of my family read my fledgling attempts to write about teaching and encouraged me to finish what I had started: my mother and father, my parents-in-law, and especially my wife. I also received advice and encouragement from many friends, especially David England, Gretchen Schwarz, Jim Scarpino, Steve Delacroix, Jim Babin, Martha Stroschein, and Meg Watson. Conversations with Tim Fuller led me to read Michael Oakeshott and thereby many long-held ideas about motives and about teaching came together in a new way. Lisa Luedeke, my editor at Heinemann, has been invaluable in shaping this book.

The Council on Research at Louisiana State University granted me a sabbatical, enabling the completion of this book. Dr. Billy Seay, Dean of the Honors College at LSU, has supported my interest in asking questions and leading discussions in many ways, not least of all by having me teach freshman seminars. Dr. Jane Collins, Dean of the College of Arts and Sciences, also encouraged my way of working with students and supported this project. But I learned the most about leading discussions from my colleagues at The Springside School twenty years ago, especially from Sarah Allen and Deborah Dempsey; what is written here I first attempted there. They guided this novice teacher with a light but sure touch, and I have been working with what they taught me ever since.

THINKING ABOUT
LITERATURE

Questions About Motives

1. ACT. What does the character do?

2. SITUATION. How does the character understand the situation in which she acts?

3. AGENT: (a) MORAL CHARACTER. What is the character's general moral character (disposition, temperament, values, habits, beliefs, sentiments, and so on)? (b) SELF-UNDERSTANDING. How does the character understand herself as the agent of this act?

4. PURPOSE. What does the character intend—aim to gain or accomplish—by this act?

5. ATTITUDE. With what feelings, in what manner, does the character perform this act (for example, eagerly or reluctantly)?

Questions About Any Work

A. What goes with what? (Identification; Association)

B. What versus what? (Contrast; Opposition; Conflict)

C. What follows what? (Progression; Sequence)

D. What becomes what? (Change; Transformation)

Examples: What has this character learned? How are things different at the end of the work than they were at the beginning?

Evaluative Questions

TRUTH. *Examples:* Is this character's understanding of her situation true or false, and why? In what ways is it true (accurate, adequate, valid), and why? In what ways is it false (inaccurate, inadequate, invalid), and why?

GOODNESS. (a) MORAL CHARACTER. *Examples:* Is this character a good person, or a bad one, and why? In what ways is this character a good person, and why? In what ways is he a bad one, and why? (b) ACT. Is this act good or bad, and why? In what ways is this act good, and why? In what ways is it bad, and why?

Consider (1) the agent's purposes (or intentions): Are her purposes good or bad, and why? In what ways are her purposes good, and why? In what ways are they bad, and why?

Consider also (2) the consequences of the act: Are the consequences of this act good, or bad, and why? In what ways are the consequences good, and why? In what ways are they bad, and why? Should the agent (the character) be praised for these good consequences? Why or why not? Should she be blamed for these bad ones? Why or why not?

1

Asking Questions to Explore Motives for Acts

Literary works, especially stories and plays, are a laboratory for understanding the thoughts and feelings, characters, and acts of human beings. We are interested in literature because we are interested in ourselves. "Why did he say that?" and "Why did I do that?" make us wonder at the variety of human beings and the complexity of each one of us. A novel or play mirrors this complex variety in a kind of controlled experiment. It heightens our natural interest in motives by crisis and conflict between characters, by the intensity of its plot, and by the beauty of its language. By giving us vivid and articulate vicarious experience, it moves us to sympathize and reflect. We are caught up in the action but at an imaginative distance, so we can think about the characters more easily than we usually can about the involvements of our lives. Literature proves a humanizing education because it explores with imaginative sympathy the variety, complexity, intimacies, and entanglements of human beings.

In reading or teaching a literary work, the question of motives often arises— "Why does Adam eat the forbidden fruit?" "Why does the prodigal son leave home?" "Why does Oedipus think Creon is plotting against him?" Rarely does an author provide a full explanation of the motives for any important act: These are left for the reader's reflection. Experienced readers do this more or less naturally, with the "second nature" of habit, as they read. Inexperienced readers, caught up in the excitement of the plot, experience sympathy with a work yet only learn gradually to reflect on it. What do experienced readers do when they reflect on characters and motives? What questions do they ask themselves, and how do they pursue them? Although there is no shortcut to mature experience, some questions can be schematized to help students think about what they read.

Let us analyze a human act by dividing it into five basic components: In a given context (Situation), a person (Agent) does or says something (Act) in a certain manner (Attitude) in order to achieve some end (Purpose). The Agent, let us say, is female. She acts in response to the Situation *as she understands it*. Other people may understand it differently and, in literature, they almost always do because stories turn on contrasts and conflicts between characters. To understand why she does what she does, we must try to understand her Situation as she does. But we must also understand *her*. The Agent has a character—a relatively stable set of habits and beliefs that make her the kind of person she is. We have many words for describing a person's character: kind or cruel, generous or stingy, energetic or lazy, and so on. Since we call a person in a story "a character," let us call this stable set of habits and beliefs her "Moral Character." This is a descriptive term and implies no value judgment by itself: A villain, by definition, would have an immoral "Moral Character." The term implies only that the Agent's acts somehow make sense: They "fit" with her Moral Character, even as it is developing or falling apart.

But the Agent also has a *Self-Understanding*, and to understand why she does what she does, we try to grasp how she *understands herself* in this particular Situation and during this Act. Different situations bring out different aspects of a person's Moral Character, and to understand her Act, we must see both the Situation and the person *as she sees them*. In addition, her Attitude, or manner of acting, is an important aspect of her Act. The Act of criticizing someone, for example, can be done gently or harshly, reluctantly or eagerly. An Agent's Attitude, how she performs an Act, tells us something important about her motives.

All told, then, we have five components: Situation, Act, Purpose, Attitude, and Agent, and the last of these includes Moral Character, which is relatively enduring, and Self-Understanding in this particular Act. Let us call them "motives" because all of them are moving components in an Act. Although we usually regard Purpose as "the motive," in a narrow sense, all of these work together to motivate what we do. These motives generate a set of questions for fully describing an Act so as to understand it. An Agent does not have to be reflectively conscious of these motives; she does not have to express any of them to herself. Rather, they are implied in what she does. A surgeon in an emergency operation, or a hostess at a party, acts without conscious reflection, but intelligently. If we read a well-constructed narrative of the surgery or the party, we can analyze why they did what they did, and why they said what they said. The questions in Figure 1–1 are tools for reflective understanding, for analysis "after the fact." An Act, remember, includes what a character says, as well as what she does.

These motives are all related to one another, and so they easily shade over into one another. They can be distinguished, but they should not be separated. The terms are not fixed, but flexible. The questions all work together to give a rounded view of what a character does and why he does it. Hence, the questions are to be *used* for understanding why characters do what they do, without worrying (for example) "Does this come under Act, or Attitude?" Skillful readers answer these, and other, questions as a matter of course while reading. They find the answers so

1.	ACT.	What does the character do?
2.	SITUATION.	How does the character understand the situation in which he acts?
3.	AGENT.	(a) MORAL CHARACTER. What is the character's general Moral Character?
		(b) SELF-UNDERSTANDING. How does the character understand himself as the Agent of this Act?
4.	PURPOSE.	What does the character intend—aim to gain or accomplish—by this Act?
5.	ATTITUDE.	With what attitude or feelings does the character perform this Act?

Figure 1–1.

habitually that they do not even notice the questions. The questions are powerful because they are simple and fundamental; they make explicit what experienced readers do. Hence, these questions prove useful in teaching less-experienced readers how to read more intelligently. In theory, they can be used to explore even minor acts and utterances. In practice, questions are best used to explore crucial acts and major speeches. A teacher may not want to use all of them even in a full analysis of a crucial Act—perhaps the Act or the Attitude is so obvious that it does not need describing. But I will use all of them in this and the other chapters to illustrate a full analysis of Motives.

✳

To illustrate their use, let us apply them to Luke's parable of "The Prodigal Son" and ask: *Why does the prodigal son ask for his inheritance and leave home?* In pursuing this question, we should keep in mind the differences between factual, interpretive, and evaluative questions. A factual question, in principle, has only one correct answer, although it may have many different components, which can be expressed in any number of ways. The question of Act—*What does the prodigal son do?*—proves a factual question, even though it demands some inferences. An interpretive question, in contrast, has many different plausible answers; some of the answers may be directly opposed, yet all are defensible from evidence in the text. The question of motive—*Why does the prodigal son ask for his inheritance and leave home?*—is clearly interpretive. The story does not tell us directly what his motives and attitudes are when he leaves home, although it invites us to reflect on them.

Naturally, the factual question needs to be answered before the interpretive question can be posed: We need to know *what* the boy does before we investigate *why* he does it.

Finally, evaluative questions are even more open-ended and complex than interpretive ones: *Is this act good or bad?* is open to the greatest variety of perspectives. One set of perspectives is offered by what may be called the "implied" moral compass of the work. But we are not limited to that, for we may criticize the evaluations implied in the work. Moreover, different people will have different senses of what is good and bad, and why. Naturally, again, the interpretive question should be answered before evaluation begins: We need to think through *why* the prodigal son does what he does before we can evaluate it. In other words, as we move from factual to interpretive to evaluative questions, the number of defensibly "right answers" increases as we explore the work's human importance and deeper meanings.

In practice, however, readers tend to assume that they grasp the facts, and then they go on simultaneously to interpret and evaluate characters' motives. When inexperienced readers do this, they tend to receive their impressions of a work uncritically: They feel their evaluations so keenly that they do not reflect on the implied interpretation of motives. Because of this, interpretive questions prove the most flexible tool in teaching. They form the bridge between fact and evaluation; they lead students to explore a fact and hold them back (temporarily) from evaluative responses. Nevertheless, facts can only be *distinguished, but not separated* from interpretations and evaluations. If I say the prodigal son asking for his inheritance is "an insult to his Father," am I making a factual, an interpretive, or an evaluative statement? A case can be made for each and for all.

With these provisos, I will try to suspend evaluative statements while interpreting the prodigal son's motives. What follows illustrates a way of using the questions just listed in a class. To be sure, a teacher will not always want to pose all of them or to pursue the questions in the ways I suggest. My treatment is intended to be suggestive, not exhaustive. Here is how the story opens (see Appendix A for the full text of "The Prodigal Son"):

11 A certain man had two sons.

12 And the younger of them said to his father, Father, give me the portion of goods that falleth to me. And he divided unto them his living.

13 And not many days after the younger son gathered all together, and took his journey into a far country, and there wasted his substance with riotous living.

14 And when he had spent all, there arose a mighty famine in that land; and he began to be in want.

Why Does the Prodigal Son Ask for His Inheritance and Leave Home?

Act. What does the prodigal son do?

This factual question proves somewhat more difficult to answer in this instance than in most stories because it requires some specialized knowledge and some inference. First, he asks for his inheritance while his father is still alive. According to Jewish law, the elder son is entitled to two-thirds, the younger to one-third, of the estate. Needless to say, the younger son's request is extraordinary because he is not entitled to his inheritance until after his father's death. Nevertheless, the father gives both sons their inheritance. Second, the younger son turns his inheritance into cash and leaves home for "a far country." Given the rural setting of the story, his inheritance comes largely or wholly as real property: land, flocks, herds. To leave home for the far country, he needs portable wealth, so he sells off his inheritance, and does so rather quickly—"not many days after" he departs.

Finally, we are given to understand that he intends a permanent break with his father, brother, and the life he has known with them. His asking for his inheritance publicly insults his father, saying (as it were) "I wish you were dead." In addition, as the end of the story shows, the two brothers have little affection for one another. Moreover, having sold all his property, rather than leasing it or putting it under the management of a steward, he has no reason to return and inspect his holdings. He insults his family and carries everything he owns with him into the far country. He repudiates his past and embarks on a wholly new life.

Situation. How does the prodigal son experience (understand) "home"?

In order to understand why he leaves it so eagerly, we need to grasp *his* understanding of "home" and the "far country." To be sure, we can only infer his sense of these. Compared with nineteenth-century novels, biblical narrative tells us little or nothing about a character's thoughts and feelings, Moral Character and Purposes, leaving these to be inferred from Acts. But because the prodigal son is so eager to leave home, we assume that "home" is loaded with negative associations, in his mind, and the "far country" with positive ones. Literary works tend to heighten and dramatize decisions by featuring contrasts between possibilities. So, too, do adolescents.

When I teach, I put the two headings up on the board and pose them as one question: *How does the prodigal son understand "home" and the "far country"? What associations does he have with each?* Every answer on either side requires a corresponding and opposing one on the other side. Sometimes an answer will begin with an entry under "home" ("boring") and an antonym must be supplied for the "far country" ("exciting"); sometimes an answer begins with the "Far Country." Hence, thinking a contrast through is good for vocabulary work, especially for antonyms, although an antonym for "sex, drugs, and rock-n-roll" is not easily found. (When there are similarities in addition to contrasts, I list them between the two columns.) I tell the students that I will list every answer they give, provided that they can defend it. No one has to agree with every answer given, and my putting it up on the board does not mean that I agree with it, only that it is plausible and worth considering. Usually the lists grow long rather quickly, filled with many different ways of "saying the same thing." But the more ways something is said, the likelier it is that the whole class will achieve a wider and deeper understanding. Also, being able to "say the same thing" in a different way encourages the diffident to speak, for they can be sure that they aren't wrong. When no one has anything more to add, and I have nothing more to ask, the list is complete. Here is a typical list:

The Prodigal Son's View

Home	Far Country
boring	exciting
dull	fun
known	unknown
work	play
hard work	sex, drugs, and rock-n-roll
under his father	independent; his own man
obedience	freedom
family	new people
country, small town	big city
virtue	vice
rules	no rules
familiar	strange, foreign, exotic
no girls	exotic dancers
routine work	adventure
safe, too safe	risky
self-denial	self-assertion
his father's little boy	his own man

After the class generates a list like this, I often give the students a few minutes to make their own short lists, abbreviating those on the board to (say) five entries, to cover all the crucial points as each understands them. This forces every student to make selections and think through the issues in a new way. You can even have some of them talk about why they made the selections they made.

Once the prodigal son's understanding of his Situation has been explored, a teacher could pose the question "Is it true?" or, a bit more complexly: "In what ways (if any) is his understanding true?" But this question, important though it is, comes too early at this stage, for it leads to a premature evaluation. (We are imagining, here, one reading of the story, with one discussion. If you were going to ask students to reread and rethink the issues, as I recommend in Chapters 2 and 3, an early evaluation would be open to revision through further discussion.) Nevertheless, we can achieve some perspective on the boy's understanding of his situation by asking, *How does the Father understand "home" and the "far country"?* Again, given the contrasts featured in the story, I infer that the father has positive associations with "home" and negative ones with the "far country." Exploring the father's point of view allows us to question the prodigal son's understanding without evaluating it prematurely. In class, I keep the prodigal son's contrasts on one board as the students develop the father's view, in a long list, on another board. Then I ask, *Are these two views just different, or do they have things in common?* Here are brief lists for both the prodigal son and the father, set up for easy comparison:

The Prodigal Son's View

Home	**Far Country**
boring	exciting
familiar (same old things/ people every day)	exotic; adventurous
restrictive	liberating
dependence; Father	independence; no Father
hard work; responsibility	leisure; play

The Father's View

Home	**Far Country**
satisfying: repose	danger
family: love	no family: loveless
order: a formed life	disorder: a dissolute life
independence: autonomy of the household	vulnerability
responsibility: real life	irresponsibility: false life

What relations, if any, do these two views have with one another? Comparing the prodigal son's and the father's perspectives in these two lists illustrates several points. First, it highlights the difference between "situation" and "setting"—the same physical place in the story is experienced in entirely different ways by the father and by the son. Nor is it hard to see why: The son is not himself a father, not the creator of a home. Home is something the father must make and sustain by his energy and insight, while the younger son simply receives it and, in the event, regards it as alien. The boy considers it his father's house, not his own. Hence, he repudiates it and his father without qualms, once he acquires his inheritance, which seems to be the only thing he cares for at home. This repudiation separates him both physically and morally from his family. But the physical separation from his father is already implied in his moral alienation, evident in the radical difference between their two perspectives on "home" and the "far country." In his departing so decisively, he deliberately "un-sons himself," as it were, in his own eyes. This break with his past, which he intends to be final, simply follows from his long-held "disvalue" for home and his dream of a completely new life far away.

Second, despite their fundamental opposition, the two lists concern themselves with the same features of "home" and the "far country." In other words, the father and the prodigal son are looking at the same things, as it were, but under the sign of opposed values. What the boy imagines as exciting, the father knows to be dangerous. The prodigal son experiences the familiar as the "same old things and people all the time"—the dull round of boring work and equally boring people— while the father understands the familiar as "the tried and true"—routines of work that proved to be productive and people who are known to be loyal. The freedom from work and obligations that the boy so eagerly seeks will lead him near to self-destruction, for these give form and meaning to life, and without their structure he dissipates himself in dissolute living.

In short, the two lists feature a fundamental aspect of literary symbolism and also of reality. Any symbol (image, act, character trait) can be taken in a good sense or in a bad sense, or in both senses but in different ways. Water can symbolize not only death (chaos, destruction) but also life (nourishment, birth); and in the Bible, it often symbolizes death-and-rebirth, as in baptism and the Israelites' passage through the Red Sea. A mother's hug can be experienced as supportive or as smothering; "escape" can have the positive note of eluding danger or the negative one of fleeing responsibility; a passion for justice can be noble or vengeful; and a laid-back style can be wisely tolerant or merely lazy. Because we are possessed of the vices that accompany our virtues, it is often hard to tell when the positive slips over into the negative, in literature as in life. If we enjoyed both the wisdom of serpents and the innocence of doves, we might be saved from the folly of being merely as cunning and cruel as a serpent or as sweet and vulnerable as a dove. A literary work frequently turns on ambiguities like these, as it explores the complexity of our moral characters, judgments, purposes, decisions, acts, and destinies.

Finally, the story as a whole shows how and why the younger son learns a new sense of values. It would be excessive to say that he comes to adopt all of the father's values within the course of the story, although bitter experience does bring him to the father's understanding of the far country. But after nearly starving to death, he associates "home" only with "bread." Nevertheless, the story implies that over time he will learn to see the fuller implications of "bread" as life, sustenance, and the common labor that sustains and nourishes life in the fullest sense. The journey home symbolizes a journey toward all of the father's values, even though that journey is not completed within the story.

I have taught this story to classes of adolescents and to adults, and I always have the class make lists like the preceding ones. Needless to say, the adolescents, not having created their own homes, tend to have greater difficulty imagining the father's view than do the adults. They often need hints and questions to help them along. Interestingly, once the two lists are on the board and have been considered, adolescents are able to see some of their commonality even in oppositions (for example, the boy's "adventure" and the father's "danger" with respect to the far country). Again, not only is making a list of contrasts from the father's view a fine exercise in interpretive sympathy, but comparing the two lists proves an intellectual challenge that students can meet and master, with perhaps a little help.

Attitude. What are the prodigal son's attitudes and feelings as he acts?

The prodigal son's Attitude or manner in asking for his inheritance and leaving home has already been suggested. From his perspective, he is eager (although a critic might call him hasty or even rash). Because he sells off his property quickly, leaving home "not many days after" receiving his inheritance, he probably does not get the best price. It seems unlikely that he seeks advice about the sale—he "knows it all" already. He could have put his property under management or entrusted the sale to an agent after receiving an advance, but either of these would have meant keeping his ties with "home." These ties he is eager to sunder, and so he makes the best deal he can, prepares for the journey, and leaves, all within a few days.

This interpretation focuses on the implications of "not many days after" and labors to view the prodigal son as sympathetically as he sees himself. This is less easy to do when we consider him asking his father for his inheritance. So brazen a request implies a brazen manner, one he doubtlessly considers "bold" but which others might call "shameless." I cannot imagine him hanging his head as he asks, and though I can imagine him wheedling and flattering, the request implies such cock-sure self-confidence and such disrespect for his father that he must be pretty sure of getting what he wants.

Asking students to imagine a character's attitude involves them more deeply with the work. It thereby extends their powers of imaginative sympathy, that is to say, their ability to imagine and understand what other people are feeling. Literature is a school of compassion for others, for understanding them "from the inside." Moreover, understanding others in this way enables us to understand ourselves better.

Sometimes this can best be done by feeling one's way into the postures and tones of an encounter. How, for example, would they illustrate the prodigal son's farewell scene with his father? They need not be artists to do this: Students can be assigned roles to play in a "tableau" of their own design. One plays the father, another the prodigal son, and perhaps a third acts as the older brother; two or three different teams could be assigned the same scene. How would an illustrator, imaginatively interpreting the farewell scene, reveal the characters' thoughts, feelings, and relationships? The students must work this out and present it to the class in a tableau lasting (say) fifteen seconds, with posture, facial expressions, and total composition (arrangement in the "frame" at the front of the class) that reveals their understanding. For me, the farewell scene with his father is painful to imagine—the old man sad but warm-hearted, the boy ebullient yet cold, the older brother standing off and scowling, only there because he has to be. Does the father attempt to embrace his son before he is gone forever, and how does the boy meet his attempt? How might this action be captured by the "illustration" of a tableau?

Agent: Moral Character. What is the prodigal son's Moral Character?

What are his fundamental values and beliefs in leaving home so hurriedly? Here, the border between interpretation and evaluation, always slender, proves unusually thin. Instead, we might begin by thinking about his age. To receive his inheritance and leave home, he must be a legal adult. In contemporary America, he would have to be twenty-one or perhaps eighteen; in ancient Rome, aristocratic youths received the toga of adulthood at age sixteen. In Luke's story, the prodigal son must have completed his bar mitzvah and been at least thirteen. Chronological age matters here only as an index of maturity. He must be old enough to act legally and young enough to make his immaturity plausible. He appears to be the kind of person who asked for his inheritance and left home as soon as he could. Do these acts show him to be independent, or cocky? bold, or shameless? daring, or foolish? Premature evaluation endangers sympathetic interpretation of the prodigal son's Moral Character, so let us turn to his Self-Understanding.

Self-Understanding. How does the prodigal son understand himself in asking for his inheritance and leaving home?

His Self-Understanding can best be envisioned by contrast with his older brother because his words at the end of the story imply a history of sibling rivalry, and rivalries give rise to contrasting self-definitions, at least so far as the rivalry is concerned. The prodigal son acts without hesitation at the beginning of the story and appears to have little self-doubt. Hence, I assume that he possesses the natural self-love of human beings in no small measure. He therefore understands himself and his values as "good," unconventional though they are, in opposition to his stay-at-home, goody-goody older brother. In addition, literary works tend to feature contrast and conflict: They clarify issues by highlighting differences in ideas through characters' opposing views. Consider the following list of answers to: *How does the prodigal son understand himself, when leaving home, in contrast to his older brother?*

Prodigal Son's View

Older Brother—Bad	Younger Brother—Good
wimpy	gutsy
always does what he's told	has a mind of his own
daddy's boy	his own man
dependent	independent
easily ruled, like a slave	not easily ruled, free
withdrawn	bold
passive	active
"a nice, sweet boy" (sneer)	a strong man
conventional (bad)	unconventional (good)
plays it safe	takes risks
cautious	adventurous, daring
narrow, closed mind	open mind
no future	open future
narrow view of life	broad view of life

Here, again, a teacher could ask, "Is the prodigal son's self-understanding true?"; however, that issue can be addressed better indirectly. That question, as posed, leads to a premature evaluation of the prodigal son's character and acts, and since most adolescents are involved in some form of sibling rivalry, students tend to weigh in "for" or "against" the prodigal son depending on whether they are younger or older siblings. The indirect approach asks, *How does the older brother understand the contrast between himself and the prodigal son?* Keeping the list for "the prodigal son's view" at one end of the board, develop a list for his older brother at the other end so that the two lists can be compared. Here are two brief lists, one for each brother.

Prodigal Son's View

Older Brother—Bad	Younger Brother—Good
dependent	independent
easily ruled	has a mind of his own
passive	active
afraid, overly cautious	bold, daring, willing to take risks
conventional (bad)	unconventional (good)

Older Brother's View

Older Brother—Good	Younger Brother—Bad
obedient	disobedient
honors his father	dishonors his father
hardworking	lazy, shiftless
prudent, responsible	foolish, irresponsible
normal, conventional (good)	abnormal, unconventional (bad)

What do these two views tell us? What relations, if any, do they have with one another? I have constructed these brief lists of the two brothers' opposing self-understandings so as to feature their contrasting views of "the same thing." Where the older brother sees his own obedience and respect for his father, as opposed to the prodigal son's disobedience and disrespect, the younger boy sees his own daring independence against his older brother's dependence on his father and conventional values. Here is the same kind of "doubleness" or ambiguity we saw earlier when comparing the prodigal son's and the father's understandings of "home" and the "far country." Surprisingly, in my experience, students grasp the two brothers' doubleness of perspective while the class is developing the second list. Their understanding of sibling conflict enables them to appreciate the validity of both perspectives, even if they prefer one of them. Although understanding any literary character can potentially give rise to new insights into oneself, leading adolescents to come to grips with these two brothers' Self-Understandings directly illuminates their familiar experience. You can see in their eyes the light dawn in their minds.

Purpose. What does the prodigal son aim to accomplish by leaving home?

This is the only motive left to be considered, and it proves the most difficult. The story only tells us what, in the event, occurs: He dissipates all his inheritance in dissolute living. Surely, when he leaves home, he does not aim to ruin himself financially. Even though the boy does pursue a headlong course of self-destruction, I cannot believe that he *intends* to destroy himself. Indeed, I have suggested that he finds home "deadly," boring, and constricting, and ventures into the "far country" in search of a new, greater, more intense life. At the same time, the human heart is folded together with complicated twists and turns. The intentions at the forefront of the prodigal son's mind may well be only those that best suit his vanity rather than the darker purposes he resists recognizing.

Certainly, the boy's intention to gain financial independence and physical separation from his father implies his search for other kinds of independence, which may be termed "moral" or "spiritual." Does he aim to live dissolutely? Does he tell himself, "When I get far from home, I am going to sin"? I tend to see him phrasing it differently; perhaps, "I will prove my father's ways are too limited for me," or even "I will prove my father wrong." What we think he tells himself depends on our sense of his sophistication and character.

Moreover, the question arises, "Is there any meaningful difference between these formulations?" On the one hand, it might be argued that deliberately aiming to challenge his father's ways is no different from intending "to sin." On the other hand, an intention to sin makes him self-consciously wicked, while aiming to prove that his father's ways are too limited for him might make him merely foolish. We tend to consider wickedness a fault of character and folly an error of judgment, two rather different evaluations. In this line of thinking, folly tends to be comic, a means toward self-understanding and mature self-control. On the other hand, some folly proves tragically self-destructive. The prodigal son manages (barely) to survive his moral adventure and learn something about himself and his father. Does this happy ending make his folly comic? Or is his folly so self-destructive as to be tragic, and the happy ending mere good luck? *Should the prodigal son be praised or blamed for the consequences of his leaving home, and why?* The narrative opens itself to a wide variety of evaluations.

Young people often prove themselves surprisingly adept at thinking through the moral complexities of these issues. I have had students defend the prodigal son as "intending to sin" yet "good," because though it leads him to disaster, he thereby learns a valuable lesson about himself and about life. "Better to learn by making mistakes than by being like the older brother, obedient and resentful." A counter-argument must be made to this, distinguishing good *intentions* from good *consequences* and pointing out that the prodigal son is lucky to survive his moral adventure. Usually another student will do the work for you, with less sophistication but with greater initial effect—for example, "Is becoming a crack addict the best way to learn about drug addiction?" You manage the discussion as indirectly as possible until the full range of possible purposes has been considered. Then you might ask each student to decide his or her own view of the matter, writing it down and defending it in a paragraph.

Evaluative Questions and Discussion

Once a class arrives at a discussion of the character's Purposes, evaluation can hardly be avoided, nor should it be. For this reason, I have saved Purpose for last, after developing as fully as possible the prodigal son's other motives, his understanding of Act, Situation, and himself from his own point of view. Evaluation is based on interpretation, and students should arrive at as clear an understanding as they can of a character's motives before evaluating his Moral Character and action.

Fundamentally, two different kinds of evaluative questions emerge. The first considers the *truth* (and error) of a character's understanding. It can be posed in different ways: *Is the prodigal son's understanding of his Situation true? Why or why not? In what ways is his understanding true, and in what ways is it false, and why?* Other words could be substituted for "true": accurate, valid, adequate, and so on. The second kind considers the *goodness* (or badness) of an agent's moral character. It, too, can be posed in different ways: *Is the prodigal son a good person, or a bad one, and why? In what ways is he a good person, and in what ways is he a bad one, and why?*

An Act can also be evaluated for its goodness (or badness): *Is this Act good, or bad, and why?* General evaluative questions like this tend to stimulate the most responses. Sooner or later in the discussion, however, you will probably find it useful to distinguish between the act's *intentions* (the agent's purposes) and its *consequences: Are the prodigal son's intentions good, or bad, and why? Are the consequences of his leaving home good, or bad, and why? Should he be praised or blamed for the consequences of his leaving home, and why?* Again, other words can be substituted for "good"—admirable, noble, virtuous—and the last can be specified further: brave, generous, moderate, kind, and so on.

When a class has finished a novel or a play, evaluative questions can generate lively reflections on work as a whole: *Who is the best (most admirable) character, and why? Who is the worst (least admirable) character, and why? What is the most admirable act, and why? What is the worst act, and why?* Questions like these open up the work and students' memories of it to a great variety of responses. Everyone can have different anwers and, in principle, no one can be wrong. Nevertheless, in fact, students can make mistakes, and one student's memory of an act often differs from another's, leading the class to examine anew the relevant passage. If you give these questions to the class the day before you discuss them, they can prepare their responses and you thereby will lessen the likelihood of student chagrin. Students will still have differing views, and relevant passages can still be consulted and explored.

Evaluative questions generate the liveliest discussions for several reasons. First, students feel sure that their evaluative judgments cannot be wrong—each person's sense of what is good and bad has equal validity. The fear of "being wrong" in front of other students stifles discussion, but students feel that their "opinions" about right and wrong cannot be wrong, so they express them more freely. In general, the narrower the possibilities of answers to a question, the deadlier the question falls on the class. Conversely, the more open a question is to a variety of responses, the more willingly and energetically the students will take it up. Interpretive questions generate keener responses than factual ones, and evaluative questions stimulate a class even more.

Second, evaluative questions touch us more closely than intellectual ones. La Rouchefoucauld said, "Everyone complains of his memory, but no one of his judgment." We feel that our ability to remember something says less about us as human beings than does our judgment about the moral character of a person or an act. We commonly believe that intellectual ability, like athletic ability, does not reveal a person's character, her inner depths, while her evaluations and actions do. Hence, evaluative questions on literary characters arouse the hearts of students. Moreover, they do so in a doubly nonthreatening way: Not only can their evaluations not be called wrong, but the people and deeds under discussion are "not real" but fictions that, however lively, live at a distance from themselves.

Finally, good discussion is often assisted, in its beginnings, by a certain vagueness in the terms of the question. Asking "Is this act good, or bad?" will lead some students to speak about the agent's intentions, others about the act's consequences, others still to reflect on the agent's moral character. The students will respond at cross-purposes to one another, until the teacher begins to help them sort out the different kinds of responses. I have seen this happen often, and not merely with young people. Adults also generally grope about in the parliamentary dark, discussing what they take to be one issue, only to discover slowly that two or three issues are actually involved. Faculty meetings often testify to this process.

Reflective Assessment

Having completed this exercise of interpretation, let us consider what we have accomplished. First, we have achieved a rounded view of the prodigal son's motives, for asking for his inheritance and leaving home. His motives are complex because they are many faceted, but they are not complicated because he has no doubts or hesitations about his course of action. We have explored his motives in all these facets and we have done so *from his perspective*: We can only understand why he does what he does by exploring his point of view. At the same time, to clarify his perspective, we have explored the perspectives of other characters on certain issues—the father's understanding of "home" and the "far country" and the older brother's understanding of himself in contrast to the prodigal son. Hence, without leaping to premature evaluation of the prodigal son's character and motives, we have explored his limitations in a way that illuminates the story as a whole. We entertained a variety of perspectives *within* the story before we began to formulate our own in any detail.

Second, these questions about motives form an interlocking whole. Hence, they enable a multifaceted and coherent exploration of motives. A line of answers to one question implies a line of answers to another in a mutually reinforcing way. The process of exploration thereby corrects itself. For example, if answers to the agent's understanding of his situation prove incomplete, exploring his self-understanding or his purposes should reveal what was missing. Moreover, because the questions interlock, they can be taken up in any sequence. Although Act comes first logically, in most literary works it proves so obvious as to need little definition, and from it one may move to Moral Character or Situation or Purpose as seems fit. Because the answers to these interlocking questions imply one another, you do not need to explore all of the questions in order to lead a satisfying class discussion about a character's motives. The set of questions forms a useful toolkit for teaching, but you do not always need to use all of the tools.

Third, we have explored the prodigal son's motives in a way that has illuminated aspects of the whole story, such as the moral characters and values of the father and the older brother. For this, there are three reasons. First, we have investigated a significant act: it motivates the story as a whole, for it sets in motion a series of complications that does not end until the story itself ends. Granted, the story is so brief and so highly charged that every act in it might be considered significant. But most novels and plays work differently, featuring some acts as crucial and others as minor. These crucial acts warrant the greatest attention, and investigating their motives, ramifications, and consequences sheds the greatest light on the work as a whole. Second, a literary work is a coherent whole, and the interlocking questions about motives draw attention to interlocking components in the whole. One of these we customarily call "foils" in a work: two characters whose contrasts mutually illuminate one another. In "The Prodigal Son," a brief work with only three characters, each character acts as a foil for the other two, albeit in different respects. In addition, "home" and the "far country" also function as foils, in one way for the prodigal son, in another way for his father. Pursuing the prodigal son's understanding of his situation and himself, we were bound to examine certain aspects of the other characters in the coherent whole of the story. Had we not done so, our investigation would have been faulted for being too limited and unenlightening.

Finally, in order to shed this light on the whole story, I confess to having bootlegged into the discussion four other fundamental questions about a literary work, drawn from Kenneth Burke's *The Philosophy of Literary Form*. These are more general than questions concerning motives for acts, so they can be applied to any work of literature, including the essay and the lyric poem, and even to works of history and philosophy. I list them by capital letters to distinguish them from the numbered questions about motives explored earlier. Burke argues that understanding any written work will involve answering, in some degree, the questions in Figure 1–2.

The first two questions go together, as do the last two. The first two deal with relatively stable elements in a work, with foils (What versus what?) and the associations that each foil has (What goes with what?). Although the word *foil* applies properly to literary characters, the notion of mutually illuminating contrasts also applies to other elements, such as the symbolism of "home" and the "far country" in Luke's story. In principle, any two elements may not only be contrasted for their oppositions but also compared for their similarities; and "What versus what?" could also generate relations between three or even four elements (characters, acts, sym-

> A. What goes with what? (Identification; Association)
> B. What versus what? (Contrast; Opposition; Conflict)
> C. What follows what? (Progression; Sequence)
> D. What becomes what? (Change; Transformation; How are things different at the end of the story than they were at the beginning?)

Figure 1–2.

bols). Nevertheless, it proves easier to grasp the relations between two elements at one time than between three or four. For example, even though I led the discussion of Situation in Luke's story to consider four columns of material—the prodigal son's view of "home" and the "far country" versus the father's—I worked toward it by means of one set of contrasts at a time. In teaching and in writing, compare and contrast two elements at a time, not three. When the mind has to juggle too many balls at once, they all fall to the ground.

The second two questions deal with the temporal movement of a literary work, its progression from scene to scene and the changes that the action brings about in the characters. This last question has long and rightly been favored by teachers: *What have the characters learned? How are things different at the end than they were at the beginning of the work?* Oedipus, the self-ignorant king in happiness, becomes Oedipus the self-knowing beggar in misery; Elizabeth Bennet, with no marital prospects and disdainful of Mr. Darcy's pride and prejudice, learns to know her own pride and prejudice in the course of falling in love with Darcy and becoming his wife. Identifying, defining, and evaluating the important changes in a literary work are crucial to the full experience of reading. While it may be obvious that Elizabeth Bennet is better off at the end of *Pride and Prejudice* than she was at the beginning, exploring precisely how and why she is so calls for careful assessment. And the question, "Is Oedipus better off at the end of the play than he was at the beginning?" may yield some surprising affirmations.

Question C, in contrast, proves rather difficult for young people. When a story "flows" (their word), they experience it as one thing after another in the "natural order." They do not normally think about the structure of a plot, and they generally resist thinking about artistic contrivances. Students prefer "realistic" stories and films, failing to recognize that they experience as "realistic" only what is most conventional in an art form, only what they have come to expect as normal. Yoko Ono's eight-hour film of a man sleeping is entirely realistic, but not what they want to see. Hence, getting students to attend to *What follows what?* in a disciplined way requires a teacher's persistence and patience, for they must learn not to see the work as natural but to understand it as deliberately constructed. Nevertheless, the rewards can be great, as I hope to show.

To answer *What follows what?* we must break the work down into its parts and see how they go together. The first of these is often done for us in a literary work: the poem has stanzas, the play comes in Acts and Scenes. Defining the relations between these successive parts, however, involves inquiring into the design of the work and how it has designs on its audience. In other words, a literary work is designed to work on its audience, and exploring the relations between its parts involves defining the effects that these parts are intended to produce. It requires exact attention to the structure and rationale underlying a literary work.

Next, I will briefly do what I assign students to do to illustrate the results of attending to "What follows what?": (1) Divide "The Prodigal Son" into Episodes (or Scenes), (2) give each one a title that summarizes its essence, (3) describe the action briefly, and (4) show how each episode connects to its neighbors to form a meaningful Progression. I will only go as far as the prodigal son's return home (Luke 15:11–24), starring (*) in advance comments that bring out the rationale of its Progression. To be sure, the episodes could be further subdivided and described somewhat differently. I am not claiming to present *the* analysis of this story's progressive structure, only to illustrate how it might be explored.

Episode I, "The Departure" (Luke 15:11–16) The prodigal son asks for and receives his inheritance, turns it into cash, journeys to the far country, spends everything, experiences famine, and becomes someone's servant as a swine-herd, so hungry that he would gladly "have filled his belly with the husks that the swine did eat." (*) The plot curves in a continuous movement: The boy's physical movement *away* from his father proves simultaneously a moral or spiritual movement *down*, for no task could be more degrading to a Jew than to be in service to "unclean" (forbidden) animals like swine. The story also contains, but does not develop, a meditation on friendship, for where are all the "friends" with whom the prodigal son partied away his money? The final words of this episode, "and no man gave unto him," imply that the "friends" on whom he spent his inheritance do not return his liberality when he is impoverished.

Episode II, "The Return" (verses 17–20a) Having hit bottom, the prodigal son decides to return home and ask his father to make him a servant in the household, for he is "no more worthy to be called [his] son" (17–19), and he makes the journey (20a). (*) The physical return home begins with the boy's returning to himself: "And when he came to himself" (17). The phrase implies that he had lost himself in the adventure of his "Departure"—departing from home, he departed from his real self, and coming to himself again, he recognizes his plight and decides to return. (*) His morally downward movement in Episode I is implicitly recognized in the way he expresses his decision to return, "I will *arise* and go to my father" (18). His return, therefore, is represented as a moral ascent. (*) Note that the story cares no more for the arduous journey ("And he arose and came to his father") than for the lurid details of his "riotous living" (13). Not events but moments of decision are given the greatest attention—"inward" attitudes and choices prove more important to this story than "outer" happenings as consequences. Imagine how different would be "The Prodigal Son: The Movie."

Attempting to define the character of the prodigal son's change, as with any literary character, leads to the borderland between defining and evaluating. Is the boy repentant? If so, what is the character of his repentance? Does repentance demand sorrow? Is he sorry for what he did, or for how it turned out? If the boy merely regrets the consequences of his foolishness, is he "repentant"? Does his return imply a moral conversion? Has he had a "change of heart"? Or is he merely desperately hungry and in need? In other words, is he still the opportunist he was earlier? Is there some third option between "change of heart" and "still an opportunist"? And so on.

Episode III, "Celebration" (verses 20b–24) The father sees his son while the boy is still a great way off, has compassion for him, runs to him, and embraces him joyfully (20b). The boy begins the speech (21) he planned earlier (18–19) but does not get to the request he intended ("Make me as one of thy hired servants," verse 19), for his father commands that he be given the signs of sonship (the best robe, a ring) and that a feast be given to celebrate his return home.

How should we define this episode? Because the theme of this story is often said to be "forgiveness," this episode is often considered a scene of forgiveness. In my view, however, "forgiveness" radically misses the point of this particular episode, apt though it may be for the story as a whole. From the boy's perspective, forgiveness is out of the question—he admits to his father that he is "no more worthy to be called thy son" (19, 21). At the beginning of the story, he took and wasted his inheritance and repudiated all relations with his father; having "un-sonned" himself, as it were, he only seeks work as a servant. From the father's perspective, on the other hand, *forgiveness is also out of the question*—his son may have repudiated him, but he has never repudiated his son. The father does not say, "I forgive you; from now on, be a good boy." After all, at the beginning of the story, he responded to the boy's extraordinary and insulting request for his inheritance by giving it. He has forgiven the boy's insults all along. In this episode, he does nothing but welcome, rejoice, and celebrate.

(*) In other words, familiarity with this story perhaps leads us to miss its most important feature, *surprise*, and pursuing "What follows what?" points it up. The prodigal son's resolution to return leads us to expect a scene of forgiveness—surely the father will not allow his destitute son to starve to death. The story has kept our attention on the boy, on his acts, words, and hopes: It leads us to see the father, as it were, from the prodigal son's perspective. Hence, when we do see the father, we should experience astonishment. Literarily, the father acts in a way that quite exceeds our expectations, yet his acts make sense in light of his understanding that his son, who was dead, is alive again (24). At the same time, the father's welcoming the prodigal home offends the older brother's conventional sense of right and wrong.

Now "What follows what?" is closely linked with the other three questions, for the story is a coherent whole and the questions aim to help us reflect on its coherence. I have already raised questions about how to define the prodigal's change or transformation (question #4) and will not pursue them further. Instead, I wish to point out a recurring image that further defines the differences between "home" and the "far country" in the story as a whole—the image of eating. When the boy wastes his inheritance with "riotous living" in the far country, he engages in wild revelry, and it leads to his ruin, morally, financially, and physically. As a result, he nearly starves to death. The progress of the narrative links "wild revelry" and "famine" with the "far country." Although the famine may seem a kind of accident (14), the boy's wasting all his resources is not—his destitution is self-imposed. He grows so hungry that he would gladly "have filled his belly with the husks that the swine did eat" (16). In other words, the far country is the land of riotous living and starvation, where excessive eating and drinking lead to famine, where disorderly feasting verges on death.

The feast of the fatted calf on his return, in contrast, presents an orderly celebration, a merrymaking. This feast, like all feasts, partakes of a certain excess, not wild but measured, for it expresses joy, not the pursuit of novel pleasures. Here again, putting two columns on the board for the two kinds of "festival" proves a valuable exercise in interpreting and vocabulary. Young people intuit something of the difference between carousal and merrymaking, between a wild party and a good one, and this exercise asks them to find words for their intuitions.

✸

This chapter has presented an array of questions to be used in understanding and teaching a literary work. They are listed right before this chapter for easy reference. The first set of questions is numbered and deals directly with a character's motives for an act; these are primarily interpretive. A second set of questions is designated by letters and is designed to clarify the structures of any written work, thus it proves both factual and interpretive. A third set of questions is explicitly evaluative. Nevertheless, we would do well to remember that these three kinds of questions—factual, interpretive, and evaluative—can be *distinguished, but not separated*. Because interpretation provides the bridge from fact to evaluation, the questions easily lead readers to both factual and evaluative issues and prove useful as guides, as rules of thumb.

These questions do not constitute a complete method of interpretation. They can get you started, and even take you quite a way, but they cannot replace your own desire to understand. You can use them in any order or in any combination. Rarely will you want to use all of them in reading or, especially, in teaching. Still, as we have seen, these are *sets* of questions, and each set of questions interlocks, and all three sets are related. Hence, pursuing one or two questions will soon implicitly bring the others into play, which is quite good enough. In this way, they help you generate material for reflection, but the questions do not tell you how you should reflect on a literary work. Let me say again: These questions simply make explicit what skillful readers already do habitually. They will help you teach your students how to tap into their own experiences and intellectual resources as they read. As they learn to think more carefully about what they read, students will care more deeply about what they read. They will be meeting real people in books, and these real people will help them to understand themselves, their friends, and the world.

Provocation #1

Leading a Discussion: Asking Questions

Leading a discussion is not hard, at least in theory. All you have to do is ask a real question and let the students answer it. Yet many of us struggle even when we attempt just one of these. Sometimes a teacher asks a real question, but the students let him answer it. They just wait him out—they do not answer, because they know he will, once the silence gets to him. In other cases, they do not answer because they think he likes to answer his own questions, because he prefers his answer to theirs. The teacher may admit this to himself, but not to others. To his colleagues he complains that his students just will not participate in discussions.

But he is rare. Many teachers are forced to answer their own questions because they have not yet learned how to formulate real ones. We have all done this and have experienced the deadly silence that follows. In my case, I was so oriented toward certain answers that I could only formulate what I now call "pseudo-questions." The ways to botch a question may be infinite, but the types are few. A brief survey of botches may help us to sight the target.

The first type fails through excessive generality. It is the professorial question: "What's going on in this text?" If you are teaching graduate students who have thoroughly prepared their work and lust to display their learning and acumen, this question may occasionally work. But not always, even then. The professor pictures himself as broad-minded, open, nondirective, and inviting. But students soon discover that his protested ardor for discussion proves insincere. He really wants to be the main show, and his slovenly question is a way of holding center stage. Even professors who select students to start class with a brief report on the reading often fall victim to fascination with their own voices. As one student told me, "The report only has to be two minutes, and then Dr. X goes on for half an hour."

A good question is a specific question, though not one with a specific answer. Now a factual question is a specific question with a specific answer. A well-prepared student will usually answer it, but it will not generate discussion. In general, because students tend to be afraid of being wrong in public, they shy away from any question with one right answer. For this reason, an interpretive question, which can be answered in several different defensible ways, generates a real discussion because it is a real question. But when the teacher poses a good interpretive question, she must learn to let the students answer it in their ways and work with the answers they give; otherwise, she has only posed a pseudo-question.

One specific pseudo-question is the "answered question," also known as the "Isn't it" question or the non-question. To consider its various forms, voice the following:

Does the prodigal son leave home to discover his identity?

Isn't it true that the prodigal son leaves home to discover his identity?

Doesn't the prodigal son leave home to discover his identity?

The prodigal son leaves home to discover his identity, doesn't he?

Few things oppress a class like the answered question. The sham is so blatant. This pseudo-question announces to the class the subject of the teacher's following remarks. No one will answer such a question. No one has ever answered such a question. Yet I have seen teachers pose the non-question, look expectantly at the room for ten seconds, then breathe a sigh that is supposed to mean, "Well, I've tried again," before going on to say what they always knew they would say.

Another specific pseudo-question is the "fishing for an answer," or the "Read my mind" question:

T: Why does the prodigal son leave home?
S1: He doesn't like his father.
T: Well, maybe. (*Hmmm. I hadn't thought of that.*) But probably not. (*And I don't want to think about it now.*) Why does the prodigal son leave home?
S2: He doesn't like his brother.
T: No. (*That's not the answer I'm looking for.*) Why does the prodigal son leave home?
S3: He wants to be independent.
T: (*brightening*) Close. (*You're getting warm, class.*) Anyone else? (*If no one else speaks, I can now legitimately supply the correct answer.*)
S4: He wants to find himself.
T: Yes. (*At last!*) He leaves home to Discover His Own Identity. (*That's a better way of phrasing it. It's the way I phrase it myself.*)

And now that the class has successfully read the teacher's mind, and he has (as he phrases it to himself) "had some discussion," he can go on to talk about Discovering Your Own Identity. ("After all, this is a highly relevant topic for my students. They can benefit from my wisdom on this subject.")

The problem here is that this teacher has an agenda. He conceives teaching, not as an exploration with students that begins from their nascent understandings, but as "communicating knowledge," which means talking about his own understanding. Hence, though he has asked an excellent question, in his mouth it is not a real one, for it has a specific answer—the Answer He Is Looking For.

Let us imagine a dialogue beginning with the same words but asked as a real question. The teacher recognizes that the prodigal son has many possible motives for leaving home, and she is willing to work with the answers that students give. She does not need to foresee all of these. She may be pleasantly surprised by a valid insight she has not considered. She may be unpleasantly surprised by an off-the-wall answer. But she has follow-up questions that enable her students to "winnow the wheat from the chaff":

> T: Why does the prodigal son leave home? Bill.
>
> BILL: He doesn't like his father.
>
> T: Why do you say that?
>
> BILL: I don't know. (*I don't like my father, and I'm thinking about leaving home.*)
>
> T: Is there any evidence in the story for the boy not liking his father?
>
> BILL: I'm not sure. (*I spoke too soon. I'm going to duck this one.*) It just seemed that way to me.
>
> T: Does anyone agree with him? Can anyone help him out? Jane.
>
> JANE: Well, the father runs the whole show at home. If the prodigal son doesn't like home, he doesn't like his father.
>
> T: Couldn't he like his father but still need to leave, Jane?
>
> JANE: Not really. Leaving home means rejecting the father. At some level or in some way, he doesn't like home or father, and that's why he leaves.
>
> T: Bill, what do you think of that?
>
> BILL: It sounds good to me. (*Whew.*)
>
> T: It sounds good to me, too. I hadn't thought of that idea before. Because the father gives the boys their inheritance, he seems quite generous to me. But the prodigal son still might dislike him. Thank you, Bill and Jane, you taught me something new about this story. Is there anything else the prodigal son doesn't like about home?
>
> JILL: His older brother.
>
> T: Who agrees with Jill? (*Many hands.*) Okay, Jill, tell us why you think he doesn't like his older brother, and Jack, you comment after her.

JILL: The older brother drips with jealousy when the father throws the party for the prodigal son's homecoming. That jealousy has been around for a long time?

T: Jack?

JACK: I agree. Look at verse 29, all that resentment: "Lo, these many years *I* have served *you*, and I *never* disobeyed your command; yet you never gave *me* a kid, that *I* might make merry with *my* friends." He's whining.

T: Do you blame him?

JACK: No.

T: Why not?

STEVE: Jack is an older brother.   (*Everyone laughs.*)

T: All right. Jack, I'll come back to you in a moment. How many in here are older siblings? How many are younger? How many of you, like Jack, do not blame the older brother for resenting the prodigal son?

This teacher speaks as little as possible, but not because she has nothing to say. She wants to discover what her students think and aims to help them think more deeply. She takes a student's answer and turns it either back to the student or to the class. "Why do you say that?" and "What is your evidence for that?" compels a student to support his answers. Often, however, an insight exceeds a student's capacity to state precisely what gave rise to it. Rather than provide the answer herself, the teacher asks the class to provide one: "Who agrees with him? Can anyone help him out?" This teacher turns every question back to the class. She has a rule for herself: Never answer a question unless no one in class can answer it; or: Never do for students what they can do for themselves.

Moreover, her final questions in this dialogue move toward setting up a minidebate between the students favoring the older brother's perspective, resenting the feast for his scapegrace brother, and those supporting the father's point of view, that such a celebration is right and good. Both sides will explain and justify their perspectives. Perhaps the two halves of the blackboard will record the evidence for both sides. Certainly the minidebate will sharpen and clarify the students' understanding of the characters and the perspectives involved. Should one side flag, the teacher will ask a leading question or two to help it.

At the end, the whole class will be asked to vote in favor of the father's or the older brother's view (no abstentions allowed). Perhaps the students will then be asked to write three good sentences summarizing the reasons for their views. This will fix the discussion in their minds and compel them to write as specifically as they can while the issues remain fresh. The intellectual exercise of oral discussion will be completed by the more exacting labor of writing. This pause for silent work also gives the teacher a breather. She then asks some students to read their sentences aloud. This reviews both sides of the discussion briefly and perhaps allows her to make some helpful and encouraging comments about the students' writing.

Teaching in this way proves exciting and tiring. The excitement comes from the students' interest and involvement in the discussion. They are led to feel that their ideas are valuable and that their participation is essential to the class. The fatigue emerges from the excitement. You can never predict what direction a discussion will take, and two different discussions of the same work on the same day will rarely unfold in the same way. Your lesson plan may go out the window, depending on what the students have to say. Or it may not, but at least it becomes subject to negotiation. On the other hand, how many teachers keep control of a class and of its content by boring the students into a stupor?

You can teach in this way and still keep a hold onto your lesson by some advance planning. You can tell students ahead of time what your opening question will be for the next class, assigning two to three students to prepare opening remarks. If you use Reading Journals (see Provocation #10), you can give the opening question as a Study Question to the whole class. In either case, you need a good interpretive question—one that has several possible answers about which students may disagree.

Another way involves trimming your lesson plan back to one or two essential foci for discussion and making sure that each class spends some time on one or both. In other words, you plan only half of the period. For example, for a single period on "The Prodigal Son" you decide that your two foci will be (1) the boy's motives for leaving home and (2) the differences between the two brothers. Other possibilities you let go or save for another day: the father's motives, feasting imagery, the question of whether the prodigal's "conversion" is sincere or not, and so on. These may come up in the time you have left unplanned, or they may not.

You begin the period by probing for the students' insights, interests, questions, and problems. One of your set topics will soon emerge and then you can become more directive—make two columns on the board for a compare-and-contrast, or make a list of possible motives for a character's actions. Anything on the board is the property for the whole class and test-eligible, and students take things down. But the list of points comes from *their* answers, perhaps prodded and elaborated on by means of your questions and comments. Each of your several classes working on the same piece or story will come up with the same lists, though not in the same sequence. If your students compare classes, they will think each one is different; however, you will have some common material to put on a test, so school will still be "the way it spozed to be." At the same time, your students will be involved in discussions and debates, with you moderating and fomenting. They will be practicing the arts of English—thinking, reflecting, discussing, with perhaps some writing added.

Now this scenario assumes that students have done the assigned reading and, hence, it may assume too much. That is why I recommend Reading Journals, though you may prefer written or oral quizzes. Perhaps you begin class with some factual questions, to gauge the students' grasp of the reading, and then move on to interpretive and evaluative ones. This hierarchy of three levels of question proves useful, as a theory. Students must first grasp the factual details of a work in order to interpret them, and they must interpret the characters and their acts in order to evaluate them. It seems to make sense to progress from factual to interpretive to evaluative questions, and some textbooks now compose study questions according to this scheme.

But the theory should be considered only a rule of thumb. Useful as this hierarchy of questions is, the mere definition of an act implicitly contains, or inclines toward, an evaluation. Certainly adolescents tend to become aware of their evaluative responses first and then construe both "facts" and interpretation to be in accord with what they know they feel. They are much better at evaluating character and act than they are at supporting their evaluations by pointing to factual details interpreted in a certain way. Contrary to the hierarchical sequence of questions, adolescents begin with evaluations, locate some "facts" to justify them, and either neglect the mediating interpretation or presume it to be obvious. How often does a boy—and it is almost always a boy—assert, with brash assurance, an evaluation that he considers obviously true, only to find it a minority opinion of one.

Perhaps my experience with adolescents, even though long, has been unduly limited, or I have not understood it correctly. But because I find them quick to evaluate and to justify their judgments by an appeal to "facts," I emphasize the interpretive question. For one thing, it draws their attention to the middle ground that they tend to ignore. For another, it allows for easy movement to both the factual details of the work and to students' evaluations of character and act. Hence, interpretive questions open up the work and the class to the kind of engaged, exacting, open, yet probing discussion I have been recommending.

Perhaps you never had a teacher who led discussions in this rather open-ended way—I did not either—and you hesitate to begin the adventure of teaching in this fashion for lack of a model. But you are in luck: There is a master teacher, expert in the art of asking questions, still working with students, and the technology is available for you to participate in his discussions. You can attend them, listen to his questions, answer them yourself, and listen while others try to answer. He has an international reputation for excellence in teaching by posing apt questions—his name is Socrates.

Plato's Socratic dialogues remain unsurpassed as representations of teaching and learning. Learning, broadly conceived, may be shown in any number of literary works, for we often talk about what a character learns from her experience in a novel or play. But representations of successful teaching occur far less often. Plato's Socratic dialogues—the shorter ones usually considered his early works—are exquisite little dramas, where intellectual give-and-take reveals the characters of the participants. If you think of Socrates as merely the mouthpiece for Plato's views, you have never read these dialogues, or you have studied them under someone who did not understand them. Socrates' art of questioning is brilliantly displayed in the *Laches*, *Lysis*, *Charmides*, *Crito*, *Alcibiades I*, and *Gorgias*. If you find fallacies in the arguments, you should assume that Plato put them there for a reason. If you find the characters funny or odd, they are meant to be. Study one of these dialogues. They are all beautifully constructed literary works, and they deserve the close attention of every teacher who wants to learn how to lead a discussion by asking real questions.

2

James Joyce's "Eveline": A Summary and Analysis of Characters and Motives

James Joyce's "Eveline" tells the same story as "The Prodigal Son," but with a few twists. Eveline is a nineteen-year-old Irish girl in Dublin, circa 1900, standing at the crossroads of her life. Should she stay at home with her father, who is often drunk and threatens her with violence? Or should she go off to Buenos Aires with Frank, a sailor who has promised to marry her there? When her mother was dying, Eveline promised her that she would "keep the home together as long as she could," and two children are in her care, probably orphaned relatives. She earns a small salary as a shop girl and keeps house for her father and these children—a hard life, but a familiar one. The prospect of a new life in a far country attracts her, but she hardly knows Frank at all and remains unsure of her feelings for him, and of his for her.

This story is divided spatially into two unnumbered parts. ("Eveline" is printed in its entirety in Appendix B at the back of this book.) The first and longest part takes place at home: Eveline is sitting and reminiscing about her life, trying to decide whether she should stay with her father or leave with Frank. It ends with her recalling her mother's death "in final craziness," and she stands up, determined to leave. The second part takes place at the harbor station, where Eveline remains rooted to the spot as Frank boards the ship, deaf to his calls, refusing to leave. She turns out to be, not the prodigal son who leaves home, but the dutiful daughter who stays, with her prodigal father.

This structure gives rise to two main questions about Eveline's motives, because she decides in favor of two different Acts. *Why, in part 1, does she decide to leave home? Why, in part 2, does she decide to stay?* The story is told by an omniscient narrator—I will call him "Joyce"—but largely from Eveline's point of view. In part 1, we enter into her reminiscences, her process of thought, and often into snatches of her speech. We thereby see the limitations of her perspective as she struggles to make a decision. Joyce puts us at a sympathetic, yet ironic, distance from Eveline—we feel the narrowness of her situation, even as we see how little she understands. But would our decision be any easier, or better, than hers? This beautiful and troubling story works wonders of complexity in very few pages. For that reason, it is a joy to teach.

Teaching "Eveline"

I taught this story to ninth graders for several years, and I want to recommend my way of teaching it because "Eveline" empowers the students to use their own intellectual resources. In general, I teach the story by leading my students further and further into it, explaining only what they cannot understand on their own (see Provocation #3). I have them read and reread the story during three to five class periods, guiding them with questions. The story is so brief that it can be reread easily, and so complex that it rewards rereading. At the end of this process, the students will have understood a complex story "on their own," with only a little direct help from you.

This process empowers students in several ways. First, it encourages open discussion. On their first reading, the students respond to whatever they find interesting and they discuss it, with you managing, but not directing, their discussion. They generally head for the central issues of interpretation and evaluation, where they will disagree with one another. All you need to do is keep them on one topic (more or less) at a time, call names, and let them argue their views. Because they will be rereading the story and rethinking these issues, a student can be wrong and you need not correct him. Perhaps the classmates who disagree with him will change his mind, but rereading the story also enables him to rethink his earlier view. Subsequent readings are a bit more directive for homework, but not for discussion, as you will see.

Second, my questions about motives deal with fundamental human realities. Even students who do not care about literature care about people: their values, feelings, choices, decisions, acts, and consequences. The questions about motives are what I call "real questions" (see Provocation #1): They demand attention to factual details but always lead readers beyond the facts to interpretation and evaluation, where there is no unambiguously right answer. Hence, the questions give rise to discussion and debate. Even when students agree about the facts, they will understand their meaning (or significance) differently, because their different life experiences have led them to different values and beliefs. As a result, class discussion proves an indirect means of self-knowledge. By the way, it is best to keep it indirect, for there is no better discussion-stopper than saying to a class of teenagers, "Your views on Eveline's Moral Character and your evaluations of her Act say a great deal about the kinds of persons you are."

Finally, the questions used in this book deal with fundamental literary patterns—they point to "how stories and plays work." For that reason, regular practice in using these questions makes students more skillful readers because it clues them in to the sorts of things to look for. But these patterns rarely emerge clearly on a first reading, even for experienced readers like ourselves: We find it easier to grasp "how a story works" on a second reading. Hence, I recommend that students read some short stories two or more times. In that way, they will acquire reflective familiarity with these fundamental literary patterns. In other words, experience with second and third readings makes them far better at reading a new story for the first time.

I realize that five readings seems excessive, but if you read "Eveline" yourself two or three times in conjunction with this chapter, you will see how rich it is. Because it concerns themes close to adolescent hearts, it excites lively discussion and debate. Hence, a sequence of classes will enable you to assign an analytical essay and receive very good work: Students already understand the issues thoroughly, so they can concentrate on organization and expression. Also, their familiarity with the work may lead to several other exercises in speaking and writing, with good results (see Provocation #2). The sequence to use is described briefly here, but it also provides the framework of my analysis throughout this chapter.

Reading #1. Getting Acquainted

This is a "get acquainted" reading—you want the students read the work and respond to it. You might ask them to write a two-page (handwritten) freewriting response because this ensures their thoughtful preparation for discussion (see Provocation #10, "Reading Journals"). You might tell one or two students ahead of time that they will begin the discussion by choosing one issue and summarizing their ideas. (This is one good way of involving shy students in discussion; when they know ahead of time that they will speak first, they get ready.) Then you manage a discussion in whatever way you think best. Keep debate orderly, but let students agree and disagree about whatever seems important to them; you will then have a good sense about how much they have understood. Because you are going to have them reread the story, premature evaluations and even misunderstandings do no harm. (I have had a class of ninth graders insist that "Eveline's father is a nice man and he really loves her." A second reading took care of that.) The level of discussion should be "a first take on plot and characters." Students generally go straight to the central issues, interpreting and evaluating Characters and Acts. Hence, they typically raise questions like these:

What do you think of Eveline's father?

What do you think of Frank?

What do you think of Eveline?

Why did she decide to leave? Why did she change her mind and decide to stay?

Did she make the right decision? Why or why not?

What is different at the end of the story than at the beginning?

Students will raise most of these questions on their own, and you will have no trouble filling a 45-minute period with discussion.

Notice that these questions mix interpretation and evaluation: "What do you think of Eveline's father?" asks for an evaluative description of his Moral Character. Although I suggested in Chapter 1 that premature evaluation should be avoided, we were working there on the model of "one reading, with one discussion." Here, in contrast, the first discussion is preliminary, and all the crucial issues raised by these questions will be revisited, in greater depth, after students have reread the story. Students' answers to these questions let you know how well they have understood the story, what details they have missed or misunderstood, and so on. Above all, since evaluative questions excite the most interested responses, debating them—for students will disagree—imparts energy to the work of rereading and reconsidering.

They are likely to raise one question that they cannot answer on their own, because they know too little about Ireland in 1900: *Why doesn't Eveline just leave home and live on her own?* Aside from her promise to her mother, "to keep the home together as long as she could," she cannot support herself on her own. She earns seven shillings per week, a pitiful wage, and she does not have the education to earn more. With seven shillings per week, she could not even afford rent and food, much less anything else. In the United States today, young women often share an apartment, but this was unheard of in Dublin in 1900. She might have left home for a job in service, as a maid or a cook for a wealthy family but, aside from breaking her promise to her mother, she seems to have no special aptitude for these jobs. There are only two other options for an unmarried girl: to become a nun or a prostitute. Both are unthinkable for Eveline. Behind Joyce's story lies English colonial rule over Ireland and its exploitation of the Irish economy. Eveline must live at home, in order to live at all, as long as she stays in Ireland. Her one hope of liberation lies in Frank's offer to take her to Buenos Aires and marry her there.

The sequence of questions I suggest for subsequent readings is based partly on the story itself, and partly on what young readers are inclined to notice. The story itself turns on Eveline's choice between two alternatives: staying at home with her father or going away with Frank. These alternatives represent her Situation, and they are explored fully in part 1. Note that part 1 is four-times longer than part 2— it sets up not only Eveline's decision to leave home, at the end of part 1, but also its reversal in part 2. Hence, when students read the story for the second and third times, they should focus on part 1, even though they should reread the whole story. We need to understand *Why, in part 1, does Eveline decide to leave?* before we come to grips with *Why, in part 2, does she decide to stay?*

Reading #2. Eveline's Situation: Father versus Frank

To understand Eveline's motives in part 1, we must understand her Situation from her perspective. Because students notice characters more readily than they do patterns of imagery, I suggest that the second reading focus on the contrast between her father and Frank. They are character foils, and we explore them by asking *What goes with what?* (Association) for each, and thereby discover *What versus what?* (Contrast). The contrasts between them are extensive, and exploring these leads students to rethink their first impressions of the characters.

Reading #3. Eveline's Situation: Home and Away—Patterns of Imagery

Prominent as the contrasts between Eveline's father and Frank are, her Situation cannot be grasped clearly without exploring the imagery of "home" and "away." Joyce associates "home" with patterns of imagery crucial to the story, and these are not easily seen when attending to characters. For a third reading, then, I suggest that students gather up the images associated with "home" (*What goes with what?*) and think about what they mean. By this time, they are well acquainted with the story, and you might ask them to think about other patterns of imagery, especially music and religion. These recurrent patterns work closely with the father/home versus Frank/away contrasts to illuminate Eveline's Situation. They help students grasp what is at stake for her in this decision.

Reading #4. Eveline's Moral Character, and Her Motives in Part 1

With Eveline's Situation thus fully explored, you might then ask students to describe and evaluate her Moral Character for the fourth reading. This description and evaluation should make sense of her Moral Character in both parts of the story. Because the story is told through her consciousness, her Moral Character is presented indirectly, while her father and Frank are presented directly. Hence, it takes considerable acquaintance with the story before young readers can articulate their sense of Eveline as a person. To be sure, they will have strong impressions of her in their very first reading, but these tend to be summary judgments—"She's a wimp, she should have left with Frank" or "Her father needs her and she stays because she's good." They do not begin to understand the complexity of Eveline's Moral Character until they come to feel the pulls of both alternatives sympathetically. But once the students have debated their evaluative descriptions of her Moral Character, the components are in place for an understanding of all her motives for leaving in part 1.

Reading #5. Eveline's Motives for Staying in Part 2

Because part 2 is so much shorter than part 1, its action is swift, and students often have trouble picking up the clues that reveal why Eveline suddenly decides to stay, reversing her decision in part 1. In the discussion of part 2 that follows, I suggest a set of questions that will help students grasp what is happening. Now that they understand the story thoroughly, they enjoy debating—*Did Eveline make the right decision in the end?* As adolescents experiencing the tension between attachment to family and the desire for independence, they tend to argue for one side or the other; few are inclined to sit on the fence.

❈

This suggested sequence of rereadings is not a blueprint, only a plausible sketch. Different teachers and different classes catch on to things in different ways, and English teachers cannot always devote a whole period to discussion of a story. In my experience, students are more attracted to characters than to recurrent patterns of imagery, and they understand direct presentation (for example, father and Frank) more readily than indirect presentation (Eveline herself). One of my tasks is to help them understand how recurrent patterns of imagery help all of us grasp Situation and Moral Character (see Provocation #6). Another is to show readers how point of view, voice, and tone give them a powerful sense of Eveline before they begin to think about her (see Provocation #4). But because students respond to characters and their acts as "real," and think of recurrent images and point of view as "merely literary," I begin with the human realities of a story and later connect its "merely literary" aspects to persons, motives, and acts.

Some teachers may want to spread these readings out through more than five classes, perhaps using some of the exercises suggested in Provocation #2. Others may recognize that their students do not have the patience for five readings of one short story, and they will want to cut back to, say, three. In any event, students will be astonished by how close-knit the details of the story are—"Did Joyce really *intend* all these things we are finding?" If you later assign students to write their own short stories (see Provocation #5), their close study of "Eveline" should help them write more close-knit stories, and ones that are more finely crafted than you or they would have expected.

Why, in Part 1, Does Eveline Decide to Leave Home?

Situation. What is Eveline's Situation, as she understands it?

Father versus Frank The students' first reading of the story has acquainted them with the characters. To be more accurate, a first reading acquaints students *with their impressions* of these characters rather than with the characters themselves. Their impressions are not wholly wrong, but they do tend to be one-sided—Frank is usually romanticized, and Eveline's father sometimes is. The second reading is designed so that students can understand Eveline's perceptions, not their own impressions, of these two men, an understanding that is well-founded in the story's details. Eveline is facing a choice between her father and Frank, and we want to know what she thinks about each of them (*What goes with what?*). She does not find it an easy one. Hence, *both men have good points and bad points*. Moreover, they are character foils (*What versus what?*), so their character traits are opposed to one another. Sometimes the opposition becomes explicit: Eveline recalls her father's verbal abuse of her, and a page later she remembers Frank's kindness. But often the contrasts are implied—her father is often intoxicated, yet there is no mention of Frank's ever being drunk.

If your students are unfamiliar with character foils, you might prepare them for the next assignment by explaining why literature so often works with oppositions. In the real world, when we have to decide between two choices, we tend to look for their differences and what these differences mean, or add up to. We have a natural tendency to turn these differences into contrasts, to make our choice easier by making it clearer. Literary works do the same thing, but more intensely. They usually concern crisis situations because these excite our interest—so much is at stake in the decision. Hence, literary works not only heighten differences into contrasts but even into opposition and conflict. The oppositions represent contrasting values, contrasting ways of living, loving, acting. Eveline's father and Frank, then, are not merely two guys in a story; they do not symbolize Eveline's life choices so much as *embody* them. She must decide between them "now," this evening, when the story is set. No compromise is possible because Frank leaves this evening. And there is no third option: She either goes with him, or she stays with her father.

Hence, we want to understand Eveline's Situation in this choice: *How does Eveline view her father and Frank?* This involves gathering together the factual details about each *in order to see what they mean to Eveline*. Because the story is told through her consciousness, we do not need to make a special effort to adopt her point of view. But we can and should attempt to evaluate it. I suggest, then, that you link the following two assignments to a second reading:

1. What is Eveline's Situation? How does she view her father? How does she view Frank? Because these two men are character foils, make a list of eight to ten contrasts between them, based on details in the story. Because her decision is not easy, some contrasts will favor Frank, and some her father. Then write two to four sentences explaining what these contrasts mean as life choices for Eveline. What does life with her father mean to her? What does life with Frank mean to her?

2. Is Eveline's understanding true? She knows her father very well, of course. How well does she know Frank? Are they in love, or not? Should she trust him, and why, or why not? Answer these questions in a short paragraph.

As you will see, these two assignments lead us more deeply into the complexity of Eveline's Situation.

You might begin a class by assembling a master list of contrasts between Eveline's father and Frank, discussing their meaning for Eveline as the list develops. Because students tend not to separate their "positive" from their "negative" details, you might also find it useful to divide the board into two halves: Father (–) versus Frank (+) on one side, and Father (+) versus Frank (–) on the other. (For your convenience in checking details in the story, I have put quotation marks around phrases taken directly from "Eveline.")

Father (–)	**Frank (+)**
violent	not violent
unkind	"very kind"
stingy, mean	generous
selfish	unselfish
unmanly	"manly"
a closed heart	"open-hearted"
"strutting," proud	natural, normal
no music in him	"fond of music"
Irishman in Ireland	Irishman, a "sailor"
dislikes foreigners	an outsider

Father (+)	**Frank (–)**
well-known	hardly known at all
old and deep family roots	no roots
loves her, in his way	E. unsure of his love
"becoming old lately, he would miss her"	young, doesn't need E.

What do these contrasts mean for Eveline? Clearly, her father is emotionally unstable and often drunk and violent, yet Eveline struggles to think well of him. Her life at home is familiar, and she believes that her father "would miss her" if she left. She knows that he is attached to her, by some kind of affection or need, and so she recognizes—or tries to recognize—a certain attachment to him. (You might draw students' attention to Eveline's euphemisms in describing her father, which is part of her effort to think well of him, and so to the role of euphemisms in speech generally.) Her father is a bad man, and his violent abuse is damaging to Eveline's heart, physically and spiritually. Nevertheless, she feels the pull of family attachment and duty toward him.

Frank, on the other hand, is young, generous, kind to her, even affectionate, and he offers her a new life. He is everything her father is not. Yet Eveline does not "fly" from her father to Frank. For one thing, she remains unsure of their feelings for one another. He sings her a song about "the lass that loves a sailor," not about a sailor who loves a lass. As for her own feelings, she admits that at first it was "an excitement for her to have a fellow and then she had begun to like him." She never says to herself that she loves him. For another, she has no rooted attachment to Frank, precisely because he is new, unfamiliar. He is something of an unknown, and going away with him is risky.

This leads naturally to the second group of questions: *Is Eveline's understanding true? How well does Eveline know Frank? Are they in love, or not? Should she trust him, and why, or why not?* After thinking about these questions during a second reading, students are less eager to project their own romantic longings onto Frank. It is clear that Eveline and Frank do not know each other well. He has come to Ireland only for "a holiday," and they met only "a few weeks ago." After her father and Frank quarrel, the young couple can only meet "secretly," as when Frank walks her home after work. They have not spent very much time together. But romantically inclined readers often counter that you can know a great deal about a person in a short time. True as this may be, Eveline does not know whether she and Frank love one another. She calls him "her lover" because he is paying attention to her, "courting" her. (It does not suggest that they have gone to bed together—this is Dublin 1900, not the United States 2000, and Eveline is a good girl by the standards of the time.) In her moment of decision at the end of part 1, she thinks that Frank "would give her life, *perhaps love*, too" (my emphasis). She remains unsure of his feelings and of her own.

Should Eveline trust Frank, or not, and why? In other words, is Frank really frank—honest and sincere? On the one hand, he has paid her a great deal of kind attention, and she finds his manner genuinely frank, "very kind, manly, open-hearted." Eveline finds nothing to suspect in his manner or his actions. On the other hand, her father does—"I know these sailor chaps." But what does he know? He only "knows," of course, what is said proverbially about a sailor—he has a girl in every port, his life is roving and rootless, and so on. For these reasons, it is often felt that sailors make unreliable husbands. But how reliable is such "knowledge"? And why does her father forbid Eveline to see Frank? Is he trying to protect his daughter, or keep an unpaid servant? On the one hand, his motives are suspect; on the other, he might be right about Frank, even with wrong motives.

In other words, "Eveline" is like real life, where decisions must be made on the basis of limited knowledge, often of other people and always of the consequences. Moreover, Eveline is rather naïve. Anyone can call himself a sailor and describe a faraway home. What Frank tells her about "the terrible Patagonians" sounds like something out of a boy's adventure book, and his mention of "the Allan Line going out to Canada" might have been gathered from the shipping pages of a newspaper. On this evidence, Frank might well be a fraud. But Eveline does not consider this possibility, so she is not frightened of being raped and abandoned in a faraway place. After all, she has spent time with him: Shouldn't she be able to sense whether he is sincere? Maybe yes, maybe no. The story invites us to question Frank's frankness, but even though we may ask suspicious questions that Eveline does not ask, we cannot answer them. In the end, we cannot be sure that we know more than she does.

Hence, you might consider asking your students, *Based on all this, what should Eveline do, and why?* By the end of the second reading and discussion, all the students will understand how dangerous Eveline's father is (he is not "a nice man"), yet also how uncertain is her relationship with Frank. Good as it may be for Eveline to get away from home, going away with Frank may well be worse. On the other hand, it may be better. Her father is undoubtedly an evil in her life, but a known one, a familiar evil. Moreover, she has a duty to him, for she promised her dying mother to "keep the home together as long as she could." But how long is that? Her mother, knowing the kind of man her father is, did not ask her to "keep the home together always." Her father's threats of violence have given Eveline "the palpitations"—what we call "panic attacks." Perhaps she has already kept the home together too long, longer than is good for her, and her duty to her father is over. Even so, is Frank trustworthy enough to risk going away with? After a second reading and discussion, all the students will see how difficult it is for Eveline to make a decision.

Eveline's Situation: Home and Away—Patterns of Imagery The third reading is to be oriented primarily to the symbolism of "home" in this story, and so to patterns of imagery that characterize Eveline's Situation and its alternatives. Her Situation cannot be fully understood simply on the basis of contrasts between her father and Frank. There are other aspects of her Situation, especially her sense of home and the place of religion in her life, and Joyce uses patterns of imagery in part 1 to develop these. Students have been responding to the patterns without noticing them. This assignment aims to make them aware of these patterns. As you will see, it also helps them understand why she decides to leave so suddenly, at the end of part 1, and why she stays, in part 2.

But this assignment has another aim as well. Like most Americans, our students think that people and things are real, but symbolism is not. They think they live in a world of things, not reflecting that things are important to them because they have meaning and value, which are not "things." In other words, things are not merely things—they have significance because they participate in patterns of meaning, and *meaning* is fundamentally *symbolic*. A home is not merely a physical space, a background setting—it is filled with objects that are important to us because they have memories and meaning, "sentimental value." Students might think about their own rooms in this regard: "What does your room say about the kind of person you are?" (see Provocation #6). When a writer like Joyce constructs a scene, everything in it is significant. On a third reading, the students, now familiar with the complexity of the characters, can begin to grasp how patterns of imagery relate to the story as a whole.

To help your students grasp these issues in the story, you might give them an assignment like this:

1. What does "home" mean to Eveline? What is "home" associated with in her mind, whether she knows it or not? Reread "Eveline" and keep a running list of everything she mentions in her home. Begin with "dust" and look especially for repeated words or images. Do the same with "away," though the list will be shorter. (Why?)

2. Can you find any larger patterns of imagery in this list? "Home" has deep meanings for everyone, and we are looking for connections between images to understand what "home" means for Eveline.

You might want to prompt them further in various ways, for example: (1) Because "home" is well known to Eveline, it has many more details than "away"—students should list at least fifteen. They should begin with "dust" in the first paragraph; when a word (like "dust") is repeated, it should be recorded as significant. Every household object mentioned is (potentially) meaningful. (2) You might have someone read aloud the first paragraph and ask them to think about certain details, like "dust," "evening" (change), and "invasion" (violent change): *How do these relate to what we already know in the story?*

A more extensive prompt would involve drawing their attention to the "coloured print of the promises made to Blessed Margaret Mary Alacoque" hanging on the wall next to "the broken harmonium," perhaps explaining that a harmonium is a musical instrument. Students do not expect household objects to have symbolic resonance, but they have already noticed that Frank loves music and sings a little, while Eveline's father does not. Hence, they may understand why Joyce puts a "broken harmonium" on the wall. You might also tell them about the "promises made to Blessed [now, Saint] Margaret Mary Alacoque." She saw Jesus in several visions, urging devotion to his Sacred Heart, and promising certain blessings to those who displayed its image in the home and made certain prayers. The promised blessings include: "I will establish peace in their homes; I will comfort them in their afflictions; I will be their secure refuge during life, and above all in death; I will bless every place in which an image of My Heart shall be exposed and honored."

Why did Joyce put these next to "the broken harmonium"? Because the students are familiar with the story, they recognize that these "promises" are broken in this broken home, where there is no peace or comfort or blessing, just as the harmony in this home has long been broken. You can thereby alert them to look out for other images (or key-words) relating to religion and to music in the story. In any event, you understand your students' abilities, so you have a sense of whether they need some hints to get them going, which ones will work best, and of how deeply you want to take them into the story.

"Home" Here is a list of details for "home" in "Eveline." As in the preceding question #1, I have arranged them in running order, not in order of importance, and the list is more detailed than we would expect from our students. In class, however, I ask students for the most important images and patterns first, and why they are important (question #2).

Home (Setting)

evening is "invading the avenue": twilight

curtains are "dusty"

(past) change outside: new bright brick houses built in the field

(past) change "inside": brothers and sisters all grown up, mother dead

imminent change: E. "going to leave her home"

Home (physical): "familiar objects dusted" weekly, so much "dust";
> yellowing photograph of a priest gone to Melbourne;
> "broken harmonium";
> "coloured print of the promises made to Blessed Margaret Mary Alacoque."

"shelter and food: those whom she had known all her life"

hard work "in the house and at business"

(no respect)

"struggle to keep house together": "hard work, a hard life"

evening darkens: she can barely see the whiteness of (farewell) letters in her lap

dusty curtains

mother's death (E. reminded of it by music from a street organ):
> her promise to her mother to keep the home together;
> "close dark room"
> mother raving nonsense near the end:
>> "a life of commonplace sacrifices closing in final craziness"
> E. "must escape"

(home is death): Frank will "save her"

What images in this list are related to one another to form a pattern? What does this pattern mean—how does it work—in the story? The first thing students usually notice are all the images of Eveline's "hard work," "struggle," and fatigue. They are not much younger than she, and they sympathize readily with her burdens: a full-time job outside the home, plus cook and housekeeper inside it. This understanding fits with what they already know of her father's drunkenness and verbal abuse. They easily feel how much Eveline struggles to keep things at home together, and how unfairly her father treats her despite all her hard work.

They also notice how often "dust" is used, and you can help them think about its symbolic resonance beyond "hard work"—"What does 'dust' mean as a symbol for human beings and human life?" For one thing, we associate "dust" with "decay": Not only is the photograph of the priest "yellowing," but this whole home is in decay. The relationship between Eveline and her father is getting worse—he threatens her more often, and she is so frightened that she gets "the palpitations." Indeed, everything in the home has gotten worse since her mother died.

"Dust" also symbolizes human fragility, mortality, death. According to the Bible, human beings were created from "the dust of the ground" (Genesis 2:7), and we return to the dust at death (Genesis 3:19); many burial services intone, "Ashes to ashes, dust to dust." Most important, part 1 climaxes with Eveline's memory of her mother's death "in the close dark room on the other side of the hall." As a place full of dust, this home is a place full of decay and death. Because Eveline has inherited her mother's tasks, she fears that she may have a life like her mother's, "that life of commonplace sacrifices closing in final craziness." By the end of part 1, "home" has acquired the symbolic resonance of a "living death."

The recurrent images of "change" and "darkness" work together with this imagery of "dust" and "death." In fact, because part 1 climaxes with the memory of her mother's death, that event gathers together these separate strands of imagery in a single significant, and terrifying, pattern. The story begins as "evening [invades] the avenue." This is the first of many images of *change* near the beginning of the story: a new house being built, someone moving away, childhood acquaintances now dead. Eveline remembers changes because she is considering a radical change in her life. Frank's coming has changed her life, at least for the time being, and perhaps permanently. At this time of change from day to night, Eveline is herself poised on a transition between the past and the future, between "home" and "away." Part 1 climaxes with her memory of her mother's death—the final transition, the ultimate change.

As she muses, we are to imagine that the room is growing darker, and toward the end of part 1, we are reminded of the fact: "The evening deepened in the avenue. The white of two letters in her lap grew indistinct." Shortly thereafter, this external darkness modulates to Eveline's memory of "the close dark room" of her mother's death. Death is the ultimate darkness. She realizes suddenly that she must "escape" because the spiritual darkness that consumed her mother's life is now consuming her. We use this imagery in everyday speech as a sign of hopelessness, or for the approach of death—"Things are looking dark for him." Eveline's life and future are going to be "dark" in many respects if she stays with her father.

Attending to these patterns of imagery and how they all come together in the climax of part 1 helps students understand why Eveline finally decides to leave so suddenly. You might walk them through the final two paragraphs of part 1; several details prove significant for the reversal in part 2: "Why does Eveline decide actually to leave only now?" She does not want to become like her mother! Thinking about her father's violence, drunkenness, and stinginess does not move her, but remembering her mother's life and death propels her from her chair. She stands up "in a sudden impulse of terror." This is her only physical movement in all of part 1, a significant fact that students generally overlook: She has been sitting and thinking the whole time—all the activity of part 1 is in her memory. That impulse of terror moves her to desire "escape" from the death-full darkness of her home and father, which consumed her mother. Frank, in contrast, is associated with salvation and life—he "would save her," "would give her life, perhaps love, too."

"Away" "Salvation," "life," and "perhaps love" are also the final images associated with "away" in part 1. While the images associated with "home" are many, detailed, and concrete, those characterizing life "away" in Buenos Aires are few, vague, and abstract: "new home," "marriage," "respect." Eveline knows nothing specific about the life Frank wants to lead her to, only that it will be "her new home, in a distant unknown country." She believes, "Then she would be married" and "People would treat her with respect then," unlike now. "She would not be treated as her mother had been." In other words, she can understand life "away" only as opposite to her life in Dublin. At the end of part 1, she suddenly feels her home as like "hell" and "death," and so Frank suddenly represents "salvation" and "life." Again, what she knows, what she could possibly know, proves limited, at best.

Religious Imagery "Salvation" and "life" are also the final religious images in part 1; they stand opposed to "that life of commonplace *sacrifices*" (my emphasis) that brought Eveline's mother to "final craziness." If you did not prompt the students ahead of time by telling them "the promises" of the Sacred Heart displayed on the wall, they might be brought into the discussion now. Students alert to religious images generally notice Eveline praying in part 2, a significant detail in understanding her decision to stay, as we shall see.

Eveline's mother displayed the promises of the Sacred Heart prominently in her home: the failure of her hopes for family harmony is Joyce's anti-Catholic irony. The story raises certain questions about religion and sanctity. Eveline's mother, and Eveline herself, could be considered Christ-like: self-denying, faithful to family, hardworking, dutiful, sacrificing her life and energies for the well-being of others. One can well imagine her friends saying, "That woman is a saint to stay married to that man." Joyce's ironies, I think, criticize sanctity—holiness in this form is "death," and only Frank can "save" Eveline and "give her life." Frank appears as her savior, not Christ, because he will take her away from "that life of commonplace sacrifices." Nevertheless, the Christian tradition has always taught that "death" is a means to "life," that suffering can purify and thereby strengthen the soul, that following Christ always involves self-sacrifice for the good of others. Joyce is deliberately using religious language and imagery to confront us with these issues.

Music Imagery There are only a few music images, and two of them are obvious: Frank loves music and sings to Eveline, and the organ-grinder's tune reminds her of her mother's death. You may need to help the students with the first one—"the broken harmonium." Most will not know that a harmonium is a musical instrument, and they probably have not reflected on the common musical metaphor of "harmony" (or "discord") in a family or group—people being "in tune" (or "out of tune") with one another, and so on. But you can lead them to discover what Joyce's images mean by asking, *When do people sing together, and why?*

This question helps them to reflect on their own experience, and the students discover that musical symbolism is not merely symbolic. Schools have school-songs, and school cheers for athletic events; nations have anthems; and people in church sing hymns together. Clearly, singing together not only expresses, but also reinforces, the unity of many different persons. The different voices come together "as one." Some of your students sing in choirs or other musical groups, and they can explain more precisely what "harmony" means: two different voices singing two different notes, both heard distinctly, yet blending into a third note, all "in tune": *What does "harmony" like this symbolize in a family?* They have no difficulty answering this, and so they grasp why this harmonium is broken.

Eveline's Moral Character. What is her Moral Character?

After three readings, students may be a little restive. They are not used to exploring a story so thoroughly and, not being geniuses themselves, they find it hard to believe that Joyce intended all these patterns of meaning, all this complexity. They want literature to be simple, and they desperately want life and themselves to be simple. I suggest that Eveline's Moral Character be explored in depth only on a fourth reading because, otherwise, students will not appreciate its complex ambiguities.

Because the previous assignments have given students a thorough grasp of Eveline's Situation, analysis of her Moral Character leads naturally into her motives for deciding to leave at the end of part 1. Hence, the assignment might be phrased like this:

1. What is Eveline's Moral Character? What is she like as a person? What aspects of her are good, and bad, and why? Your description of her Moral Character should fit—should make sense of—both her decision to leave in part 1, and her decision to stay in part 2.

2. Why, in part 1, does she decide to leave? What is her Purpose, her Attitude, her Self-Understanding? How does she understand her Situation at the moment of deciding? How does this decision fit her Moral Character?

3. Is her decision to leave good, or bad, and why? Do you approve of it, or disapprove, and why?

Description and evaluation necessarily go together because there can be no "neutral description" of Eveline's Moral Character (or anyone's, in my view). You might ask the students to summarize their views in two or three paragraphs. Or you might ask them to make a list of, say, four to eight points, with a sentence or two explaining each. Perhaps you could select two students ahead of time to begin the discussion, one for "opening remarks" and one for "first reply." This topic generates a vigorous debate: Students know the story well, and so their descriptions are well-grounded, and they also know their evaluations cannot be wrong. They are eager to go.

Let me sketch my understanding of her Moral Character, emphasizing its ambiguity. On the one hand, Eveline can be understood as active, strong, and good: dutiful, self-sacrificing, hardworking, faithful to her family, full of grit and determination "to keep the home together as long as she could." She wants to be "a good girl" and, especially, "a good daughter," and this desire drives her to live up to her responsibilities. As we have seen, these qualities can be illustrated and amplified by many of the details in part 1.

On the other, she can be understood as passive, weak, and therefore bad: dutiful only from social conventions, not from love, and faithful to her family in a bad cause. In this line of argument, her sense of duty arises, not from "strength of character," but from weakness and fear, and so does all her hard work. She is also oppressed by her religion: In part 2, she "[prays] to God to direct her, to show her what [is] her duty." She has no "duty" to Frank, so she stays. She has no love for her father—why should she?—nor any affection for "the two young children who had been left to her charge," yet she chooses loveless duty over the chance at a new life. The story as a whole shows her deep passivity. In all of part 1, she makes only one movement, when she stands up, moved by "a sudden impulse of terror." She does not really "decide" to leave—she is merely passive to fear. In part 2, she never moves at all—again, passive to fear.

Clearly, even though these two evaluations exclude one another, both account for Eveline's Moral Character. Every "strong" quality in her can be explained as "weakness," and every "weak" quality can be characterized as "strength" (for example, devotion to duty). Because the story emphasizes her passivity in part 2 as a kind of increasing paralysis, Joyce seems to be criticizing "duty" and "religion" as forms of oppression, and adhering to them as weakness. But we do not have to accept his critique, and in my experience many students find Eveline admirable, albeit in a terrible Situation.

The other motives in her decision are fairly obvious. The story describes her *Purpose* as "escape" and her *Attitude* as "sudden terror." Her *Self-Understanding* at the moment of decision might be phrased: "I will not be like my mother!" In the moment of decision, she recognizes her *Situation* at home as a living death, or even hell, for she sees Frank as her savior, who will give her "life." Naturally, all these can be expressed differently, elaborated more fully, or explored in other ways.

Is Eveline's decision to leave good, or bad, and why? You will find that this question generates a wide variety of views, all defensible, depending on what students think of Frank's reliability, of duty to family, and so on. If you enjoy moderating passionate debates between students (and I do), you will enjoy using this question.

Why, in Part 2, Does Eveline Decide to Stay? *What becomes what?*

Because part 1 is so much longer than part 2, the previous readings (2–4) have emphasized part 1. The students' description and evaluation of Eveline's Moral Character have led to some serious thinking about part 2, and they are now well prepared to consider why she reverses her decision and whether her decision is good. Eveline changes her mind because her sense of her Situation has changed, and therefore she has a changed view of Frank. Because part 2 is so brief, these changes are registered quickly and may be easy to miss. To be sure, students will be quite familiar with part 2, but familiarity sometimes leads readers to overlook what, precisely, is going on.

Let me suggest a four-part assignment for the end of the story:

1. What is Eveline's Situation in part 2? She feels differently than she did at the end of part 1 because she acts differently. Pick out five key phrases or images from the first paragraph that suggest her mood, her feelings, her state of mind. Pick out three more key phrases or images from the rest of part 2. What is happening to Eveline, and why? What do the key phrases tell us about her state of mind? (Picking out key phrases is a useful exercise for helping students grasp the "tone" of a passage. This question will also reveal Eveline's *Attitude* and *Purpose*.)

2. Her new sense of her Situation involves a new sense of Frank. What is it? How is it different from that at the end of part 1? Answering these two questions should enable you to understand fully why Eveline reverses herself and decides to stay.

45

3. Is her decision to stay good, or bad, and why?

4. What, if anything, is different at the end of this story than at the beginning? Has Eveline learned anything from this experience? If so, what has she learned? If not, why has she failed to learn anything? (*What becomes what?*)

You might begin class with the first assignment by making a master list of "key phrases" from the first paragraph in part 2 on the board and then asking what they reveal. The paragraph evokes Eveline's fear without ever using the word; students usually grasp it first in the description of "her cheek pale and cold." Students also respond to "the mournful whistle," the "mist," and the images of darkness—"the black mass of the boat" and "soldiers with brown baggages." Eveline's fear disorients her, and you might appeal to your students' experiences of being afraid to help them notice this—"What happens to you when you're *really afraid?*" Frank is speaking to her, but she cannot understand him. She is in "a *maze* of *distress*" (my emphasis), and the paragraph evokes this by unfolding in a series of disconnected perceptions. Eveline's *Attitude* is a sickening fear—more a feeling that grips her, than an Attitude she possesses and shapes.

If you have previously discussed religious imagery, someone will notice that Eveline "[prays] for God to direct her" to do "her duty." This crucial moment clarifies Eveline's new *Purpose* and *Self-Understanding*, and if students miss it, you should direct their attention to it: *What does this sentence tell us about Eveline's Purpose and Self-Understanding in part 2?* Once Eveline conceives her *Purpose* as "duty" to her family rather than "life" for herself, she is bound to stay, for she has no duty to Frank. (Does she have a duty to herself? You might pursue this question with your students, if it interests you.) Her *Self-Understanding* returns to being "a good girl, a good daughter," even if it means she will live and die as her mother did. On the other hand, it could be argued that Eveline is so overcome by fear that she can have no real Purpose or Self-Understanding. In other words, she has become so passive with terror that she cannot genuinely make a decision on her own. Her "*Act*" in part 2, then, is a non-Act. This ironic view of Eveline becomes even clearer as part 2 unfolds, and it may attract some students.

Once the key phrases in the first paragraph have pointed to Eveline's Situation, it can be further clarified by listing the key phrases students have selected from the rest of part 2. If you list them in their order of occurrence in the story (*What follows what?*), students will see clearly how her "disease of fear" progresses, and what it does to her (*What becomes what?*). At first, her "distress" gives her "nausea," and then her perceptions are disoriented by a sense of drowning. She grips the iron railing, holding fast and refusing to move. Then she "[clutches] the iron in a *frenzy*" (my emphasis), feels "anguish," and at last is "passive, like a helpless animal" caught in a trap.

What is happening to Eveline? What do these images tell us directly? What do they suggest indirectly? Students readily understand the "spreading" of Eveline's fear into disease, insanity ("frenzy"), and paralysis or immobility. They know what it means to "freeze up" from fear. They respond powerfully to Eveline's finally becoming "like a helpless animal," and of her giving Frank "no sign of love or farewell or recognition." They may need your help to verbalize their responses, though question #4 has already led them to sense how reduced Eveline is here—speechless, an animal caught in a trap, awaiting her death.

By this point in the discussion, the class would have registered the answer to *What is Eveline's new sense of Frank?* At the end of part 1, he "would save her" and "would give her life, perhaps love, too." Now, in part 2, he "would drown her." Eveline's sense of values has undergone a reversal: Now that her *Purpose* is to do "her duty," rather than "life" or "love," Frank is no longer her savior, but the bringer of death.

·*Is her decision to stay good, or bad, and why?* Students generally maintain the same positions they held in evaluating Eveline's decision to leave at the end of part 1. If they approved of that, they disapprove of this, and vice versa. In my experience, they are ready to renew the debate, partly because they know the moves, partly because they enjoy the contest with their classmates. If you think this discussion is simply going over old ground too often, you might push them on to question #4—a version of *What becomes what?*

What does Eveline learn from her experience? This has a range of possible answers, but it seems to me that they run chiefly in two directions. The first is ironic—she does not change and she learns nothing. She is passive at the beginning of the story and passive at the end. She has experienced some powerful feelings, but she has decided nothing new and done nothing new. She will go home to her hard but familiar life. The second is tragic—she has rejected her one real chance for life and love. At the beginning of the story, she has hope; in the end, she has something worse than despair. In part 1, her mind is full of memories and hopes; at the end, she is "like a helpless animal." Even if everything is the same at home, she will not be. She will be more miserable than before.

A different way of pursuing this question is to ask, *What happens when Eveline goes back home?* The ironic interpreters will say, "Nothing. Life goes on as before." You might suggest that her father has returned home and read her letter by now. What will their meeting be like? Although several different scenarios can be imagined, the poles of the spectrum seem to be two. Her father is filled with remorse and embraces her tearfully, vowing to reform. Or, her father is drunk and filled with rage, and when Eveline returns, he beats her for the first time.

"Eveline" is a beautiful work of art, for Joyce, like a poet, makes every image work, every phrase count. The story deserves study and repays it. It also works well in high school classes because it concerns situations and emotions that strike close to home. Even if their homes are happy, adolescents know about alcoholic and abusive parents. They also have direct experience of confusing emotions in romantic love and of their desire for independence. Still, it takes more than one reading for them to enter Eveline's world, empathize with her Situation, and evaluate her Character and Acts. But once they do so, students learn something that we cannot tell them, because they have worked through the details themselves, argued their views, heard the counterarguments, and worked toward the largest understanding each can manage.

Provocation #2

Eighteen Exercises for "Eveline" or Other Works

The motto of this book might well be "Doing More with Less." Chapter 2 suggests a series of five classes on "Eveline," five readings of the story that lead to more detailed and deeper understandings through class discussion. Here are eighteen exercises of a different sort, drawn largely from various Provocations in this book. They all involve oral or written presentations, and they use "Eveline" merely for concrete illustration. They attempt to involve students with a literary work, not by reading and discussion, but by creating their own performances, usually in words, but sometimes in other media. Consider them as suggestions to stimulate your imagination for assignments.

1. Assign each student a paragraph or section to prepare for reading aloud well and dramatically (with accents and voices, if possible). Assign two students per section for Comparative Performances so that students can hear different voice interpretations of the same passage. (See Provocation #8.)

2. Look closely at the narrator's voice in the first three paragraphs. That voice always renders Eveline's point of view, but it does so sometimes in the narrator's language ("She sat at the window watching evening *invade* the avenue"), sometimes in snatches of Eveline's own colloquial speech ("usually little Keough used *to keep nix* and call out if he saw her father coming"). Rewrite these two paragraphs (a) solely in the narrator's language and then (b) solely in Eveline's own speech. (What does each lose from Joyce's story?) (See Provocation #4.)

3. Writers often make Profiles of their characters before creating a story around them. Make a Character Profile of Eveline, imagining her *in*

complete detail. Use everything you can find in the story in your file but you should also imagine other things appropriate to her character. Among these would be her height, weight, build, and looks; characteristic gestures, acts, mannerisms of speech, her way of walking; her fantasy life; crucial memories; and so on. (See Provocation #5.)

4. Do the same thing for her father or Frank.

5. Imagine that you are Frank or Eveline after the story, writing a letter to someone about what happened. You may write to a third party or you could be Eveline writing to Frank, or vice versa. (See Provocation #4.)

6. Imagine that you are Eveline. What did you say in the letter you left for your father when you left home to run away with Frank? (What happened when you returned home?)

7. Write the first two paragraphs of Frank's story, as he prepares to leave or is waiting for Eveline. What does he see, feel, hear, think at the station from which his boat will depart? Write it in Joyce's manner (omniscient third-person narrator, writing from Frank's point of view and using bits of Frank's voice here and there). (See Provocations #4 and #7.)

8. Did Eveline make the right decision? You are an attorney addressing the class as a jury. They have studied the story and have heard the evidence. Make your case for Eveline—she made the right decision—or against her. You must use both reason and emotion in your speech, for you must *move* the jury to vote your way.

9. Write an argumentative essay (not a speech) to prove that Eveline did (or did not) make the right decision. Do not make oratorical appeals to emotion; confine your presentation to reasoned argument.

10. Write a "sermon" using Eveline's story to make a specific point or points to a specific audience (e.g., fathers, alcoholics, young men, young women, reforming child abusers). You do not have to be a preacher, of course: You could imagine yourself as a psychologist, a counselor, a doctor, a reformed alcoholic, or anything you like. You must make clear (a) your role, and (b) the audience you are imagining. You must persuade your audience to think and to feel as you do on some point or points. Two minutes minimum, five maximum.

11. The name "Eveline" means "little Eve." Study Genesis 2–3 and chart the similarities and differences between the biblical story of "the temptation in the Garden" and Joyce's "Eveline." Do they add up to anything, or to several things? Did Joyce intend the allusion to Genesis? Give reasons for your answer.

12. Write a scene for a play, rendering something in Joyce's story or implied by it. Your scene should include detailed stage directions (position of actors and actresses, gestures, tone of voice, and so on) so that it could be readily acted by your classmates. Some possible scenes: Eveline and Frank together, perhaps when he asks her to go away with him; Eveline trying to get money out of her father for the week's groceries; a family dinner when Eveline's mother was still alive. (Or the scene can be derived from a student's modern transposition of "Eveline.") (See Provocation # 13.)

13. Write a movie script for "Eveline" or for some section of it. The script should include information about each shot (close-up or middle or far-away; camera angle) and about the pace of the cutting, as well as dialogue. (Or the script can be derived from a student's modern transposition of "Eveline.") Students should be led to understand how and why dialogue in a play and in a film differ, what can be accomplished through camera work and what cannot. (See Provocation #12.)

14. You are a professional illustrator and you must illustrate the story, creating a single image that somehow reflects either the story as a whole or a crucial moment that implies the whole: (a) Draw your illustration; (b) alternatively, use a tableau with a few classmates to create your illustration. The illustration should be so effective that the audience can interpret it without your explanatory comments. (See Provocation # 7.)

15. Transpose Joyce's story to a modern setting. You may change the genders of the story's characters in any way that stimulates your imagination but you should keep the same basic Situation. You must decide what voice to use in telling it, whether the character's own voice, or an omniscient narrator's voice, or some combination of the two, as in Joyce. (See Provocation #7.)

16. Transpose the story to Frank's point of view or her father's. That is, tell the story of "Eveline" from the perspective of one of the other characters. (See Provocation #4.)

17. Write a poem derived from some moment or mood or sequence of feelings in "Eveline" (or from a student's modern transposition of it). You do not need to refer to the story unless you wish to do so. Rather, you should aim to create an independent work, your own poem, that poetically accomplishes something that Joyce does in prose. (See Provocation #17.)

18. Alternatively, write the script for a film poem that would evoke, through a sequence of images, a moment or mood or sequence of feelings derived from the story. Your script should mention not only each image but camera angle, camera movement, pace of cutting, and so on. (See Provocation #17.)

Provocation #3

Rereading, or Teaching Students to Do What We Do

Our courses enact an elaborate pretense: Students should aspire to a teacher's understanding of a book, even though they are reading for the first time what the teacher has read often. The teacher guides them through the book, points out significant moments that could not be seen on a first reading: here is a crucial moment, a significant image, an important paragraph, a verbal exchange that foreshadows the climax of the play; let us pause to examine, analyze, explore, reflect on it. The teacher controls the process of discovery; his students "discover" the book according to the map he gives them. They may notice a stream here or a burial mound there that he has not seen before, but the significant landmarks of the journey are his, and students are wise not to wander too far from the path he has charted. In truth, what we teach is not so much a book as *our* understanding of a book.

Some of this is inevitable. After all, we cannot teach what we do not understand. Nor would any of us teach a book we had not read before. Inevitably, we can only teach what we know, and a student's first reading proves fruitful for her only because the teacher guides it. If he were not guiding her, he would be useless—he would not be teaching.

In the present book, I am trying to describe a different kind of guidance, one that assists discovery rather than directs it. This requires, as we have seen in the chapter on "Eveline," that students read and discuss a work, and then reread and discuss it again. When we teach a story with only one reading, we necessarily have to be more directive and corrective, because first readings—even teachers'—generally miss a good deal of what is going on. Young readers, being inexperienced, tend to overlook important details, project their own desires and feelings onto characters and situations, and make other kinds of errors. But when we have students read a work more than once, we can allow errors, because a second reading and discussion will enable them to arrive at a better understanding. In that way, *the students correct themselves as they learn*, and we simply help them along. My ninth-grade students all believed that fathers should be nice men (and so do I); hence, many of them thought that Eveline's father was "a nice man," after their first reading. None of them thought so after their second. Their first reading also tended to romanticize Frank's relationship with Eveline, giving it a soap-opera aura—"They love one another *deeply*." But once the students were asked to read it a second time and reflect on certain questions—*How well do they know one another? Do they love one another? Should she trust him?*—they toned down their previous view.

If we teach students to read, we also should teach them how to reread, and we should teach them to ask questions about their reading. To be sure, we could hardly teach every work with multiple readings, but we can do so more often than we do now. Evaluative questions excite us the most, and rightly so, for these touch our values and our responses to the work most deeply. They generate the liveliest discussions: *Is this character a good person, or a bad one, and why? Is this act a good one, or a bad one, and why?* We cannot do without them.

To answer these evaluative questions well, however, we should first grasp why the character has done what she has done. Interpretive questions, it seems to me, are the keys to deeper, more careful understandings of a work, and of ourselves: *What is Eveline's Situation in part 1? Why does she decide to leave? Why does she make that decision so late in part 1, and not earlier?* The "what?" and "why?" questions open up our understandings of people and Situations in literature, and in life. We cannot ask them too often in class:

"What is this person thinking?" (*Situation*)

"What is he trying to accomplish?" (*Purpose*)

"How does she see herself, in this relationship?" (*Self-Understanding*)

"What is her *Attitude* when she makes that request?"

"What does this Act tell us about the kind of person she is?" (*Moral Character*)

When we teach students how to reread and ask questions, we open to them the pleasures of discovery and so help them cultivate one of the mind's greatest pleasures. Students enjoy making discoveries no less than we do, and we should design our courses, or parts of courses, to foster that enjoyment. But to do that, we must assist more and direct less. We should try to ask more questions, and give fewer answers. We should try to ask more open-ended questions, interpretive and evaluative ones, because these are real questions—that is, debatable ones. In this way, students will not only learn what we know but also discover what they know.

What they discover for themselves, they will not easily forget. You will also have the pleasure of being taught new perspectives and insights by your students. Just as parents enjoy rediscovering the world through their children's wonder at it, so you will enjoy rediscovering stories as your students are excited by your questions.

When rereading a work with students, the teacher should try to resist the urge to be knowing and helpful. She assists more by asking questions than by answering them—"Turn all questions back to the class" is a useful maxim. The teacher aims to foment inquiry and stimulate dialogue, to foster the students' exploration of problems rather than state her own solutions. There are two governing principles. The first is: "What students can do for themselves, they must"; in that way they discover their own powers. The other is: "Let them express their understandings in their own ways." In open discussion, they learn a great deal from how their fellow students express their understandings. Let many expressions of "the same thing" flourish.

One of my teachers liked to say, "Anything worth reading is worth rereading." This may be an exaggeration. But it had better be true that "Anything worth teaching is worth rereading" because we reread it every year. When we teach students how to reread a work, we are simply teaching them how to do what we do. As we assist them with rereading and rethinking, we convey the discipline of our disciplines to them. We all know that only by rereading a work can we begin to think fully and carefully about it. When we teach students how to ask questions and pursue them, we are teaching them to become active inquirers. Thereby, we give them the keys to discovery and self-discovery, and they experience the pleasure of newly won powers. If we would open to them the delights of the mind, we must teach them to do what we do.

Provocation #4

Rewriting and Reimagining for Voice and Point of View

High school teachers, it seems to me, understand how to teach their students about point of view in narrative, for my college students can identify the point of view in a story, and sometimes they even say something significant about how it affects the story being told. Yet many teachers have never tried this wonderful resource for teaching writing and point of view at the same time: having students rewrite parts of a story.

Consider the narrative voice in Joyce's "Eveline." The story is told in the third person by an omniscient narrator, yet he writes consistently from Eveline's perspective in part 1 and often uses fragments of her speech for her thoughts and feelings. The first sentence is, "She sat at the window watching the evening invade the avenue." It seems from this that an omniscient narrator is telling the story in his own voice. But in the second paragraph, as Eveline remembers her father hunting them home from their outdoor play, we read "usually little Keogh used to keep *nix* and call out when he saw her father coming." "To keep *nix*" is an idiom from Eveline's world, quite unlike the narrative voice that describes her as "watching the evening invade the avenue." Perhaps other phrases should be understood as coming from Eveline rather than the narrator. But which ones? And why does it matter?

Thinking through these issues in an analytical way proves laborious, and I am not suggesting that you try. You can accomplish the same thing with more work for your students and more enjoyment for you all. Simply ask them to rewrite Joyce's first two paragraphs (1) wholly in Eveline's voice, first person; and (2) wholly as an omniscient author, with no trace of Eveline's speech.

In this way, the students learn to make the same kind of fine discriminations that Joyce did, and *in the same way*—not by laborious reasoning, but by acquiring a feel for the job he wanted to do. Although they cannot be expected to write in the idiom of a poor Irish girl in 1900, they are close to Eveline's age: They can rewrite Joyce's paragraphs in their own first-person words and still see where and what kinds of changes have to be made. They will not all agree on what is properly the narrator's and what is Eveline's, nor does that matter. The exercise forces them to see that an omniscient narrator can suggest certain things that a first-person narrator cannot, and vice versa. They will then see how Joyce has combined the two to obtain the advantages of both. At the same time, they will have probed the prose of a great stylist in detail.

There is no story for which this exercise cannot be adapted. Consider "The Prodigal Son," whose narrative voice has none of Joyce's complexity. Nevertheless, that story may give rise to several analogous assignments. Students can be asked to rewrite the story from the prodigal son's point of view. They must first decide at what point in his life the ex-prodigal is telling his story, for an old man looking back after many years will convey different attitudes than the recent returnee. Similarly, they may want to give him a particular audience, for he would tell it differently to a wild young man tempted to a similar adventure than he would tell it, say, to his aunt and uncle.

The assignment can be further complicated by having it told at two different lengths. First, the student would write it at the same length as the parable, or as close to it as can be done. Then he would write it at a length that will enable him to tell the story as fully as it needs to be told, given the age of the ex-prodigal and his audience. That would involve expanding different parts of the story as appropriate. As the student imagines the ex-prodigal's audience, point of view, and voice, a new version of the great story unfolds.

A similar assignment involves "modernizing" a story, and this may involve a different point of view. Consider the following possibilities:

1. Rewrite "The Prodigal Son" as a short story set today. You may make him a daughter, if you wish.
2. Rewrite "The Prodigal Son" as a short story set today, but from the point of view of either (a) the father or (b) the elder son.
3. Rewrite "Eveline" as a story set today. You will have to change many details so as to make the choice between "home" and "away" interesting, and this may mean inventing a whole new story. Feel free to change whatever you need to (even making the main character male if you prefer).
4. Rewrite "Eveline" from the point of view of either (a) Frank or (b) her father.

Another way of teaching students about voice and point of view is to have them write letters as though from a character in a story or a play. They must try to adopt the voice, values, perspective, attitudes, and so on of the character (or a modernized equivalent), and it is often helpful to require two letters from one character but to two different people. In this way, students fully experience what they already know from their own lives, that they talk about "the same thing" differently to different audiences (for example, their parents and their friends). Consider the following possibilities:

1. Frank writes letters to his best guy-friend and to his mother about what happened with Eveline. Or, Frank writes to Eveline and to his best guy-friend.

2. Write Eveline's "farewell letters" to her father and to her brother.

3. Imagine a modern "prodigal son" writing (a) to his father for money to come back home and (b) to his best friend about his adventures. (The writer can be a prodigal daughter.)

4. Imagine the prodigal's older brother writing about the whole story (a) to an uncle and aunt who live far away and (b) to his best guy-friend.

The two audiences for each assignment are different enough to warrant different treatments. In #4, for example, I imagine that the elder brother can pour forth his resentment in writing to his best friend, while he will restrain that in writing to his aunt and uncle, who would want to hear that their other nephew had returned home safely. Similarly, in #1 Frank can write about Eveline as coarsely as he wants to his best friend, but not to his mother. And so on.

You can generate any number of assignments in these ways, and each of them exercises the imaginations and verbal abilities of students. Yet let me remind you that even though you assign writing, you do not have to grade it. Make the due date Performance Day: more work for students, less work for you (see Preface). They will come to enjoy reading their work aloud in class, and it teaches them to be at ease in front of a group. Performances also give rise to discussion as, for example, different Franks have different understandings of what they did with Eveline and write to their two audiences in different ways. Put two students at the front of the room at the same time and, after their readings and applause from the class, let them be the first discussants of their differences.

In the exercise of "rewriting paragraphs in 'Eveline,'" you can have different groups of students rewrite different paragraphs so as to review the whole story. In this way, the class as whole rereads and rewrites the whole story, thereby rethinking it in all its details. A public reading of the rewritten story follows, with whatever discussion you find appropriate. A useful opening question is, *What did you learn by rewriting this paragraph?*

You might give different versions of different assignments for several stories, and have the students keep Portfolios of their work. When these are fat enough, collect them. As with Reading Journals (Provocation #10), you count assignments and read only one, perhaps selected by the student, for the grade, penalizing heavily any missing assignment. In addition, you can create small groups in the class so that students read a few friends' Portfolios and help their classmates choose their single best one for you to grade. You might even ask the student to write a paragraph on why it is their best work, comparing it to their other pieces. At the end, you can have a Writers' Festival, where every student reads his or her best piece to the class. Create prizes and have an Academy Awards for Fiction in each class, with categories like "Best Letter," "Best First-Person Rewriting," or "Best Eveline" and "Best Frank."

The kinds of assignments recommended here deepen a student's understanding of the fine points of narrative without dismaying them with critical complexities. The laborious explanation of why a writer chose to write these words in this passage, or chose this voice and point of view, is replaced by the insightful labor of rewriting a passage or reimagining a character's voice in the different literary form of a letter. It is harder to say why you chose certain words than it was to actually choose them. These assignments work more with the choices a writer made than with explanations of why he made them. They increase students' feel for language, exercise their skills in writing, and stimulate their imaginations. Let English class make all students be writers. Those who have a knack or yen for explaining can go on to become critics.

Provocation #5

The Character Profile and the Short Story

When I teach the short story, I want my students to write one of their own. Making them struggle with the literary form increases their appreciation of narrative artistry. This assignment is best given near the middle of a long unit on the short story, or at the end of a relatively short unit. The students need a few weeks of studying short stories before they are prepared enough to write one; but if you give this assignment in the middle of the unit, you will be amazed at what they notice in stories after they have written their own. Here is a sequence of assignments that prepares students to write fairly good short fiction.*

One: Imagining the Crux

First, the students must imagine a main character in a serious situation demanding a decision. Does he run away from home, or not? Does she throw over her boyfriend for someone else, or not? Does he take revenge on a friend who has injured him, or not? Does she get an abortion, or carry the baby to term? Does he give evidence against a friend who has done wrong, or not? Does she tell her mother that she thinks her father is seeing another woman, or not? Does he join a gang, or not? If the situation is not serious, the story has no interest. If the situation cannot be affected by the character's decision, it has no drama.

Having chosen a character and a situation, the student must develop, in writing, as many reasons as possible for *both* choices. This assignment first revealed to me that students think stories are about "action"—events, things happening—rather than experiences, decisions, and their consequences in the making or

---

* *Note:* The "Character Profile" can also be used to stimulate their imaginative involvement with other works (for example: Write a Character Profile of Eveline in Joyce's story).

unmaking of a person's life. The first time I gave this assignment, the reasons given leaned heavily to one side. The character's choice was obvious, and the only thing left for the story was to narrate the events surrounding the obvious choice. It took me some time to persuade the class that an obvious choice has no dramatic interest. A short story is not an action movie; it builds its drama around a moral struggle, as a human being decides a crucial issue at a crucial point in her life. The consequences of deciding one way or the other must be nearly equal, for without moral tension the story lacks dramatic tension.

In sum, then, for the first assignment the students must write three paragraphs. In the first, she describes the main character's situation and the two options for the decision that must be made. In the second two paragraphs, she gives the reasons for one option, and then the other, in as much detail as possible.

Two: The Character Profile

The second assignment is a full Profile of the main character. The student must get to know the character intimately and in writing, imagining her in as much detail as possible. To make the character come alive in a story, the student must first make her come alive in her own imagination and writing. This writing proves especially important when the student is featuring herself, or a part of herself, as the main character: The writer needs to acquire some imaginative distance on this image of herself in order to make the character live on the page.

Students need some guidance for this exercise, so let me suggest that you give them an Information Form to fill out: name, date and place of birth, height, weight, hair and eye color, distinguishing marks, general physical appearance, and so on. You might include a section on the family: parents' names, dates and places of birth, brothers' and sisters' names and their ages, and so forth. Including this kind of information helps a student imagine the whole life of her character. Then list a series of questions, each of which requires a short paragraph. Here are some examples:

1. Describe the character's physical appearance, including clothing (jewelry, tatoos, perfume, and so on).

2. Describe the character's walk, favorite postures (sitting, standing), and characteristic gestures.

3. Describe the character's tastes in food, music, friends, books, movies, and so on.

4. Describe the character's most important childhood memory, and tell why it is important.

5. Describe the character's favorite good dream, and what it tells us about him or her.

6. Describe a characteristic nightmare, and what it tells us about him or her.

7. Describe the character's values, beliefs, habits, dominant emotions—all the important good points and bad points of his or her Moral Character.

8. Describe the character's hopes for the future.

9. Describe the characters fears for the future.

The Character Profile proves to be a substantial writing assignment. The more thorough it is, the better the writer understands her main character, and the better her short story. With a little luck, your students will become so involved with the characters they are imagining that they will talk about them with one another as though the characters were real people.

Three: Background of the Crux

The third assignment asks the students to describe the relationship that the main character has to the other significant figures in the story. For example, if a girl is trying to decide whether to leave her boyfriend or not, the writer should narrate the history of this relationship. If the character is trying to decide whether to leave his home or not, the writer needs to imagine the boy's problems with his parents or siblings, and so on. This assignment proves an extension of the first one—the description of the character's Situation and choices. Now that the writer has imagined the character in detail, she is ready to imagine that crucial situation more specifically and to narrate its history over three to five paragraphs.

Four: Technique and Outline

By this point, the students have thoroughly imagined the worlds of their stories. The next step asks them to decide how they plan to tell it: first person, or third? How much flashback will they use to develop the dramatic context of the decision? How will they show or suggest what happens after the decision is made and acted on? Also, each writer needs to list, for her own use, a brief outline of her story—what she will tell first, second, third, and so on. This outline is not etched in stone, just a plan from which to begin writing the story itself.

Fifth: Writers' Conferences

The fifth assignment is group work. Each student's prewriting is read by two other students, and the writer explains to them her rationale for Step Four, how she plans to construct her story, and why she thinks it the best possible way. By this point, the group should be fairly eager to talk about their work. The consultation group gives every writer the chance to hold forth and to listen to questions and comments, enabling each to see the work more clearly. Students should be told that their main role here is to listen and to encourage one another, to act as sounding boards, to help the writer get clear about the story *each person* wants to tell. Advice tends to be less useful than a good question, because advice tends to arise from the story the advice-giver would write, not the one the writer wants to tell. A little guidance from you on listening sympathetically to one another will go a long way here. Simply requiring a writer to show and discuss her prewriting with others involved in the same assignment enables her to see *her* story in a new light. Students can help one another a great deal simply by appreciating a friend's work. For some useful guidelines for peer writing conferences, developed by Nancie Atwell, see Appendix J in Atwell's *In the Middle*.

Six: *The Story Itself*

The last assignment is writing the story itself and the due date becomes Performance Day. The sequence of five preassignments generates tolerably good stories and considerable demand for their reading, so you should not have any trouble finding volunteers to read stories aloud. The students do pages and pages of prewriting, with all the imaginative thinking they involve, to produce stories generally running three to six pages. Although you assign, oversee, and encourage the whole process and require all prewriting to be turned in at the end, you need only read and grade the story itself. In short, properly managed, this sequence of assignments demands a great deal of thinking and writing by the students, culminating in well-crafted stories, and relatively little work by you as you grade work that is enjoyable to read.

Provocation #6

Setting as an Index to Character and Feeling

In high school and college courses, setting remains the most underinterpreted aspect of narrative. It is less obvious than character and plot, so it seems less important. Our preference for naturalism (or realism) in literature leads us to think of setting as "mere background." We forget that the mere backgrounds of our rooms and homes say a great deal about us: our tastes, our habits, our attitudes, the ways we order (and fail to order) our lives. I want to tell a true story to illustrate how important setting is and suggest two imaginative exercises for your students that will illuminate this importance.

Rick's first job as a professor was a one-semester stint at a small college in the Los Angeles area, replacing the chairman of the English department who was in England on sabbatical. The college gave Rick the chairman's office to use—a corner office, the largest in the building, filled with natural light from many windows. During the semester, a Hollywood crew came to shoot some scenes for a "college film," and they commandeered his office for a few student-meets-with-professor scenes. They moved out all of the professor's bookshelves and books and brought in bookcases with leaded-glass doors, filled with leather-bound books with gold-tooled titles. They took out his wooden desk and brought in an elegant mahogany library table. They took down his theater posters and put up fine antique prints, adding a bust of Shakespeare for good measure.

"What are you doing to this office?" Rick asked, incredulous.

"We are making it look like a professor's office," he was told.

"What do you mean 'look like'? It *is* a professor's office."

"So it is," Rick was told. "But it does not *look* like one."

As it turned out, not too surprisingly, the professor-in-the-film looked like his film office. He wore $1,000 worth of clothes: soft leather designer shoes, shirt of fine Egyptian cotton, Brooks Brothers suit. Office and professor were designed to evoke a mood of highly cultivated assurance, to contrast with the (carefully arranged) slovenliness of the student. The set and clothing people knew exactly what the director wanted, and they delivered it on schedule. The contrasts between student and professor were already embodied in the scenery and clothing.

This is what art does: makes every detail count. Every detail need not "have a meaning," but every detail makes a point. Often this point will appear in an ensemble, like the film professor's office, where all the details were carefully combined to evoke a unified aura, mood, or quality. Similarly, writers describe settings so as to give cues or clues to the reader, and the setting can also acquire significance or symbolic value as the cued associations accumulate. For example, in James Joyce's "Eveline," the first image of "home" comes in the first paragraph, in the smell of dust in the curtains. The word "dust" is soon repeated as Eveline thinks of her endless housework; and by the end of the first part of the story, it is associated with darkness and death. The "realistic detail" comes to have deep symbolic resonance for Eveline's whole life.

Here are two writing exercises that will help students to understand how even realistic details express aspects of a life. The first is derived from a standard scene in mystery novels and films. The detective–hero goes to the house of the dead or missing person and tries to get to know him by looking at what is there.

> Imagine someone your age who is missing from home. The detective–hero of your novel goes to this person's room and spends time looking around. You must describe what the detective sees, and your description must give your readers a sense of what the missing person is like as a person. Every detail you set forth should contribute something to our sense of this person through his or her room. You will read this aloud to the class *twice*. The class will then discuss what kind of person is revealed by this room. Hence, your room description should be detailed enough so as to lead your classmates to understand clearly the kind of person you have in mind.

If you enjoy mysteries, you might photocopy a description of this kind to discuss in class before the students write. Or you might show them an equivalent scene in a film. I also like to tell students that their rooms at home say something profound about the kind of person each of them is. The silence after that remark has a unique quality.

The second exercise involves two different descriptions of a place, one neutrally factual, the other evoking the thoughts and feelings of a particular person. Here is one way of giving such an assignment:

1. Write a neutral description of this classroom, just the facts: number of desks and how they are arranged, color of the walls, and so on. Write the kind of description that would go in an official report.

2. Then, imagine this room from the point of view of a character in a situation loaded with feeling and meaning. Here are some possibilities: (a) a transfer student on the first day of school; (b) a freshman on the first day of school; (c) a senior, on the first day she realizes she will soon be leaving school for who-knows-what; (d) a senior on the last day of school. *You may not name the feelings.* You must evoke the feelings by your description of the room.

Here again, you can have students read their descriptions aloud to the class, twice. The students then interpret it, discussing the kind of person and feelings the description evokes.

This exercise helps students see that settings in literature, like spaces in reality, are rarely neutral. The neutral description of "facts" in an official report gives the familiar classroom a completely different flavor. Students have perhaps felt that the room is "just another place," not realizing that their familiarity with it makes it *not* "just another place." Moreover, making them imagine the classroom from a new and feeling-full perspective defamiliarizes the familiar in a different way. Like any exercise of the imagination, it leads them to see and feel the world anew. It also helps students become aware of how writers *use their settings* to evoke point of view, attitude, feeling, and meaning.

Provocation #7

Transpositions

Transpositions take a work from one genre or medium or setting to another. From a poem, for example, the students derive a prose narrative or a play in miniature. The poem can even be transposed into a nonliterary medium: an illustration, a tableau, a work of art, a film. Or a short story can be reworked for a different time, place, and characters—as Alice Walker reworks "The Prodigal Son" in the modern American context of "Everyday Use" (See Chapter 3). Transpositions exercise the students' powers of imagination and deepen their engagement with a poem. Literary transpositions foster imaginative use of language, while nonliterary ones enable less verbally gifted students to display their understandings in an artistically significant way.

Because some Transpositions for "Eveline" are suggested in Provocation #2 (exercises 14–18), let "The White Rose" (see full text of this poem in Provocation # 14) serve as an example here for possible assignments. The following suggestions presume that the class has discussed the poem and understood something of the variety of possible motives in the man and the greater variety of possible responses in the lady.

I. Narrative
   A. Write a mini-story (two pages minimum) focusing on the man who sends the flower and poem: his decision to act this way; his thoughts, feelings, hopes, fears, acts; and so on.
   B. Write a mini-story (two pages minimum) focusing on the woman who receives it: her thoughts, feelings, and so on when she receives the gift and how they change while she considers it and decides what to do about it, if anything.

II. Drama

Write a miniplay in which the man and the woman meet one another after the rose and poem have been sent. Each character may speak *no more than five times*, so make every exchange count. You must decide the circumstances of their meeting: Does she send for him? Does he come calling? Do they meet by accident and, if so, is it where they can be alone or, say, at a party? Is it soon after he has sent the poem? Or has he waited for several days with no reply?

III. Film

A. Write a film script for this meeting. You must rely less on words than in a minidrama and more on visuals to create the feeling of the situation: camera angles, camera movements, background (white and red roses on the drapes?).

B. Write a film script that conveys the meaning of the poem in a series of visual images only.

IV. Visual Art

A. The poem will appear with a single illustration, which will illuminate the poem visually. Draw that illustration.

B. Tableau: Perhaps you lack the artistic talent to draw that illustration, but you can act it out in a tableau scene for the class. Recruit a partner if you need one; bring whatever props are absolutely necessary (for example, something to serve as "the rose").

C. Draw, paint, or sculpt an image that conveys the same meaning (or feeling) as the poem. Or create an artistic response to the poem. In this case, you should be able to explain how your work of art responds to the poem, for you might be asked to do so.

Except for the final assignment, all of these can be completed overnight and some of them presented in class the next day. If you wish to grade presentations in class, rather than papers at home, you can assign Transpositions for several poems in a unit and then assign them only to a handful of students each time. Over the course of the unit, each student will have done the same number of them.

Presentations in class are like "Performance Day": The presenters may not state their interpretations explicitly (see Preface). Rather, they present their ministories or miniplays or tableaux (held for five seconds, at least) and then, after a round of applause, the class interprets them. What kind of relationship between the man and the woman did the class hear or see in this Transposition? Was the Transposition a successful work of art in its own right? Why, or why not? Even though students shy away from criticizing one another's work, you can encourage them by saying that your grade-giving depends on your evaluation, not theirs—their comments may change your mind positively, but cannot influence it negatively.

Not all lyrics can be transposed to all other media. "The White Rose" implies a social context that enables its Transposition into drama, unlike a meditative poem like "Stopping by Woods on a Snowy Evening." Still, Frost's poem can be turned into a short story or a dramatic monologue in prose: "What is the speaker thinking and feeling as he watches the woods fill with snow?" Students can imagine the situation for themselves, take what the poem hints, and elaborate on it, all in good prose. Granted, ninth graders will wax adjectival on "the beauty of Nature," neglecting the insinuation of a death wish in the final stanza. Why shouldn't they? Nature attracts them more than Freudian psychology. Saturnine scholars, on the other hand, plump for the death wish, being too sophisticated to be moved by "the beauty of Nature" in print. Students will not say all that you want them to say. So what? What they want to say, let them labor to say well. Transpositions urge them to be literary artists in their own right, with the poem and assignment simply guiding and spurring their work.*

Among the many oddities in teaching English is this: We study literature yet assign essays. Students read one kind of writing but write another. We do not ask them to read literary interpretation, but we do ask them to write it. We ask them to read literature, but we do not make them write in literary forms.

Now I am not suggesting that we abandon the teaching of exposition and argument, nor do I want works of literary criticism read in high schools. Rather, I want students to write more, to write in literary forms, to present them to the class, and even to perform them. Writing in literary forms fosters the zestful use of language; it leads students into pleasures of writing akin to the pleasures of reading. Interpretive essays emphasize "getting it right"; literary forms demand "doing it well." When students grow accustomed to performing their works in class, to the applause of their classmates and perhaps even their real delight, they begin to read literature with a new eye and ear. You can see the light there, and hear the resonance.

---

*Turn Whitman's "When I Heard the Learned Astronomer" into a rap song—Would this assignment be a Derived Poem (Provocation #17) or a Transposition?

3

Alice Walker's "Everyday Use": A Summary and Analysis of Characters and Motives

Whereas "The Prodigal Son" is the story of "a certain man [who] had two sons," Alice Walker's "Everyday Use" tells of an African American woman who has two daughters. The story is told by the mother, whom I will call "Mama." Mama and Maggie, her younger daughter, live in a three-room shack in a pasture. The story begins with them waiting for a visit from Dee, the older daughter who has made a successful life for herself far away and who has not been home in years. The story turns on the contrasts between Dee and Maggie. Maggie suffered severe burns as a small child when their previous house was destroyed by fire. She is ashamed of these scars and shy, and she views her sister with not a little jealousy (47).* Dee, in contrast, is good-looking and self-confident, and from her worldly success she looks down condescendingly on her mother and sister. As she sees it, she has made something of her life and thereby liberated herself not only from rural poverty but also from her family's past. Walker's subtle and powerful story reveals the ambiguities of Dee's self-liberation.

The story builds to a climax in which Mama, as though inspired, does something that surprises her and her daughters. Not long after Dee arrives, she asks to be given certain handcrafted household objects. She has never been interested in such things before because her whole aim in life has been to escape the world she grew up in. But now she finds them picturesque, for they have become fashionable antiques. Mama allows her to claim the top and dasher of the butter churn, which were whittled by her uncles, even though the churn will be useless until new parts can be made. But when Dee asks for two handmade quilts, Mama tries to resist, for

---

*All page references to the story are taken from Alice Walker, *In Love and Trouble* (New York: Harcourt Brace Javonovich, no date). Ms. Walker does not allow her work to be excerpted, so there are no quotations.

she has promised the quilts to Maggie for her upcoming marriage. Dee is furious, arguing that Maggie will simply use the quilts and soon they will be worn through. Dee, in contrast, plans to display them as wall hangings and thereby preserve them. The forceful Dee holds the quilts possessively, and Maggie comes to the door to say that Dee can have them, like someone always defeated. Mama, looking at Maggie, suddenly feels a thrill run through her from head to toe, and surprises everyone by seizing the quilts from Dee and thrusting them into Maggie's arms. Dee leaves abruptly, and Mama and Maggie spend the rest of the day sitting outside together.

The *climax* is the high point, or plot-center, of a story. Everything in the story leads up to it, and so it "contains" everything that has come before. Hence, we want to understand and evaluate Mama's motives for her climactic Act, for the climax contains almost the whole story. Then we want to understand the rest of the story: the consequences of that Act, its effects on the characters (*What becomes what?*). Having explored the climax and its consequences thoroughly, we grasp the story as a whole. In other words, just as every story coheres around its climax, understanding that climax forms a coherent goal for teaching the work. *Why does Mama take the quilts from Dee and give them to Maggie?*—This is the question at the heart of the story and, hence, the primary focus of my following sequence of classes.

Teaching "Everyday Use"

As in Chapter 2, I will describe a sequence of classes for teaching this story, in which students first read and respond to it, and then reread it in order to think about it more clearly and fully. Because "Everyday Use" is twice as long as "Eveline," and I want students to respond to it by writing, the first reading takes place over two classes, instead of one, and so does the rereading. You might prefer to stop after these four classes, but I project a fifth one because the story's climax and aftermath raise so many questions that it usually takes two days of discussion to explore them.

"Everyday Use" presents itself in five unnumbered parts and divides itself into two halves: parts 1 through 4 (47–51) anticipate Dee's arrival, and part 5 (51–59) records her visit. Parts 1 through 4 present the characters and their relationships in the past, and Dee and Maggie emerge clearly as character foils (*What goes with what?* and *What versus what?*). Part 5 carries these contrasting relationships into the present and climaxes in Mama's taking the quilts from Dee and giving them to Maggie. Hence, I recommend assigning parts 1 through 4 and part 5 for separate classes. With a class of able readers, of course, the first reading could be given as a single night's homework, with a general discussion on the following day. But even those students might be asked to reread the story in two stages so that they can explore it carefully.

The next sections contain a brief description of my sequence of five classes for teaching "Everyday Use." More detailed assignments and analysis follow.

Class #1. Parts 1 through 4: Get-Acquainted Reading

The best discussions occur when students are well prepared, and nothing prepares them so well as writing about what they read. Writing always leads them to express and, thus, clarify their impressions; and it often brings them to reflect further and even to change their minds while scribbling. Hence, I suggest that you ask students to write a two-page (handwritten) freewriting response to what they read. They should write about whatever they think is important, in full sentences, but informally. (That is, they need not worry about spelling or writing coherent paragraphs, for they are "thinking out loud" in their writing. You do not need to read all this writing—see Provocation #10, "Reading Journals.") Normally, they record their sense of the characters and plot in general; sometimes, a particular situation or issue will lead a student to reflect (or vent feelings) more personally.

You might also tell two students ahead of time that they will open the discussion on the following day. One gives opening remarks, and the other gets first reply. In that way, the discussion begins with what they think is important, and moves on from there. Once a class is used to this way of proceeding, the relevant questions will be raised in a period with only a little guidance from you. These questions include the following (unnumbered because they can arise in discussion in any order):

What do you think of Dee? Is she a good person, or not, and why? Is she a good daughter, or not, and why?

What do you think of Maggie? Is she a good person, or not, and why? Is she a good daughter, or not, and why?

What do you think of Mama? Is she a good person, or not, and why? Is she a good mother, or not, and why?

What do you think will happen with Dee's visit, this family reunion? Will it be happy, or sad, and why?

In my experience, students head directly to interpreting and evaluating the Moral Character of the characters. As students discuss the characters, agreeing and disagreeing with one another, you will have a sense of how much they have understood. You need not correct their errors, because they will reread the story and make corrections themselves. The final question helps to prime them for the next assignment. They cannot be wrong in their answers, and the answers reveal some of the expectations roused in them by parts 1 through 4.

You might save the last ten minutes of class for a reading aloud of the first five paragraphs of part 5, because your students will probably need a little help to understand what is going on. It turns out that during Dee's years away from home, she has become a Black Muslim and embraced her African heritage, even to changing her name to Wangero. Alice Walker expected her readers to grasp all this before Mama does. Mama and Maggie live in a shack without electricity, without telephone, radio, or television. Hence, Mama, though a reliable narrator, proves something of a naïve one: She has no sense of what the new fashions in clothing and lifestyles are in the great world where Dee lives. She registers Dee's unusual new clothes and foreign greeting, but does not grasp immediately what has happened in her daughter's life; our students do not, either. A little bit of help with part 5 from you can get them past this barrier, which might otherwise distract or confuse them. Nevertheless, I recommend as little help as possible, with no evaluations of Dee/Wangero's change from you. The students will come to their own evaluations soon enough.

Class #2. Part 5: Get-Acquainted Reading

If you ask the students to prepare for this class as for class #1, writing informally about what they have read, you will probably find that they want to begin by discussing, "Did Mama do the right thing in giving the quilts to Maggie?" I suggest that you let them, even though they will not yet have grasped certain crucial details about Dee/Wangero. Again, because they will be rereading the story, errors and oversights at this point will not create a problem. They will discuss the story all the more energetically, knowing they will not be brought up short by the teacher, even though their classmates will disagree with them. Hence, the following questions form a likely sequence for the discussion (unnumbered because they arise from the students' remarks and need not be treated in this order):

> Does Mama do the right thing when she takes the quilts away from Dee and gives them to Maggie? Why, or why not? (This evaluative question involves some consideration of Mama's motives, *why* she does it.)
>
> What effects does this have on Dee/Wangero? Are they good, or bad, and why? (The consequences of Mama's Act, and a version of *What becomes what?*.)
>
> What effects does this have on Maggie? Are they good, or bad, and why?

These questions can easily take up a whole period, especially since they can involve rereading and exploring specific passages.

Class #3. Parts 1 through 4: Second Reading

The second reading of the story is oriented toward a clear and full understanding of Mama's motives for her climactic Act. To be sure, the students have already discussed her motives, more or less indirectly, in evaluating her Act and its consequences. But they have probably done so with a very imperfect understanding. All first-time readers, even skillful ones, miss a good deal of what is going on in a story. Even when our responses are apt, we need a second reading to clarify our perceptions of what we responded to, and why. Students, not being as skillful as we are, need a second reading even more than we do. Now that they are familiar with the story as a whole, they not only notice details previously overlooked but they also revise, and sometimes reverse, their understandings and evaluations.

To understand Mama's Act, we need to explore her Situation and Moral Character. Because Mama's Act involves a decision about her daughters, her Situation turns on the contrasts between Dee and Maggie, who are character foils. Hence, we need to assemble the contrasts that Mama develops between the two sisters and try to understand what these contrasts mean to her.

You may want to remind students, now and again, that assembling contrasts is no mere exercise, like a puzzle, but a way to understand the people in the story and, in this case, Mama's decision near the end. The human mind works by comparison and contrast: We understand our experiences of people and things by comparing and contrasting them. Comparison and contrast—looking for similarities and differences and understanding what they add up to—are the natural way we make sense of our experiences. Moreover, whenever we have to choose between two things, we look especially at their differences. Literature tends to heighten contrasts in order to convey the drama of decision and to clarify the significance—the meaning and value—of the choices. Dee and Maggie represent two kinds of people, two different kinds of living. What are they (the interpretive question), and what are they worth (the evaluative one)? These issues will need further attention in part 5, but most of the details are set forth in parts 1 through 4.

Mama's Moral Character, in contrast, can be discussed and evaluated rather fully on the basis of parts 1 through 4. All of what she tells us directly about herself occurs here, and what she conveys indirectly about her attitudes and values fits with her actions in part 5. A description of Moral Character implies certain evaluations, and these are useful even at this stage because they involve students in making inferences. Nevertheless, their first task is to achieve clarity about what Mama reveals about herself, directly and indirectly, and the significance of it.

The students usually want to evaluate, as well as understand, the Moral Characters of these people, as they did in class #1. Some will have revised their views since then, and even those who have not now have more evidence with which to argue them. In general, as students notice precise details on their second reading, their evaluations of Maggie tend to improve, and they grow more critical of Dee. If you wish to pose a new question, you might try, *Does Mama treat both daughters equally, or does she favor one over the other?* There is evidence for both alternatives, and since adolescents are often involved in similar issues at home, it excites keen interest. This question specifies the more general one from class #1, "Is Mama a good mother, or not, and why?"; plus, it pertains directly to Mama's Act in part 5.

Class #4. Part 5: Second Reading

I like to gather together all the motives for Mama's Act and explore, and set these motives forth in class before returning to the question of whether it is a good or bad Act, and why. The first task is to complete our understanding of her Situation, by carrying forward the Dee versus Maggie contrasts into part 5. Similarly, we should also look for any new insights into Mama's Moral Character in part 5. Then, we can examine her Act closely to discover and define her Purpose, Self-Understanding, and Attitude.

Because the whole story comes together in Mama's Act, an entire class period can easily be devoted to understanding its various aspects. Normally, this will involve discussing specific passages. Students then can begin to reconsider their earlier evaluations of Mama's Act in itself, as distinct from its consequences: *Is Mama's Act good, or bad, in its intentions?* The end of this story is so subtle and so rich that, in my view, it needs one more class; otherwise, the consequences of Mama's Act will not be fully explored.

Class #5. Rereading the End of the Story

There may not be enough time in one class period both to understand and to evaluate Mama's Act, and in that case the evaluation can continue on into the next class. Moreover, its consequences—for Dee, for Maggie, for relationships in the family—are conveyed so swiftly, and so suggestively, that another class is needed to understand them, much less to evaluate them. It would be all too easy to "under-read" the end of "Everyday Use," so swift and understated is the aftermath of Mama's Act. Let me suggest that you ask your students to reread the last half page of the story, asking themselves how Mama's Act affects Dee and Maggie, and whether its consequences are good, or bad, and why. A more detailed set of questions is spelled out in the analysis that follows.

This analysis unfolds according to the sequence suggested for classes 3 through 5. Even if you are unfamiliar with "Everyday Use," the analysis should help you understand how you might use these questions to teach this story, and how you might use similar questions in teaching any story. Nevertheless, the better you know this beautiful and compelling story, the better you can evaluate my analysis, and the extent to which my recommendations for teaching may work for you and your students.

Why Does Mama Take the Quilts from Dee and Give Them to Maggie?

Parts 1 through 4. Mama's Situation: Dee versus Maggie

Because the students have already read the story, they know that Mama's climactic Act involves deciding between her two daughters: which one should get the quilts? Hence, to understand Mama's Situation, they need a detailed, in-depth understanding of the differences between Dee and Maggie. I suggest an assignment like the following for class #3, directed to Mama's Situation and Moral Character in parts 1 through 4.

1. What is Mama's Situation in her climactic Act? She makes a decision about her two daughers: How does Mama understand Dee? How does she understand Maggie? Reread parts 1 through 4 and make a list of ten contrasts between Dee and Maggie. Then write three sentences summing up the basic differences. Which woman do you think is better, and why?

2. What is Mama's Moral Character? To understand Mama as a person, make a list of five to eight points about her in parts 1 through 4. Then write a paragraph on what these tell us about Mama as a person. Is Mama a good mother or not, and why?

If your students have little experience working with character foils (*What goes with what?* and *What versus what?*), you can explain that contrasts between characters are often implied or suggested rather than stated outright. Hence, if one is called "shy," we know that the other is "not shy, outgoing, bold." Because they have read the story and are familiar with the characters, the students are already aware of many contrasts between Dee and Maggie, and they can therefore gather a great many more on their second reading. In other words, experience with second readings familiarizes them with basic literary patterns and helps them become more skillful readers in general.

You might note how vaguely the evaluative question is posed, *Which woman is better, and why?* so that it does not tilt students prematurely toward one or the other sister. "Which woman is the better person?" or "Which is the better daughter?" might incline most of the students toward Maggie, while "Which one do you admire the most?" might incline them toward the ambitious and successful Dee. Asking "Which one do you think is better?" leads each student to a free and genuine response, while "and why?" asks for the reasons, the criteria, for their evaluations.

I suggest that you begin class discussion by creating a master list of contrasts on the board. It might look something like this:

Dee	Maggie
bold, confident	shy
lives away	lives at home
independent	dependent
good-looking	not good-looking
full-figured	skinny
poised, smooth	awkward
not afraid of anyone	afraid of her sister
sense of style	no style
loves nice clothes	dresses plainly
loves city life, hates country life	knows only country life
fault finding, bossy	accepting, humble

ambitious	not ambitious
successful in the world	not successful in the world
not happy at home in the country	happy at home in the country
well-educated (college)	not well-educated
reads aloud well	does not read well
loves fiction, "make-believe"	(?)
strained relations with Mama	gets along well with Mama

Such a list might grow longer as students find other ways of "saying the same thing." For example, the final entry for Maggie could be elaborated—loves Mama, loyal to Mama, close to Mama—and appropriate opposites discovered for Dee. Discussing appropriate opposites raises crucial issues about the characters and about how students understand and evaluate them. "What is the right contrast for 'loves Mama'? Does Dee 'hate Mama'? 'dislike her'? 'disapprove of her'?" Different students will have different views and reasons for their views.

As you can see, developing and discussing the master list of contrasts leads naturally to the explicitly evaluative question: *Which woman is better, and why?* In my experience, students usually want to debate this issue before the list is finished, because they have already *committed themselves in writing* to an evaluation—they know that no one can prove them wrong, and their hearts and values are in it. Good! Nevertheless, I usually hold off the debate on evaluation until the contrasts are fully surveyed. This gives students the opportunity to rethink their views, and while few reverse themselves at this stage, many understand that the issues are more complex than they first thought.

Hence, before beginning to discuss *Which woman is better, and why?*, you might give them a few minutes to review the three sentences they have written, suggesting that they can revise them, if they wish, and can write one or two more to express their fuller understanding. This gives everyone a few moments of quiet in which to gather old thoughts and new ones together before the evaluative discussion begins.

Because classes are so different, I can give little concrete advice about how to manage the evaluative discussion beyond "let students agree and disagree freely," yet "keep order" and "insist on civility." I do have a goal for this particular discussion, which, if you agree with it, you might help your students to grasp: the ambiguity in both characters. Dee has achieved success in the world partly because she hates home so deeply; Maggie remains with Mama in loyalty and love partly because she does not have Dee's intelligence and ambition. In other words, Dee's success in the world and failure as a daughter are inseparable, as are Maggie's success as a daughter and failure by worldly standards. To be sure, this ambiguity can be expressed in many other ways, but essentially the good and bad aspects of each character are thoroughly interwoven. This ambiguity does not necessarily imply that Dee and Maggie are "equally good in the end," although an argument could be made for that too. The goal in this discussion is for students to see how complex each character is, how the positive and the negative aspects of each are inseparable from one another.

Parts 1 through 4. Mama's Moral Character

What is Mama's Moral Character? Having read the story once, students are familiar with Mama's Moral Character and they have views on the kind of person she is, whether they like or admire her or not, and so on. But this familiarity is rather impressionistic and vague. The assignment suggested before leads them to become more fully aware of the facts that Mama reveals about herself, helps them to make clear inferences about what these signify, and thereby leads students to a deeper and clearer understanding of her. Students almost always like and admire her on a first reading, and this assignment does not change their minds. It does give them a more detailed and, hence, a better grasp of Mama's personal history and qualities of character. They need this grasp in order to understand fully her climactic Act.

The assignment suggested earlier asks for "five to eight points about Mama in parts 1 through 4." You might explain that the five to eight points include the facts Mama reveals about herself, but every fact has meaning for her Moral Character, and that students need to put *fact* and *meaning* (or *significance*) together. (I prefer to say "points," rather than "facts," because some students limit "facts" to the most explicit statements.) Given the story, we are especially interested in Mama as a family member; hence, the evaluative question—*Is Mama a good mother, or not, and why?*—proves part of the assignment. Their paragraphs should describe and evaluate Mama's Moral Character based on the five to eight points they list.

You might consider adding a further question: *Is Mama a reliable narrator, or not, and why?* This leads students to state their sense of Mama from the way she tells this story. Relevant subquestions include: *Does she know what she is talking about? Does she understand her daughters? Is she honest? What about the story leads you to say this?* Students rightly find Mama a reliable narrator, yet asking them to explain why leads the students to become conscious of the inferences they have already made about her Moral Character from her style of narrating. You might prefer simply to pose these questions orally, as a follow-up to the assignment suggested earlier.

I suggest you begin class discussion by making a master list of the points they have discovered about Mama, asking what each means (suggests, implies) as it is presented. Here is a sample list, with the meaning (or interpretation) of each point suggested in parentheses:

Mama's Moral Character

1. A big woman who can do a strong man's work outdoors in any weather. (Physically strong, tough, enduring. Suggests that she is morally strong and enduring.)

2. Only had an education through second grade because white authorities closed down the school for African Americans in 1927 (50). (Not educated, so she has to live by manual labor. But she values education, because she helped Dee go to college.)

3. Mama and the Church raised money to send Dee away to college. (Mama loves Dee, and even though Dee is a difficult daughter, she wants Dee to be happy. It must have been hard work for poor country people to raise all that money, but Mama got it done. Mama is loving and unselfish.)

4. Mama's television-show fantasy in part 2: Dee seems not to be grateful for all Mama has done for her. But Mama does not accuse or blame or resent her for ingratitude. (Mama cares for others, not for herself. Unselfish, no self-concern.)

5. Dee often made Mama angry with her sarcasm and selfishness (love for fancy clothes), but Mama, though often tempted, did not scold or threaten her. (Mama is patient, enduring, unselfish, caring.)

6. Mama had one husband who made the benches. He must have died a while ago because Mama mentions him without sadness. Mama raised the girls by herself. (Hard work, but Mama loving and enduring. Mama is the backbone of this family.)

7. Mama could not look a white man in the eye, though Dee could. (Mama is oppressed, for all her physical and moral strength: shy, a bit afraid. Contrast Dee's boldness with respect to white people.)

8. Mama lives in a shack, has no electricity (no telephone, radio, television) and no car, for she walks wherever she has to go. (Very poor in material goods, yet she does not complain, does not even notice. This is her life, and she is OK with it. Maggie is the same, but not Dee. Mama has spiritual or moral wealth, but not material wealth.)

9. Mama must be pretty old: left school in second grade in 1927, so she must have been born about 1920. Dee is grown up, Maggie about to be married. Yet Mama still going strong: enduring.

10. Mama belongs to a church and goes to church. (Mama is a Christian, and a highly moral person. Raised her children by herself. After her husband died, she did not marry again, or take up with another man. Believes in marriage: approves of Maggie's upcoming marriage. In part 5, Dee is not married.)

11. Mama watches out for Maggie, feels special affection for her, but she does not need to protect Dee. (Mama is a good mother: Maggie is shy and awkward, so she needs some special care. Sometimes people give special attention to the child or pet who seems to need it more.)

Students generally reach a consensus about the qualities of Mama's Moral Character, differing largely in emphasis and in the ways they express their understandings. They also tend to admire her as a mother. Hence, you may need to push some classes to think fully about the detailed points they have gathered because there may be little debate to excite them.

Differences of opinion, however, emerge when they are asked: *Does Mama treat both daughters equally, or does she favor one over the other?* In one sense, she has done more for Dee, while in another, she seems to love Maggie more. The crux of the question, which gives rise to the debate, lies in the difficulty of treating two such different daughters "equally," for to treat them "the same" would be unfair to one. Here again, because most students are involved in sibling rivalries, this question often provokes a lively discussion.

Students will rightly connect the honesty of her storytelling to her good Moral Character—her love for her daughters, her Christian beliefs, her unselfishness and patience as a person—if you ask, *Is Mama a reliable narrator, or not, and why?* She knows her daughters well, and she speaks straightforwardly about them. Her record is not self-serving and seems balanced, for she even presents the difficult Dee in some positive ways. Her narration is artless, "natural," as she recalls now one thing about one daughter, now something else about the other; it is governed by factual details, not by Mama's attitudes or feelings. In her selflessness, Mama tells things as she sees them. Her understanding may be limited, but it is not wrong or insincere or dishonest.

Part 5. Why Does Mama Take the Quilts from Dee and Give Them to Maggie?

In class #4, we reread the climax of the story, and we want to understand Mama's motives in detail and depth before evaluating her act. "Everyday Use" is a masterpiece of subtlety and indirection, especially so in part 5. The basic questions about motives lead us into the heart of the story and help clarify the human realities at its center. When Dee and Maggie stand before Mama, Dee claiming the quilts for herself and Maggie giving them up of her own free will, the whole story comes to a crux: Mama sees her daughters' whole lives and values, as it were, gathered together in a single moment, before she acts.

The following assignment focuses on each of Mama's motives in turn; it thereby leads students to pull all of them together into a full understanding of why Mama does what she does:

1. Mama's Situation. What new contrasts emerge between Dee and Maggie in part 5? Make a list of five to eight new contrasts; include, especially, their contrasting views on the quilts. Write two to four sentences explaining what these contrasts mean. What do they signify? Why are they important?

2. Mama's Moral Character. Do we learn anything new about Mama's Moral Character in part 5? If so, record the new insight or insights. What aspects of Mama's Moral Character are important in her Act?

3. What is Mama's Purpose in this Act? Self-Understanding? Attitude? Describe each as precisely as you can.

4. Are Mama's intentions in this Act good? Is it the right thing to do, or the wrong thing, and why?

In my view, these questions require a full period of discussion. Hence, the consequences of Mama's Act will be explored after briefly analyzing the issues raised by the questions.

I suggest beginning class with the students' responses to the first question, generating a master list on the board and discussing the contrasts as they arise. Consider the following list of contrasts:

Dee	Maggie
new name, new identity	old name, same identity
convert: now a Black Muslim	still a Christian
does not remember family details	remembers all family details
does not care about family history	cares deeply about it
cannot quilt:	can make a quilt: Grandma Dee
did not want to learn	taught her
will use quilt for decoration:	use it for marriage bed:
wall hanging	warmth in winter
the quilts belong to Maggie,	they belong to her, but she'll give
but she'll take them anyway	give them up
selfish	not selfish, selfless
doesn't care about family harmony	wants family harmony
quilts are antiques:	quilts are part of family
fashionable, stylish	
doesn't care about Grandma Dee	remembers Grandma Dee with them
hence, not a true Dee: rejects family	hence, the true Dee: cherishes family

You will note that some of these are factual, some interpretive, and most are both. Often, their significance for the story is briefly suggested, an "on-the-board note" abbreviating a point made orally by a student, or by several students. Such a list practically shows, all by itself, why Mama gives the quilts to Maggie.

On their first reading of the story, students do not pick up all these details or their implications. Then, they generally insist that the quilts rightfully belong to Maggie because Mama promised, and "a promise is a promise." A second reading allows them to explore the contrasts between the two sisters and so discover that

Maggie deserves the quilts for other, deeper reasons as well—she has embraced the family's traditions, while Dee has rejected them. Dee does not want to be a Dee in the family line of Dee's, for she changes her name to Wangero. Maggie is the true Dee, for she maintains the family's memory and heritage. To be sure, a teacher could point out reasons like these to students reading the story only once, perhaps by pointing to specific passages and asking leading questions. But that practice, useful and even necessary from time to time, keeps from students the pleasure of making their own discoveries.

Making this list also helps students notice the value that Mama, as well as Maggie, places on family tradition in part 5. Most find this a new aspect of her Moral Character, even though some say it is implied in her devotion to family, already clear from parts 1 through 4. In either case, it becomes important in Mama's Act, for she recognizes that Dee has no love for the family and its traditions, while these are deeply important to her and Maggie. Hence, her giving the quilts to Maggie keeps them in the family. Dee has rejected the family in so many ways that letting her keep the quilts would be like giving these family heirlooms away to an outsider.

The other components in Mama's Act can be described in any number of ways. Her *Purpose* is, evidently, to do what is right, to do justice, to maintain the family traditions, which Maggie loves and Dee hates. Her *Self-Understanding* in this Act is similar: Mama is the kind of person who tries to do what is right even when it costs her. (For example, she worked hard to raise the money for Dee to go to college because it was right for Dee to go.) Here, it is right to defy Dee—something she has never done before—and to affirm Maggie. Moreover, Mama does this at the risk of further alienating Dee. It would be natural for her to let Dee claim the quilts, as she had already given her the parts of the butter churn: Mama would like her daughter to visit more often. But when Dee claims the quilts, Mama's love for her comes into conflict with both her love for Maggie and the claims of justice. Mama is a highly moral person, and this proves a deeply moral Act.

Still, the Act astonishes Mama even as she does it, and it astonishes Dee and Maggie too. It is perfectly in character, yet utterly unforeseen, because Dee has always gotten what she wants before. Mama's *Attitude* in doing it is ecstatic, and she describes it as just like experiencing the touch of the spirit of God in church: joyful, ebullient, happy, strong, inspired. Once all these components are in place, students generally agree that Mama's intentions are good. Whether it is the right thing to do, however, proves a slightly different question, for there are two quilts, and some students argue that Mama should have divided them between the sisters.

The Consequences of Mama's Act: What Becomes What?

I argued earlier that after Mama's Act the story ends so subtly and quietly that it would be all too easy to miss what is going on. That is why I suggest devoting one more class (class #5) to discussing the consequences of Mama's Act in the final paragraphs of the story. We can understand *What becomes what?* only at the end of the story. What have these characters learned from these events? What is different at the end than at the beginning? Because the students know the story well after two readings, you might ease off the homework for a night and use the following questions in class to guide a rereading and discussion of the ending. But I prefer to give them these questions the night before and ask them to write down their answers to all of them, because that ensures the best discussion. It takes careful attention to the text to answer them because they all require considerable inference:

1. How does Dee feel about, and respond to, Mama's Act? How does she act toward Mama, and why? How does she act toward Maggie, and why? In your view, are the consequences of Mama's Act good for Dee, or bad, and why?

2. How does Maggie feel about, and respond to, Mama's Act? How does she act toward Dee, and why? How does she act toward Mama, and why? In your view, are the consequences of Mama's Act good for Maggie, or bad, and why?

3. Are the consequences of Mama's Act good for this family, or bad, and why?

4. What is different at the end of this story than at the beginning? (*What becomes what?*) Reread part 1 to answer this.

You might notice that these questions simply survey the consequences of Mama's Act for each character and for the family as a whole. Hence, with a class accustomed to exploring my questions about motives, you might sum them up in a single, *What are the consequences of Mama's Act for each character and for the family as a whole? In each case, are the consequences good, or bad, and why?* I need not sketch out answers to these. If you read "Everyday Use," you can explore them at leisure. But I will comment briefly on question #1 to illustrate the kinds of issues involved in all of them.

After Mama takes the quilts from her and gives them to Maggie, Dee leaves abruptly. Because Mama is telling the story, we do not know what Dee is feeling, and what we infer depends on what we think about the kind of person she is. Plausible inferences include: her feelings are hurt; she is angry because Mama has rejected her; she is angry because she has not gotten what she came for; she is not angry, but since she clearly will not get what she came for, she might as well leave; she is not really angry, but she enjoys dramatizing situations, so she pretends to be angry to get some slight revenge on Mama for not giving her what she wants. Combinations of these are possible, and other feelings and reasons might be argued too.

Dee kisses Maggie good-bye (but not Mama) and gives her a brief lecture about transforming her life, just as Dee has. Is this an act of sisterly affection? Or does she kiss only Maggie so that Mama will feel hurt? Or both? When Dee gives Maggie that brief lecture, is she motivated primarily by kindness? On the one hand, that seems unlikely, for the shy Maggie, with little formal education, can hardly imitate Dee by going to the big city and making her way independently in the world. From this perspective, Dee's brief lecture looks more like an Act of snide revenge against Maggie and Mama because she didn't get the quilts. Yet Dee might well believe that she has "made it" simply because of her own hard work and ambition, and she hopes to stir some ambition in Maggie, believing that she too can be a success. From this perspective, Dee is moved by kindness toward her sister. As you can see, Mama records Dee's acts, but what they mean for Dee and for the family are left for us to interpret. Perhaps Dee, feeling rejected by Mama's Act, may never come home again. Would that be good, or bad, for her, and why? (question #1) Would that be good, or bad, for the family, and why? (question #3)

As in the real world, we cannot see into the heart of another person, and it is always difficult to assess the consequences of an Act for the heart, and the life, of another. Mama is not an omniscient author: We are given her perceptions, as though we were there, and invited to understand them as best we can. *Yet this story, like every story, invites us to see into the inner life of its characters and to assess the consequences of their Acts.* The questions here have no single or sure answers because, even though they draw on facts, they are not factual questions. They ask for interpretation and evaluation. They pursue, with the final paragraphs of "Everyday Use," the hearts and lives, which are always somewhat mysterious, of its human beings. We arrive at different views of the hearts of these characters because we come at them from our own different lives. That is exactly how the questions raised at the heart of a story enable us to know ourselves better.

Provocation #8

Reading Aloud

The freshmen in my Honors seminar all rank above the eightieth percentile in verbal ability. They are not only among the most intelligent in their class but the most ambitious, since many eligible for Honors courses avoid them. They were the best students in their high schools, and they want to be the best at the university. They are likable and admirable young people; but, for all their high-percentile scores, they cannot read aloud.

I do not mean that they cannot read aloud well, that they shy from dramatizing a passage with their voices, although that *is* true. I mean they cannot read aloud *at all*: They skip words. They substitute prepositions. Their voices stumble. They fracture phrases into unmeaning. I am not asking them to read aloud the unfamiliar— they are not reading Thomas Browne or Edward Gibbon but passages from the *Iliad* or the Bible they read the night before. When a particular passage comes up in discussion and deserves a closer look, I ask someone to read aloud and inwardly cringe. Rarely do all its phrases receive an intelligible voicing.

The fault is widespread among the nominally well-educated, young and old alike. The lectors at my church prove uneven performers at best, and they have the chance to prepare their reading aloud. They sometimes skip words, often stumble, and nearly always fail to match the cadence of their speech to the rhythms of the phrasing, thereby rendering obscure the clear and bland the beautiful. These are people with the benefit of advanced degrees. I am not holding unreasonable standards for these adults or my students. I simply want their voices to make sense of the words on the page. Surely that is not too much to ask of the literate.

Teaching students to read aloud proves an excellent means of leading them to the pleasures of language well-used. Yet teachers seem to be embarrassed by beauty, sensual and intelligible. We do too little to help our students relish the sounds and rhythms of language or to enjoy its shapes of balance and antithesis. We really are dry-as-dusts, perhaps for fear of exposing our pleasure in something students do not yet feel. They do, however, respond to the linguistic beauties they do perceive. They recognize a certain pungency in "No pain, no gain," even though they have never heard of anaphora and isocolon. They feel a richer beauty in "When the going gets tough, the tough get going," even though they know less about chiasmus than they do about mu-mesons or *n*-dimensional spaces (see Provocation #9, "Shapes of Language"). We all love beauty when we perceive it. One of our tasks is to develop their feeling for beauty in language.

Most teachers of English do not recognize this as a proper task. They have so many things to teach that local "beauties" are ignored in favor of larger structures. Students respond more readily to plot, theme, and character than they do to imagery, tone, and sound. They prefer the familiar pleasures of literature to the unfamiliar beauty of shapes in language. That is why they like fiction and fear poetry, and also why they want their essays graded for their "ideas" rather than for what they actually write. To be sure, teaching students the pleasures of language well-used proves slow work. But the game is worth the candle. A taste acquired is a permanent possession—students soon acknowledge it's good to own a new pleasure. Plus, as they learn to attend to the shapes words make, they not only read but write better than they did.

When we teach students to read aloud well, they give voice and body to these new pleasures. As things stand, we assume that when we teach the formal analysis of poetry, students acquire new pleasures with their new perceptions. But we assume too much. Howard Nemerov writes that his students prove skillful interpreters of poems yet have little experience of poetic pleasure. The students' teachers have cultivated their knowledge and skill yet have left their sensibilities untouched. Poetry is getting something right in language, but our students have little or no feel for that rightness. Nemerov works to repair this loss by teaching students to savor the rightness of language. He reads aloud, and is silent; he teaches them to read aloud and be silent. Learning to relish the rightness of language proceeds no different from learning any new pleasure, like a taste for wines or for Rembrandt. The skills of formal analysis can be acquired by method. Sensibility requires time and silence.

Reading aloud, however, gives sense to sensibility. Skill in it can be acquired by method and practice—sensibility learned from the outside in. As the voice breathes form into the words on the page, as its rhythms strike emphasis, its tones grace meaning, the intention incarnate in an order of words is embodied in a process of speech. The reader gives to airy something a local habitation and a music. All I do to help students develop this skill is to model a good performance once in a while and make students practice. They just get better. Ask them frequently to pick a passage to read aloud and to prepare it. This gives students time to become familiar with the piece before they have to perform in front of peers.

One good way to make literature come alive is to give to it the voices of the living. When we read aloud well, we sound the meanings of a text, plumbing and impersonating them. We thereby fuse the depths and surfaces of language with the depths and surfaces of ourselves, for we give to it the resonances of mind and body, mind in body. When we teach students to read aloud well, they learn to give more of themselves to what they read, so they learn more from their reading.

Provocation #9

Shapes of Language

Doubtless your school has a weight room, and your weight room probably has a sign or two on the wall urging young athletes to work out hard. Does one of them read, "Those who do not struggle against obstacles will inevitably fail to make sufficient progress"? If there is a second, does it say, "When hardship, hostility, or adversity loom, then people prove their mettle by the vigor with which they overcome them"?

Of course not! Coaches do not speak like bureaucrats. The signs say, "No pain, no gain" and "When the going gets tough, the tough get going." Something short, pithy, direct, and memorable. The language of proverbs features its patterns. "No pain, no gain" achieves eloquent simplicity through parallel structure, repetition, and rhyme. Alter any of these and the exhortation suffers. "Without pain, no gain" achieves dullness and sing-song at the same time, while "no pain, no achievement" succeeds in being fatheadedly flat.

Everyone responds to these differences. Everyone prefers a beautiful phrase to "the same thing" said in some unlovely way. If Samuel Goldwyn had said of a star's high salary, "It's a lot of money, but we expect to make a profit on him anyway," no one would have blinked an eye because every producer thinks this of every star. But Goldwyn said, "We're overpaying him, but he's worth it," and the remark is remembered. Similarly, if Gertrude Stein, when asked why she preferred Paris to Oakland, had answered, "Nothing interesting ever happens there," no one would have remembered it, for many have felt, thought, and said such things about their hometowns. But Stein said, "There is no there there," and the pungency of the sentence pleases over and over again.

You might introduce your students to some of these verbal patterns and assign them to write some memorable sentences of their own according to these schemes. The schemes all have fancy Greek names, but you can ignore them. Start with parallel structures (A : B :: A : B), move on to chiasmus (A : B :: B : A), and then add anything you like. The exercise will create a different kind of writing exercise and help students notice these kinds of patterns when they read.

Write some parallel structures on the board so as to feature the parallelism:

1. No pain,
   no gain.

2. The bigger they are,
   the harder they fall.

3. In peace, sons bury their fathers;
   In war, fathers bury their sons. (Herodotus)

4. The world will little note
         nor long remember
              what we say here,
   but it   can never forget
              what they did here. (Abraham Lincoln)

In this way, students can *see* the parallelism of structure, underscored by the repetition of certain words in the first three examples. In the last three examples, they can also understand how parallelism can be used to emphasize *contrasts of meaning*. Lincoln's sentence is particularly fine, developing contrasts-in-parallel even down to pronouns ("we" and "they"), auxiliary verbs ("will" and "can"), and adverbs ("little," "nor long," and "never"). Examples of parallelism can be found everywhere, even on weight-room walls: Biblical poetry is based on it; the Gettysburg Address is full of it; the great prose stylists of the eighteenth century, like Samuel Johnson and Edward Gibbon, use it in every paragraph. All prose aspiring to be memorable exploits parallelism, even in advertising. Tom Wolfe uses it frequently, especially in lists; even E. B. White employs parallelism, more subtly but almost as often.

Something similar can be done with chiasmus. The word *chiasmus* comes from the Greek letter "chi"—shaped like our "x"— indicating a cross-step or crossing movement:

	A	B
1.	When the going	gets tough,

	B	A
	the tough	get going.

2. The exalted shall be humbled,
   and the humble shall be exalted.

3. Fair is foul,
   and foul is fair. (*Macbeth*)

4. Ask not what your country can do for you;
   ask what you can do for your country.

   (John F. Kennedy)

5. There were not
   forty children conducting themselves like one,
   but every child was conducting himself like forty.

   (Charles Dickens)

All of these, of course, involve some parallelism of structure and repetition of words: that is how they become pointed and memorable. Unless you plan to school your students in subtle distinctions between rhetorical schemes, do not fuss over the differences between parallelism and chiasmus. Instead, you want them to *hear* some memorable expressions and to *see* what makes them so.

But the point is aimed at their own writing. Spend some time on parallelism and ask your students to write or to find (say) five good examples. Students can choose their best ones to read aloud in class. At least some of these should be put on the board so as to feature, visibly, their structures. Every student is working to produce at least one original, memorable, and pointed sentence. Having done this with parallelism, repeat the process with chiasmus. You will, I think, be treated to a display of verbal artistry and wit that everyone will enjoy.

The question may then arise, "How do I follow up on this exercise?" To do that, you need to learn the shapes of language—some basic terms of rhetoric and how to apply them to the description and analysis of style. Although I can reasonably assume that your college courses in English have taught you about the major elements of fiction, drama, and poetry, the elements of style and rhetoric have long been neglected in English departments. I had to learn these things entirely on my own, and the books most useful to me are recorded in the annotated Bibliography in the back of this book. Do not let the labor of learning something new deter you, for you have a treat in store: Learning about the shapes of language will quicken your pleasure in words well-used and enable you to enjoy good writing in new ways. Once that happens, it will light up your teaching all by itself, even if you never plan a follow-up on the exercises suggested here.

4

Teaching Character and Motives in
The Great Gatsby

F. Scott Fitzgerald's *The Great Gatsby* transposes "The Prodigal Son" to America in the 1920s. The novel is narrated by Nick Carraway: Its action begins with his leaving his home in the Midwest to work in New York as a bond salesman, and it ends with his returning home to stay, and to tell this story. Although Nick is not himself a prodigal, he witnesses the "restlessness" and "carelessness" of others and what they cost in their lives. His return home marks his deliberate return to his roots, to tradition and order, away from the rootless life of the "far country." The story of Jay Gatsby, of his self-creating rise to wealth and of his ill-fated love for Daisy, unfolds as part of Nick's story.

Gatsby's story so dominates the novel that it becomes all too easy to neglect Nick's story framing the whole. Nick's framing presents Gatsby's story as a tale with a moral, with several morals. It thereby orients the reader to the basic concerns of the work. The first time I read it, I missed the frame entirely. The first time I taught it, we skimmed over Nick's remarks at the beginning and, consequently, short-changed the questions raised at the end. Eventually, as I learned how to ask better questions about a story, I came to understand how the story itself raises these questions through various strategies such as plot structure and framing. The present chapter attempts to explain what I have learned about teaching a novel in general, with *The Great Gatsby* as case in point. By showing how you might use the basic questions in this book to teach *The Great Gatsby*, what's here tries to illustrate how you might use them to teach any novel.

Preparing to Teach a Novel

We can legitimately ask students to reread a short story, from time to time, and thereby foster the process of discovery and their ability to ask questions about a literary work. But we cannot ask them to reread a novel, and so we must teach it differently. When students reread a story, they can see how earlier incidents foreshadow later ones, and they can pick up the story's themes by their familiarity with its keywords, recurring images, and so on. But since they read a novel only once in class, they cannot see foreshadowing except in retrospect. Given the size of a novel and the pace of teaching it, a retrospect of 100 pages may mean two or more weeks of classes—a long retrospect for high school students. Also, novels builds up their themes slowly, by incremental repetition. They are not written to be read at high school pace—at a few pages a day over a few weeks; it is all too easy to lose the thread of themes so gradually built up. Hence, we need to help students with a novel in various ways so that they can follow the threads of the work while exploring it a few pages at a time.

Your Reading

I believe the best way to prepare for teaching a novel is to read it twice. The first reading is a rapid, get-acquainted reading. The second begins right away, while the work is fresh in your mind, and moves more slowly as, pen in hand, you annotate your teaching copy of the work. It takes two readings to know what are the crucial events, where the most important passages are, and to decide what themes you may want to feature in teaching it.

In my view, a plot summary proves an inadequate substitute for a first reading, though you might use one as an aid. A plot summary can acquaint you with the action and characters of a work but only in a superficial way. It cannot introduce you to the voice of the narrator or the voices of the book's characters, so it cannot reveal their Moral Characters, except by a summary judgment. Similarly, a summary cannot reveal the incremental repetition of keywords and images that form the work's themes. At most, it can only tell you what the summarizer thinks the themes are. A plot summary, then, proves at best a poor substitute for a first reading and positively could even mislead your reading of the novel.

On the other hand, it can prove a valuable aid to a first reading, a kind of tonic for the attention. A plot summary necessarily leaves out some details, and noticing these omissions helps you grasp its inadequacy. It also cannot encompass the ambiguity of the characters' Moral Characters and Acts; a summary may so emphasize one aspect of these as to misrepresent the novel, in your view. Finally, if your students have recourse to *Cliff Notes* and their ilk, familiarity with that enemy can only help your teaching, for you will note where *Cliff* is wrong, and they will not.

Your two readings of the novel aim at the fullest understanding you can reach, given the time available, but they should be oriented toward teaching the work. For that reason, I suggest that you mark your teaching copy in whatever way you find most helpful. The following questions may be useful as a preliminary, general guide:

1. Who are the main characters, and where is each introduced? What passages reveal their Moral Characters and relationships most clearly?

2. What are the crucial Acts of the novel? What passages reveal, or suggest, the characters' motives for them, especially Situation (as each understands it) and Purpose?

3. What are the work's keywords and central themes? What passages reveal these most clearly and fully?

As you can see, there is nothing spectacular or surprising about these questions. They assume the primacy of characters, action, and themes in reading and teaching a novel, and they recognize that everything in a novel is not equally important. Some passages are more telling than others, some acts more crucial, and these you mark because you are likely to draw your students' attention to them if they do not notice their importance first.

In addition, every novelist prepares readers for the climax of the work from its very beginning, often introducing main characters in situations that foreshadow the crisis. For example, Fitzgerald's first chapter introduces his main characters, revealing Tom's infidelities and Daisy's unhappiness. Yet despite the palpable tension between them, as they say good-bye to Nick they stand "side by side in a cheerful square of light" (24), appearing, for this final moment, united and happy.* This foreshadows Nick's final view of them together in the novel (138)—sitting at their kitchen table after the accident, Tom's hand on hers, urging that they leave town together the next day. It takes most of us at least two readings of a novel before we perceive connections like this one: two periods of marital tension ending in an image of unity. Perhaps this is a connection you would prepare your class to perceive, and perhaps not. But you cannot decide what connections to prepare the class for until you have noticed them first.

Moreover, most novels contain many internal cross-references and it takes two readings to discover them, mark your teaching copy, and begin to reflect on what the connections mean. The most important cross-references pertain to the climax of the work and its resolution in the lives of the characters. *The Great Gatsby* abounds with these. Near the end of the novel, for example, Nick learns that Tom thinks Gatsby was driving the car that killed Myrtle, so he got what he deserved when Myrtle's husband killed him (169–170). Daisy has not told him of her guilt, and perhaps has not told anyone. In other words, when Tom persuades Daisy to leave with him, he uses one set of arguments, but she has a different set of reasons. We do not hear what he says to her when Nick looks through the window at them sitting together at the kitchen table: Tom is "talking intently" and "in earnestness" (138), while Daisy gazes silently downward, looking up from time to time to nod in agreement.

---

* All quotations from and page numbers for *The Great Gatsby* are taken from the Penguin Books edition. The page numbers are different in the Simon and Schuster edition.

On the one hand, Fitzgerald has given us enough information at various points to imagine what Tom says: that Gatsby is a hit-and-run murderer and deserves to go to jail for this crime (cf. 169), and perhaps others; that Daisy does not want to get mixed-up in the scandal of Gatsby's arrest and trial; that Tom has always loved Daisy "in [his] heart" (125) and will give her a new life as a faithful husband in the future. On the other hand, Fitzgerald leaves us to imagine Daisy's thoughts and feelings. She knows that she is the hit-and-run murderer and deserves to go to jail. She also knows that Gatsby will say he was the driver (137) because he loves her. Yet she abandons Gatsby to leave with Tom. How does she feel about her decision? What rationalizations does she give herself?

Fitzgerald has planted this cross-reference prominently at the end of the novel, to move us to wonder about Daisy's thoughts. Perhaps you will help your class notice an internal cross-reference like this, and perhaps not. But unless you read a work twice, to map out such cross-references and reflect on their meaning, you cannot help students in this way. Their one reading of the book will not lead them to discover such connections on their own.

It also takes me two readings to understand a book's themes: Where they are introduced and how they are developed. To be sure, a first reading reveals themes to an experienced reader, but it always does so by some form of repetition. Generally, we finally recognize a theme somewhere in the middle, or even at the end, of its development. For example, the word "careless," and its opposite "care," are used often near the end of *The Great Gatsby* (142, 143, 153, 168, 170): Nick's disgust with the "carelessness" of Tom, Daisy, and Jordan (170) leads him to return home. The word is first featured when Jordan almost hits a workman with her car (59), and "careless" does not receive the same emphasis again until the end of the novel. Yet once a reader is clued into this theme, *images* of carelessness abound in the novel: Tom's adultery and drunkenness, the casual party in Chapter 2 that ends with Tom's breaking Myrtle's nose, the "amusement park" (53) attitudes of Gatsby's partygoers.

Other themes also come into focus and their interrelations are clarified. The novel features an extravagant instance of caring—Gatsby's long devotion to Daisy—but it includes Nick's return home to care for his life, far away from all the carelessness that had disgusted him. The keyword "restless," used so often in Chapter 1 (9, 13, 15, 23), especially for Tom, is linked through him (169) to carelessness (170) near the end of the story. In fact, Tom has been restless and careless from the beginning, but the character Nick realizes this fully only at the end. Hence, though Nick as narrator shows Tom's restlessness and carelessness (his infidelities) in Chapter 1, he puts the keywords together for Tom only at their final meeting. In Chapter 1, "restless" seems to be a neutral word, for Nick uses it for himself. By the novel's end, however, it has acquired moral overtones by its link with carelessness. Consequently, Nick's return home implies his seeking of both rest, for he will remain there, and caring for others. Internal patterns like these emerge only gradually in one's understanding of a work. As I said before, it takes me at least two readings to notice patterns and to see how they function.

Designing the Unit

There is a rational, logical way to divide up the reading assignments for a novel, and I recommend that you avoid doing so. This rational, logical way works simply by numbers of pages. *The Great Gatsby*, for example, runs about 170 pages, and you know that your students can assimilate (say) about ten pages per night. Hence, you allot seventeen class days for reading the novel, plus a final discussion or two to prepare them for a test or a paper, or both. Unfortunately, this "rational way" of dividing assignments assumes that every part of the novel is equally important; that simply is not true. The important parts of a novel call for more time and attention: The reading pace should be slower so that students can think more carefully about them, and more should be done with them in class.

The important parts of a novel are its beginning, climax, and end. Often there is a turning point in the middle, and it, too, calls for careful study: *The Great Gatsby* has one in its central chapter, when Gatsby and Daisy are reunited in love. The beginning of a novel should be taken slowly because it sets up the rest of the work. It usually takes a rereading to see all that the opening pages are working to accomplish: the tone of the narrator, the framing of the story, the introduction of main characters, and so on. Our first vision of Tom Buchanan (12), for example, epitomizes his whole Moral Character, and our first vision of Daisy (13) emphasizes her delicacy, in contrast to Tom's physical power. An experienced reader knows that first visions like these are weighted with significance and reads them attentively. Inexperienced readers often need our help merely to notice these passages. They also need help getting oriented to the world of the novel. Experienced readers readily pick up the writer's opening hints, shaping the significance of his characters and action, but students often do not. Once we help them get up and running, however, they do better with the middle of a work.

Climaxes deserve special attention and usually receive it. The novel builds to its *climax*—a crisis and resolution that gathers together the work's main characters and themes. The climax often abounds with internal cross-references to other parts of the work, because that is one way of gathering its threads together. In *The Great Gatsby*, this involves the mystery of what exactly happened in the accident that killed Myrtle Wilson. Clues explaining various details are scattered over many pages (117–119, 130, 135, 137, 151–152), but they are never brought together into a single, coherent account. Nick leaves it for us to put them together and expects readers to do so.

Because the climax of a work is so exciting, it proves all too easy to under-read the ending. If we think of *The Great Gatsby* as Gatsby's story, we are inclined to see

Gatsby's death as its end (154), and the final chapter (155–172) as mere after-math. But because the novel is being narrated by Nick, we can see how the meaning of Gatsby's life is carried over into his funeral and the ironic absence of mourners. More precisely, Gatsby's story has become part of Nick's life story, and Nick's failed efforts to gather mourners for the funeral reveal Gatsby's significance for Nick and lack of significance for Daisy and for the dead man's other "friends." The novel's ultimate issues become clearest at its ending. For this reason, I recommend spending extra time on the ending of a work and will suggest some strategies for how to do this with *Gatsby*.

In short, when designing a unit on a novel, you should consider paying more attention to its beginning, turning point, climax, and end by giving shorter reading assignments and doing more with them. You also need to decide how much time you want spend on minor characters and the subplot. The romance between Nick and Jordan Baker forms a subplot in *The Great Gatsby*. Students can follow the romance rather easily, though its breakup is obscure (135–136, 147–148, 168). Do you also want them to think about the subplot? Do you want them to think about how the subplot relates to the main plot? If so, you must give time and attention to these tasks. Paying attention to subplots necessarily slows the reading pace a little and distracts students from the main line of the work. In general, the more able your students, the more easily they can reflect on minor characters and integrate a subplot with the main action. But less able students read less easily, and too much time on a subplot tends to distract them from understanding the work as a coherent whole.

Integrating the Novel with the Course

Let me begin by confessing that most teachers find this more important than I do. It takes several weeks to teach a novel well, and helping students understand it as a coherent whole proves, in my view, integration enough. They find it difficult to get their minds "around" a novel over several weeks of bit-by-bit reading, and they could care less about seeing connections between it and the rest of the course. Such connections can only be made in a highly general way and, generally, the themes tend to become too broad and vague to illuminate anything clearly; however, this is a minority opinion. I am primarily interested in helping students understand individual works, in detail and in-depth, and large themes do not give me the same kind of intellectual satisfaction.

Nevertheless, I think about course-long connections too and often tell students how what we are doing now relates to what we have done before. The present work offers one way of doing this in a course, regardless of its thematic content: The basic questions can be applied to every story and play. Your repeated use of them in class teaches students how to ask and answer them on their own. They may notice, for example, that Daisy and Myrtle are character foils and work out the details of *What goes with what?* and *What versus what?* They may go on to wonder: "Why is Tom attracted to two women so different from each other? What does this tell us about Tom's Moral Character?" The more often students learn to ask questions like these, the more reflective and skillful they become as readers. Their inquiry skills, their ability to formulate good questions on their own, build up as the course progresses.

But teachers also want thematic connections to unify the various parts of a course, and what these are depends on the course itself. While *The Great Gatsby* is always *The Great Gatsby*, it connects differently to a course on Literature After World War I than to an American Literature survey. No general advice can be given beyond E. M. Forster's, "Only connect." But if you are unhappily afflicted with a Survey of American Literature, because you have not yet read widely in it, the following remarks may help.

The following list contains a set of contrasts that recur often in American Literature courses because they characterize some central aspects of American experience. The contrasts work at a high level of generality and, naturally, they do not cover everything important because nothing does. A structural anthropologist would call them "binary pairs" and say that they reveal certain "deep structures." I would not go so far. But this large-scale *What goes with what?* and *What versus what?* may help you think about connections within your course:

East	West
old	new, young
[Europe	America]
[Eastern cities	Western frontier]
dependence	independence
civilization	nature
sophisticated	naïve, natural
corrupt	unspoiled
"experience"	"innocence"
settled patterns	open possibilities
ordered	wild
fixed, rigid	fluid, fresh
shaping force: tradition, society	individual energy, initiative
primacy of social roles, placement	self-making, self-creation

From the beginning, coming to America has always meant a new beginning, a fresh start, for social groups and for individuals. Freed from oppression in England, the Puritans would build their "city on a hill" in the new land. Later immigrants would leave behind their Old World antagonisms as they started their new life:

Poles and Russians did not make war in the streets of Chicago in the nineteenth century, any more than Jews and Palestinians do today. Moreover, in the New World, the social and economic restraints of the Old World no longer applied. You might start out poor, but you could make your own way, based on your energy and initiative. Benjamin Franklin, born in modest circumstances, became a successful businessman, inventor, scientist, politician, founding father, diplomat, and international luminary. Had he lived in England, much of his achievement would have been impossible.

Jay Gatsby stands in a direct line from Franklin, in his struggle to liberate himself from his past and to create a new life. "Self-making," even "self-creation," is a distinctively American theme—national and historical as well as individual and literary. That theme includes works as different as the Declaration of Independence, Thomas Paine's "Common Sense and the Crisis," Emerson's "Self-Reliance," Thoreau at Walden, Whitman's self-celebration, essays by W.E.B. DuBois, and much more. Alice Walker, like Fitzgerald, takes up the theme in a critical mode with Dee in "Everyday Use."

The quest for independent self-making marks the westward movement not only from the Old to the New World but also in America itself. This quest often involves preserving one's "innocence" from eastern sophistication and corruption. James Fenimore Cooper's heroes are frontiersmen, and they remain innocents even in the midst of violence. At the end of *Huckleberry Finn*, Huck heads West to avoid being civilized by Aunt Sally. Gatsby himself comes from poor farm people in the West, and therefore he remains an innocent in his love for Daisy despite his bootlegging. He stands in contrast to Tom, born wealthy in sophisticated Chicago. Similarly, when Nick Carraway moves to New York, he experiences a "fall" from midwestern innocence to eastern "experience," and he eventually returns home to recover.

To be sure, this West versus East dichotomy can also be given opposite values: The West is primitive, rude, raw, while the East is civilized, cultured, polite, learned, and sophisticated in a good sense. Henry James's fictional Americans go to Europe and encounter there a world more strangely and more deeply complex than their own. From the European perspective, America is young and callow, so even sophisticated Americans prove shallower than their European counterparts. To adapt Mark Twain's title, they are *Innocents Abroad*. James lived much of his adult life in Europe, as did Ezra Pound and T. S. Eliot, who filled their astonishingly new American poetry with allusions to very old books. But many writers have portrayed the American encounter with Europe in fiction, memoir, and travel writing. The movement from western "innocence" to eastern "experience" can mark a cultured deepening of awareness, the giving up of naïve illusions, a growth into mature responsibility.

But it can also mark a fall into corruption. The Fall is also part of the story of America. The New World may have potential, but it has to be realized by our old selves, and the realization never lives up to the greatness of the potential. *The*

Great Gatsby dwells on this theme in a particular mode—the dreams of the imagination are so extravagant that reality always falls short (92–93, 94–96, 106–107, 171–172, and others). The Christian story of the Fall is echoed often in Hawthorne's fiction, in Melville, Updike, Cheever, and others—even in Paradise an evil serpent lurked. The national "fall" is slavery and the Civil War, reflected in many speeches and literary works. But innocence is always being threatened by experience, high ideals by low realities.

On this theme, Huck Finn and Holden Caulfield (*Catcher in the Rye*) are not far away from Hawthorne's "Young Goodman Brown," "Rappacini's Daughter," and Reverend Dimmesdale (*The Scarlet Letter*). Huck would be lucky to come to terms with experience as well as Newland Archer does in Edith Wharton's *Age of Innocence*, or Jim Burden in Willa Cather's *My Antonia*. Gatsby's tragedy lies, not in his murder, but in his fall from innocence. Nick suggests (153) that untimely death was a happier end for Gatsby than being abandoned by Daisy, the source of love and meaning in his life.

Although some themes in *The Great Gatsby* can be illuminated by the preceding columns of contrasts, it clearly uses them with a twist or two. Gatsby and Nick go East, and not West, in their quest for a new life. Perhaps because the novel is set after "the closing of the frontier," the West no longer necessarily represents the pure potential for self-creation. Gatsby and Nick are mid-westerners, not far-westerners, and Nick associates the Midwest with settled patterns of living in small towns and on farms. Nevertheless, the eastern city, New York, continues to be linked with sophistication and corruption. Here, urban rootlessness, not frontier rootlessness, enables Gatsby's self-creation through wealth from bootlegging. Yet, like Cooper's frontiersmen, Gatsby remains an innocent in the midst of a turbulent world, for he is moved primarily by his dream of Daisy's love.

The Great Gatsby is a profound, and profoundly American, literary work. If you are not satisfied with these broad themes linking it to other works of American literature, you will surely find others.

Teaching *The Great Gatsby*

When I teach a novel, my primary goal is to help the students get involved with the characters and the action. The sooner they regard the characters as "real people," the more involved they are with the action, the better they read and discuss the work, and the more they learn and enjoy learning. Perhaps this marks me as naïve, but once this primary goal is reached, the rest of our work becomes much easier; for a good novel, by definition, teaches itself, once readers are involved with it. As Aristotle said, "A good beginning is more than half of the whole."

There are several useful strategies for fostering this involvement. Reading Journals (see Provocation #10) lead students to think about a reading assignment and commit their responses to writing. They think and write about what is important to them, and this both involves them with the book and prepares them to discuss it. They tend to interpret and evaluate characters and their Acts, knowing that their evaluations may provoke disagreement but cannot be wrong. This security lends them confidence, and even enthusiasm, for reading and discussing. For our part, because a novel enables continuing acquaintance with its characters, we teachers can allow interpretive evaluations that we find mistaken. After all, if a class reads "Eveline" only once, and the students think that "Her father is really a nice man," we should probably point out some passages about his verbal abuse of her. But if half the class excuses Tom Buchanan's adultery in Chapter 1, insisting that he is "just being a guy," they can still change their minds when he breaks Myrtle's nose in Chapter 2.

Reading Aloud (see Provocation #8) also encourages involvement because it leads them to realize the characters' feelings by using their own voices. "How would Daisy say this to Tom?" gives rise to several different performances, each with its own nuances, and so, naturally, does Tom's response. In my experience, students tend to recognize these nuances accurately, even if they have difficulty verbalizing what they mean. They are better at performing the characters' parts, and at appreciating their classmates' voicing of them, than in analyzing them. This bothers me not a whit: The voice has many more nuances than analysis can define.

Another strategy involves asking students to pick out a significant passage from the reading and to explain why it is significant. You can even ask them to write a paragraph on it in their Reading Journals. Several students often pick the same passage, and the ensuing discussion thereby has several experts. Again, because the students select what is important for them, they cannot be wrong, and this encourages their involvement in the novel.

All these can be used throughout your teaching of a book. The best advice for beginning a novel is: "Go slowly." The first reading assignments should be shorter so that more time in class can be spent on acquainting students with the characters and their relationships. First appearances of characters are always important, and we can help students become aware of these by keeping the assignments short and asking them to reflect on what they notice. These first appearances can also be read aloud in class and probed in a detailed discussion. The aim is to establish the main characters clearly in the students' minds. Let them disagree about their impressions of these people, so long as they are impressed. Once this happens, the students will follow the action of the characters with greater ease and interest.

Beginning The Great Gatsby

Let me illustrate this general advice with some practical details—not a prescription, because classes differ so widely, but suggestions to be used, adapted, or ignored as you see fit. For several reasons, you might begin the novel by taking students slowly through the first two to four pages in class: Nick's introduction (7–8, a distinct section) in the narrator's present, and his (past) move to the east (8–10). First, inexperienced readers tend to find novels a bit forbidding—they're so long! After all, if a student dislikes one short story, she can look forward to reading a different one in a day or so, but it takes weeks for a class to work through a novel. Second, Nick's introduction is linguistically difficult, for he uses many more Latinate (that is, polysyllabic) words than proves usual over the rest of the work. Although the narrative in *Gatsby* moves briskly and reads easily, Nick's introduction does not, and students are easily put off by it. They need help to understand his introduction, and perhaps also your promise that the rest of the book is easier to understand. Finally, the opening pages orient the reader to the novel. Inexperienced readers tend to miss the issues raised here, especially because the vocabulary is often beyond their "range." Your assistance in class will go a long way to helping students begin *The Great Gatsby* well.

You might begin by walking the students through Nick's introduction a few sentences at a time. By raising questions, you can help them see how this introduction is supposed to orient their reading. The questions might include some or all of the following:

1. Who is this narrator? What does he tell us directly about his values, beliefs attitudes, and so on? What does he tell us indirectly? Do you agree with his values, beliefs, and so on, or not, and why? Do you like this narrator, or not, and why?

2. Who is Gatsby? What does the narrator think of Gatsby? Why does he call this story *The Great Gatsby*—what makes Gatsby "great"?

3. Why is the narrator telling us this story? That is, why do you think it is important to him? What do you think he learned by living his part in this story? What do you think he wants us to learn from his telling of it?

These questions concern the Moral Characters of the narrator and of Gatsby (*What goes with what?* for each), and the narrator's Purpose in telling this story. They progress from the explicit to the implied. The first question set might be answered every few sentences. Doing so builds up a fairly detailed picture of Nick's values, as he declares them. The second question has more ambiguities. Gatsby is not named until the final paragraph, and then with some ambivalence, for Nick has "unaffected scorn" for all that Gatsby represents, and yet he "turned out all right at the end" (8). Hence, Nick does not clarify what makes Gatsby "great," except perhaps his capacity for "hope," even though other things are suggested. The final question is the most significant, yet it cannot be answered fully until the novel's end. Nevertheless, it is worth raising, I think, for the students can make some reasonable guesses based on Nick's values and beliefs (question 1). One thing, at least, is clear: This is a moral tale, for Nick has returned from the East with a commitment to moral conduct. In fact, you might help your students to see how Nick's moralizing stance, in these pages, makes his prose seem so stiff. Not a few of us grow stiff with Latinate diction when we moralize from a height.

If you begin *The Great Gatsby* in class this way, I recommend that you pace the reading and discussion so that students can read a page or two into the next section, where Nick explains his move to the East. The narrative proper begins here, and it proves much easier for students to understand. The class can read half a page, rather than a few sentences, before considering a question like: "What new things have we learned about the narrator?" They quickly grow more comfortable with the book as it becomes easier to read. They come to like Nick better as he speaks more clearly about his life, telling his own story. They also grow to accept the world of the novel, rather than resist it, as with Nick's introduction. In other words, they are growing comfortable and involved with the book.

Having begun the novel in class this way, what would make an appropriate reading assignment? Perhaps you have taken the class two pages into the second section (8–22), to page 10, and a good class could read the next twelve pages. Nevertheless, on the principle of "Go slowly at the beginning," let me recommend that the first night's reading go no further than page 17. By that point, all the major characters have been significantly introduced, Tom in some detail (11–13), Daisy and Jordan more briefly (13–14). There has also been some conversation, so their voices have been heard. The assignment could end even earlier, with the physical description of Jordan (16), and you would still have ample material for discussion. These are all significant characters in the novel, and our first glimpses of them tell us a good deal about them, if we take the time to look.

Again, the primary aim is to help students get involved with the characters and the action, to establish the main characters clearly in their minds. Because readers are first attracted to the characters and action of a work, students tend to feature these in their Journals. I suggest that, ahead of time, you name two students—one for opening remarks, one for first reply—to open the discussion on the following day. (Then, if "opening remarks" is absent, you still have a student prepared to begin the discussion.) Students always go to what is most important for them, and whatever one student finds important will have attracted several others. In the preceding proposed assignment, for example, a student will begin discussion with Tom's Moral Character almost every time, and others will be ready to add their views, agreeing and disagreeing.

Your problem will soon become managing the discussion so that it achieves some focus and clarity. You might make a master list on the board of significant details about Tom, while allowing students to debate their meaning as they describe and evaluate his Moral Character. Once all the possibilities have been covered, you might also give them a few minutes to summarize their evaluative understandings of

Tom in two to four sentences. Then, if you wish, you could have a few students read their sentences aloud as a summary review of the discussion or even a renewal of it. In any event, this exercise helps them establish their views of Tom firmly in their minds; they need not agree with one another, of course, or with you. Because each student's view is valued, students are encouraged, in this way, to involve themselves with the characters without worrying about being right or wrong.

With a shorter assignment, you can ask students to read more carefully, for they must complete an entry in their Reading Journals on the basis of fewer pages. You might suggest ahead of time that all the characters in the assignment are important, and that students need to understand them as fully as possible. Students should feel free to mix interpretation and evaluation in their Journal responses because evaluation involves them with the characters and the action. Class discussion, then, might gather together the details about each character (*What goes with what?*) and explore their meanings (*What is this person's Moral Character?*). Discussion of Tom, for example, could include the following questions:

What kind of person is Tom? What is he like physically? What do these details tell us about his personality (or Moral Character)?

What do we know about Tom's past? What do these details tell us about him?

Does Nick like Tom, or not, and why? Do you like Tom, or not, and why?

What do you think of Tom's relationship with Daisy? Do they have a good marriage, or not, and why?

Similar questions work for Daisy and for Jordan Baker, even though they encompass fewer details. In general, wherever we find a detailed set of associations in a work (*What goes with what?*), a set of oppositions is not far away. Hence, you might also pursue *What versus what?* for Tom and Daisy, for Tom's size and power clearly contrast with Daisy's delicacy, which is suggested by her name and other flower images.

On the next assignment, the students can probably finish Chapter 1, reading eight to nine pages, which are filled with conversation. They are now acquainted with these people, so students can assimilate new details more easily, such as Tom's adultery (20) and Daisy's bitterness at her own "sophistication" (22). They are familiar with the style of the work and are enjoying it. While three class days may seem like a lot to spend on eighteen pages, the investment pays off. The students will be up-and-running with the novel.

The Middle of the Novel

Once students are up-and-running with a work, you can easily give reading assignments of normal length. For example, if students do thirty minutes of homework per night for your course, you might allow twenty to twenty-three minutes for reading, and seven to ten for Journal writing. Naturally, whenever possible, it is best to adjust assignments for chapter breaks (and section breaks). Because it is always hard to consistently reach the middle of what a class can do, my tendency is to prefer shorter assignments: The less they read, the more they have to think to produce the minimum Journal entry. This means I can enforce requirements with greater assurance, knowing my demands are reasonable. But other teachers tend to require longer assignments, stretching their students in that way. Since we teachers are going to miss the middle sometimes, whether short or long, it is good to know which we prefer, and why, and to fashion assignments accordingly.

As we work with students' responses, it is useful to have several different ways of posing "the same question." Because different students view characters in different ways, some respond to some forms of a question better than others, because that particular form somehow registers with them, chimes in with their way of thinking. For example, early in Chapter 2 Tom introduces Nick to Myrtle Wilson, his mistress, before getting her away from her husband for a casual party in New York City. The following questions all concern Tom's Moral Character with respect to this affair. For us, each question has different nuances. But in class, these nuances prove less important in themselves than as ways of appealing to different students, with their different ways of responding to characters as human beings:

Interpretive Why is Tom having an affair with Myrtle? What does this affair tell us about Tom? What does this affair mean to Tom? Why is it important to him? What does Myrtle mean to Tom? Why is she important to him? In what ways is she important to him? How does Tom feel about Myrtle? Is Tom "in love" with Myrtle, or not, and why? Why does he have these feelings? What do his feelings tell us about him?

Evaluative What do you think of Tom for having this affair, and why? How do you feel about Tom's having this affair, and why? Is this a good thing, or a bad thing, and why? Do you approve of Tom's affair, or disapprove of it, and why? What, if anything, is good about Tom's affair, and what is bad, and why?

The questions can be posed in other ways. Each of us has certain ways that appeal to us, because we tend to think in certain categories. But as teachers, we work with a variety of students who have different patterns of learning and thinking, and we need to learn how to give them questions that spark responses. In that way, all the students can learn to ask not only the kinds of questions that open up their own patterns of thinking but also new questions that extend their powers.

Because a novel opens up a variety of perspectives within the work, these deserve some exploration too. Although Tom's affair with Myrtle is first presented from his point of view, Myrtle's perspective gradually becomes clearer and deserves some attention. As we all know, a relationship is not a single thing, but works both ways. Hence, Tom's affair with Myrtle is one thing, and Myrtle's affair with Tom is something rather different. Consider the following interpretive and evaluative questions about Myrtle in Chapter 2, divided into categories:

Myrtle's Moral Character What is Myrtle's Moral Character? What kind of person is she? What do you think of her? How does she look and act, and what do these details tell us about her? Do you like Myrtle, or not, and why? Is she a good person, or not, and why?

Myrtle's Marriage What does Myrtle think of her husband, and why? How does she feel about him, and why? What does Myrtle think of her marriage, and why? How does she feel about her marriage, and why? What do Myrtle's views on her husband and marriage tell us about her? What do you think of her marriage? How do you feel about her marriage? Is Myrtle being fair to her husband, or not, and why?

Her Affair with Tom Why is Myrtle having an affair with Tom? What does Tom mean to her? Why is he important to her? How does she feel about him? Is she in love with him, or not, and why? What is she getting, or what does she hope to get, by having this affair? What do you think of Myrtle for having this affair? Do you approve of Myrtle for having this affair, or not, and why? Is this affair a good thing for her, or not, and why?

Now, at the beginning of a discussion about Chapter 2, students are likely to express all kinds of views about Myrtle, interpretive and evaluative, on these three issues, helter-skelter. My practice is to allow this to go on for as long as ten minutes, letting them agree and disagree and introduce new points freely. In that way, they are encouraged to speak, and I come to understand the range of thoughts they have had. But then I say the equivalent of, "There are several issues here, so let's take them one at a time," and I try to begin with what has excited the greatest interest. On the one hand, it would be logical to discuss Myrtle's Moral Character before discussing her marriage, and logical again to discuss her marriage before her affair with Tom. On the other hand, because these issues are closely related, I am happy to begin with her affair with Tom, if the class seems to want to begin there, and let the others emerge afterward.

But you may not be. Perhaps you are teaching the novel for the first time, and lack of familiarity with teaching *Gatsby* leads you to want more control over the discussion. Perhaps you are teaching the novel to several different class sections, and you want them all to have gone over the same material in the same sequence of topics. After all, if one section begins with Myrtle's affair, and another begins with her Moral Character, the discussions will have different shapes even though both succeed in helping students clarify their understanding of Myrtle. Perhaps you will wonder, "If the discussions differ, how can I give them the same test at the end?" On the other hand, perhaps you intend the final test to be an essay, so differences here and there will not matter. In general, the more experience you have in teaching a particular work in a particular school, the more flexible you will feel you can be. In any event, you should do what is best for you as the teacher you are now.

But the questions about the characters' motives are always relevant. Naturally, everyone wonders why a person does something. "Why is Tom having an affair with Myrtle?" is a good question, directive yet open-ended, because it has many different answers. When we also ask, "Why is Myrtle having an affair with Tom?" we come to see two quite different perspectives on a single situation, and we know that conflict and disappointment are not far away. As students read through the middle of the novel, their Journals will canvass the main characters' Acts, interpreting and evaluating them. To help them think more clearly and deeply, we can always make use of the basic questions about motives, posing them in the various ways suggested before and working with students' answers.

What goes with what? and *What versus what?* also prove useful throughout the developing middle of a work. For example, if your students are used to looking for character foils, they will pick up on the contrasts between Daisy and Myrtle. Or you might point the contrast out, perhaps with reference to the passages introducing each (13–14, 28). Then you might have students work out the contrasting details, with you making a two-column master list on the board. In this way, the class arrives at a clearer understanding of the their Moral Characters—how Daisy and Myrtle each embody a way of living, thinking, feeling, and acting, with corresponding beliefs and values about love, marriage, moral conduct, and so on. As the students agree and disagree about Daisy and Myrtle, they naturally express their evaluations of which one they like better, and why. In this way, discussion deepens their involvement with the characters as it increases their understanding. The same kind of discussion could also be had as Gatsby, the faithful lover who earned his wealth illegally, emerges as a foil to Tom, the faithless husband who inherited his money legally.

Yet *What goes with what?* and *What versus what?*—Association and Contrast—can also be applied to other things. The Valley of Ashes, at the beginning of Chapter 2, can be contrasted with the mansions of East and West Egg in Chapter 1. The quiet, arranged party in Chapter 1, although it has its marital tensions, contrasts with the raucous, casual party in Chapter 2, ending in violence. Gatsby's enormous party in Chapter 3 can be contrasted with either. Gatsby himself, sober and decent, emerges in contrast to his drunk and disorderly guests, while his Moral Character, on the basis of the rumors about him, might be contrasted with that of quiet, law-abiding Nick. Because literary works feature conflict between persons to illustrate differing values, beliefs, and ways of living, writers use Association and Contrast continually in their works, not only for characters but also for settings, keywords, and images. Hence, as often as you wish, you can put *What goes with what?* and *What versus what?* to good use.

Turning Point and Climax

Because the turning point and climax of a novel are crucial to the plot, they deserve more careful attention than the rising action that leads to them. At these moments, various strands of character and theme come together, and exploring them fully takes time. As we read a novel, we are always trying to grasp "What is happening?"—the character's Acts in the plot—and "Why is this here?" or What does it mean?" for their lives and Moral Characters. These are the effective questions that underlie every student's Reading Journal on every assignment. A middle assignment normally contains only one or two significant incidents for one main character, while the turning point and climax, by definition, contain highly significant incidents for two or more main characters. Hence, I recommend that you trim your reading assignments a bit for these parts of the work, perhaps to 80 percent of what is normal. The turning point and climax raise special kinds of questions, and a slightly slower pace gives students more time to explore them.

A *turning point,* by definition, is a kind of transformation. It involves a Before and an After in the characters' lives. *What becomes what*—the master question for the work as a whole—should be applied to the turning point in order to understand it fully. After a turning point, the characters' lives are forever changed, whether for good or ill, and this seems not to be true of other significant incidents. The turning point in *The Great Gatsby* comes in Chapter 5, when Nick arranges for Gatsby and Daisy to meet again, and it runs only fourteen pages (79–93). I recommend that you cover it in two assignments, perhaps dividing it at Nick's leaving Gatsby and Daisy alone (85). Not only is it about midway in the chapter, but it also leaves the students in suspense as to how the meeting will work out.

To understand the significance of any turning point, we must assess the change it works in the characters' lives, the Before and After of *What becomes what?* In *The Great Gatsby*, we enter this turning point through Nick's awareness of Gatsby nervously anticipating his meeting with Daisy. In order to understand his nervousness, we need to have a sense of what this meeting means to him. Some of the following questions can be used with the preceding first reading assignment (79–85):

> Why is Gatsby so nervous? What does this meeting mean to him? What does he hope from it, and why? What does he fear, and why? If this meeting lives up to Gatsby's hope, how will that change his life, and why? If this meeting fails, how will that change his life, and why?

> Are Gatsby's hopes for this meeting good, or bad, and why? Do you blame him for trying to arrange a love reunion with Daisy, or not, and why?

The question of hope and fear points to the future and to the change involved in this turning point. For the meeting will be a turning point in Gatsby's life, no matter how it turns out, and he knows it.

The turning-point question of *What becomes what?* arises in addition, as it were, to the normal assignment questions—what is happening and what does it mean. That is why a little extra time should be spent on a turning point. The normal task of exploring the incidents in a work has this additional level of significance, which is manifested in new questions. By the end of Chapter 5, these questions also apply to Daisy, and to Daisy and Gatsby together. Because Daisy does not know that Nick is inviting her to see Gatsby, she has no hopes or fears, as Gatsby does. Nevertheless, the Before and After significance for her of this reunion needs to be assessed, as the following questions attempt to indicate:

> What was Daisy's life like before this reunion? That is, how did she think and feel about herself, her life, her marriage, her happiness, her future, and so on? After her reunion with Gatsby, how does she feel about herself, her life, her marriage, her happiness, and so on? How has this reunion changed her life already? How do you think it will change her life in the future?

> Is this reunion a good thing, or a bad thing, and why? (Or, in what ways is it good, in what ways is it bad, and why?) Do you blame them for beginning a potential adultery, or not, and why?

> What do you think will happen to Gatsby and Daisy as a couple, and why? What would you like to see happen, and why?

Even though a story regularly invites us to wonder "What will happen next?" it does so especially at a turning point. Because Daisy is married to Tom, this blissful reunion carries a burden, and the novel invites us to wonder how it might be resolved.

That resolution takes place in the work's climax in Chapter 7, which features a confrontation, or a contest, between Tom and Gatsby over Daisy. Here, we need to take stock of the motives, hopes, and fears of these characters as the confrontation unfolds. This is the *crisis of novel*; their Situations and Moral Characters have been carefully established by the work, and the crisis has been building ever since the love-reunion in Chapter 5. Gatsby has been actively working toward it, and once Tom realizes that Daisy is in love with him (113), the crisis arrives in full. From that point until the end of the chapter, the following questions can be brought to bear for each of the characters (though I phrase them only for Gatsby here):

> What does Gatsby want to achieve, or to have happen, overall? In a given Act, what does he want to achieve? (Purpose)

> Why does he want to achieve it? That is, what does it mean to him, for his life? (Moral Character)

> How is he trying to achieve it, and with what feelings does he speak or act? (Act, Attitude)
>
> Is his overall Purpose good, or bad, and why?
>
> Are his Purpose, Act, and Attitude (in a given instance) good, or bad, and why?

The answers to these questions shift at various points in the action. For example, although Tom's overall Purpose is to keep Daisy and save his marriage, he has more immediate ones for different Acts: to provoke conflict between himself and Gatsby; to move Daisy's love for him by declaring his constant love for her "in [his] heart" (125); to create disagreement between her and Gatsby (126); and so on. To understand and fully appreciate the dramatic action in these pages, we seek to grasp the perspectives and aims—the hopes and fears—of each character at each significant shift in their relationships with one another.

At the end of Chapter 7, when Nick sees Tom and Daisy together at the kitchen table (138), he knows that they will stay together, and that Gatsby has lost the love of his life. The crisis has been resolved, though Gatsby has only an inkling of it. For Chapter 8, then, you might return to a normal reading pace. By this point, students are eager to solve the mystery of Myrtle's death and to see how everything turns out. If you want them to explore the romantic subplot between Nick and Jordan, you should probably continue to go slowly through Chapter 8. But if you have decided to focus the students' inquiry on the main plot, you can let them "head for home."

The Ending: What Becomes What?

I suggested earlier that it proves all too easy to under-read the ending of *The Great Gatsby*: Chapter 9 seems mere aftermath, for the main events of the novel end with Gatsby's death. Nevertheless, the *significance* of these events, the *meanings* of Gatsby's life, are still important to seek. The novel raises several questions in its ending, without resolving any of them unambiguously. Insofar as we neglect them, we do not come to understand fully the meaning of the story Nick has been telling us. We want to know what each of the main characters has learned, if anything, from the tumultuous experiences they have endured. At the ending of every narrative, we can and should ask, *What becomes what?*—how are things different at the end than they were at the beginning? Some novels answer this question fully in their endings. Fitzgerald's novel does not, for he wants to tease us into thought.

Perhaps the character of this ending can be illustrated by contrasting it with that of a Jane Austen novel. Austen's final chapters typically tell us how all the characters turned out over the rest of their lives: The good and sensible people have good marriages and happy lives, while the wicked or foolish generally do not, and there may be a mixed in-between case. Austen achieves considerable closure in this way, so we who are Austen fans find her endings enormously satisfying.

The final chapter of *The Great Gatsby*, however, is more open-ended. Although from the beginning Nick presents it as a moral tale, he is not an omniscient author, like Austen, so he cannot tell us whether Tom and Daisy have a happy or an unhappy life, nor can he tell us much about his own. After all, he only returned home "last autumn" (8), so these events took place the year before: Nick is only thirty-one, and he has years to live. He does not know how everything turns out for everyone, in the Austen manner; he is not even sure about Gatsby's last thoughts, though he has his suspicions (153–154). Hence, Nick's story leads us to wonder about the meanings it has in the lives of these people, without telling us what they might be, even though he does give some hints. Where Austen's endings tend to close off interpretive and evaluative questions by answering them, Fitzgerald's ending deliberately opens them up.

Let me suggest several questions opened up by the ending of *The Great Gatsby*. These deliberately skip Meyer Wolfsheim (161–163) as a minor character, and Nick's last meeting with Jordan (168–169) as a subplot. The questions begin with Gatsby's murder at the end of Chapter 8 and move forward through Chapter 9; hence, they are sequenced, with page numbers indicated in parentheses. Even when they arise from local incidents, they are all concerned with large-scale assessments, interpretive and evaluative, of the main characters and their relationships. We would like to understand and evaluate how each main character views the others, and we also want to understand and evaluate each character for ourselves. Because Gatsby is the title-character, most of the questions involve assessments, from different perspectives, of his Moral Character and his life.

1. At the end, what does Gatsby think and feel about his life? How do you think he regarded his life—was it a success, or a failure, or something else—and why?

2. Why is it so important to Nick to gather mourners for Gatsby's funeral? In your view, what does he think of Tom and Daisy's leaving (156), and why? What does he think about Daisy's sending no message or flowers (165), and why? What does a lack of mourners mean to Nick about Gatsby's life, and why? Do you think Nick is right or wrong about that, and why?

3. What does Mr. Gatz think and feel about his son, as a person, and about his life as a whole (159–160, 163–165)? Are Mr. Gatz's views true, or not, and why? Are they good, or not, and why?

4. Why, at first, does Nick refuse to shake hands with Tom when he sees him again (169) and yet shakes hands with him at parting (170)? Would you have shook his hand in the end, or not, and why? In the end, what does Nick think of Tom as a person, and why? Do you agree with Nick's view of Tom, or not, and why?

5. Daisy has not told Tom the truth about the accident (170). In your view, what does Daisy think and feel about Gatsby's life and death, and why? What does she think and feel about her role in Gatsby's life and death, and why?

6. What do you think of Tom and Daisy's marriage in the end? Do you think their marriage is better, worse, or the same as it was in Chapter 1, and why? Are they happily married, or not, and why?

7. What do you think of Nick as a person (his Moral Character)? Nick has suggested that he is careful, while Tom, Daisy, and Jordan are "careless" (170), and he says outright that he is "one of the few honest people" he has ever known (59). In your view, how true is this? That is, is Nick always careful in his relations with others, or is he sometimes "careless"? If the latter, where is he careless, and why do you say that? Is Nick always honest in his dealings with others, or not? If not, where is he not honest, and why do you say that?

8. In the end, what is Nick's view of Gatsby (170–172, 7–8)? According to Nick, what makes Gatsby "great"? Is Nick right, or wrong, about this, and why? What is your view of Gatsby's life and death? In your view, is Gatsby's life a success, or a failure, or something else, and why?

9. What do you think Nick wants us to learn from this story? That is, what are the large lessons he has put into this book? Do you agree with them, or not, and why?

All these questions, and others, arise at the end of *The Great Gatsby*. You would probably not want to use them all, and you may prefer others. You might take the students through Chapter 9 a bit slowly, raising one or two of the questions each day as you progress. Or you might let them finish the novel at a normal reading pace, and then raise some of these questions, with directed rereading of specific pages. Or you might use the following questions to lead the class to some final assessments:

> We have four main characters: Nick, Tom, Daisy, and Gatsby. In the end, what does each of these characters think and feel about Gatsby, his Moral Character, and his life? What does Gatsby think and feel about himself? In the end, what do you think and feel about each of these characters? In what respects is each a good person, in what respects is each bad, and why?

These few questions might be given as a final Reading Journal assignment and then discussed in class. They seem to cover a great deal less than the previous nine even though, in fact, they simply abbreviate seven of them (1–2, 4–5, 7–9) without directing students to specific pages for rereading. Unfortunately, by focusing on

Gatsby, they leave out a final assessment of the marriage of Tom and Daisy. But students will head for that issue on their own anyway.

The main point is this: Even though the action may be over in a story, its significance for the lives of the characters remains to be assessed. Many modern narratives raise open-ended questions in this way—we saw something similar in the ending of "Everyday Use." For whenever a story is told by a character in it, we cannot be given an omniscient author's knowledge of how everything turns out in the end. Hence, we need to attempt some final assessments of the characters and their relationships in order to understand and evaluate the meanings of the work as a whole. Young people are attracted by action, and all the exciting action in *The Great Gatsby* ends with Gatsby's death. But the significance of the action remains to be considered, and students will not learn how to consider it without our help.

One useful way to help students reflect on a novel or play as a whole is to pose the following evaluative questions for a Reading Journal entry and then discuss them on the following day:

> Which character is the best person in this work, and why? Which character is the worst person, and why? What single act is the best act, and why? What single act is the worst act, and why?

These questions provoke the students to reflect on how the work affects them. They cannot be wrong in their opinions, yet grounding the answers with reasons leads them to reflect on their own beliefs and values. Hence, class discussion tends to be lively, and, indirectly, this also provides a way in which the students can come to know one another better—a means to know a book, themselves, and one another better than before.

Teaching the Structure of a Novel: *What Follows What?*

I am not sure why, but it seems high school English teachers and college English professors rarely help students understand the plot structure of literary works. Yet there is an easy way to do this, and it works well as one way of reviewing the work as a whole: keep a running outline of the main events in each chapter, noting when each occurs in the "real time" of the novel. The outline need not include every incident—its aim is simply to give an overview of the whole. Perhaps each student can do this, or you can help the class as a whole do it. Then make the outline of *What follows what?* available to the whole class, and ask students what they notice.

Here is one for *The Great Gatsby*, with page numbers for where the time indications occur.

Chapter 1. Nick's introduction. Party with Tom, Daisy, and Jordan. Two weeks short of the longest day of the year (17): c. June 7.

Chapter 2. Nick meets Myrtle Wilson. Casual party in New York. Tom breaks Myrtle's nose. Not long before July 4 (29): c. July 1.

Chapter 3. Nick goes to one of Gatsby's huge parties, and meets Gatsby. The three nights of Chapters 1–3 take place over several weeks (56).

Chapter 4. Gatsby takes Nick to New York and tells "the truth" about himself. Jordan tells Nick of Gatsby and Daisy being in love back in 1917. Late July (62).

Chapter 5. Gatsby asks Nick to arrange a meeting with Daisy; same day late July, at night. Nick arranges it and Gatsby and Daisy are in love again, two days later; still late July.

Chapter 6. Truth about Gatsby's past. Tom and Daisy come to one of Gatsby's parties, and Daisy does not like it. A few weeks after Chapter 5 (98); c. August 15.

Chapter 7. Tom and Gatsby compete for Daisy, and Gatsby loses; Daisy kills Myrtle in hit-and-run. One day, near the end of summer (109).

Chapter 8. More on Gatsby's past, falling in love with Daisy. Wilson, distraught, kills Gatsby and himself; next day after Chapter 7.

Chapter 9. Nick tries to gather mourners for Gatsby's funeral, and fails; next four days or so. Nick decide to return home; fall (167). Nick's last meeting with Tom; late October (169). Nick's last night there, thinking of Gatsby.

✴

A few remarks might clarify the principles of this structure. First, the turning point comes in the central chapter of the novel. Students are usually amazed when they notice this, because they are used to following a plot by reading, not to designing one. "Did he really mean to put the turning point in the middle, or did it just turn out that way?" Yet it is easy to help them understand why a turning point must be at or near the center of a novel: to it, everything leads, and from it, the rest of the book follows. Gatsby's love for Daisy proves central to the work both thematically and mathematically. In any event, a turning point always occupies the thematic center of a work, even though it may not lie exactly in its mathematical center.

Second, students notice how time "slows down" in Chapters 7 and 8 (two days) and the first half of Chapter 9 (3–4 days more), compared to how much time is covered over Chapters 1 to 3 (several weeks). They are familiar enough with film to recognize this as a kind of "slow motion"—even though the action feels fast—as the writing concentrates our attention on every remark and gesture. You can help them understand why this must be the case in almost every climax of every novel. While the turning point is the thematic center, its climax is the dramatic high point, for this is where a book first intensifies and then resolves the story's crisis in the lives of its characters. All the main characters and themes are in play here, which is why a great deal of action is concentrated in a short space of time. In one sense, the pace of the action moves fast: so many important events happen quickly, one after the other. In another sense, the writer slows time down in order to focus our attention on the details of this crisis and its resolution. A similar time concentration occurs in Chapters 4 and 5, and for the same reason: Gatsby's past and present love for Daisy needs focus and full development so that we can sympathize with it.

Third, with an outline like this, students can see at a glance the progress of Chapters 1 to 3: three parties, each one larger, louder, and more violent than the previous one. From the marital tension in Chapter 1, to Tom's breaking Myrtle's nose in Chapter 2, to the fierce quarrels between couples (52–53) and a serious automobile accident (54–56) in Chapter 3, occasions of would-be festivity turn bad. As we read through these chapters, disorder seems to grow and spread in the world of this novel.

Yet there are no deaths until Chapters 7 and 8, after the love reunion of Chapter 5. You might ask students what this means. Is the love-reunion an island of peace between the growing disorder in Chapters 1 to 3 and the outright violence in Chapters 7 and 8? Or is the love-reunion itself a form of disorder and the cause of the violence in Chapters 7 and 8? In other words, once we notice the forms of violence in Chapters 1 to 3 and 7 and 8, we want to know how they are related to one another, and how they are related to falling-in-love-again description at the turning point. What is Fitzgerald communicating by means of this structure?

Finally, we do not learn the truth about Gatsby's past (Chapters 6 and 8) until after he and Daisy are in love again. Why? I think that Nick's narrative of these truths was deliberately placed afterward so that we can understand just why Daisy means so much to Gatsby. He explains Gatsby's devotion to her with the language of the grail-quest—religious conversion and knightly dedication to her service. Daisy embodies all that Gatsby has ever dreamed of and aspired to have; she becomes the meaning of his life because she incarnates everything he has ever wanted. This can mean little to us until after we have seen him transformed by Daisy's loving him again. But once we have seen that transformation, we can understand its deep reasons in Gatsby's Moral Character and in the story of how he first fell in love with Daisy. We can also appreciate just how much Gatsby loses when he loses Daisy at the end of Chapter 7—he loses everything he cares for.

Why Does Gatsby Fall in Love with Daisy?

There is so much to cover in teaching a novel that you may not want to single out one event for an in-depth examination of motives. But if you do, it should be a crucial event. Gatsby's falling in love with Daisy stands at the center of his life; being crucial to the plot, its description contains many of the work's central themes. Moreover, being in love is an inherently interesting subject, especially for young people who are regularly falling in (and out) of love. "Why do people fall in love with some people, and not with others?" seems one of the greatest mysteries of life. Fitzgerald brilliantly manages to make Gatsby's love intelligible not only without losing the mystery of it but even while accentuating its mystery.

Let me sketch an answer to this question. The relevant passages come at the beginning and end of Chapter 6 (94–97, 105–107) and the beginning of Chapter 8 (141–146). You might have students explore the preceding question by assigning these passages for rereading. The following paragraphs do not attempt a detailed answer, just an outline of how one might approach it.

In a sense, falling in love is not an *Act* with a *Purpose*: We do not do it but, rather, it happens to us. It comes with surprising force, and with the force of surprise. This certainly proved true for Gatsby, who only intended to seduce Daisy as another conquest yet found himself feeling married to her (142). The would-be sexual seducer was seduced into enduring love, committed "into the following of a grail" (142). Hence, his *Self-Understanding* in this non-Act proved entirely unforeseen and, indeed, outside his power.

His falling in love with Daisy becomes intelligible on the basis of his *Moral Character* and his *Situation* in life. Nick relates the young Gatsby's extravagant dreams of self-creation as he sought to liberate himself from his impoverished background (95–96). Self-absorbed by these dreams and grandly ambitious, he met Daisy when he was an army officer in 1917. She was a "nice girl," the first he ever knew, and her house had "a ripe mystery about it" (141), a style and taste he admired and hungered for. She lived "safe and proud above the hot struggles of the poor" (142) he knew so well. Seducing her was a way of winning all these things, so far beyond his penniless reach. Yet he found communion with her more satisfying than mere conquest (142–143). Nick imagines their first kiss (106–107), when all of Gatsby's "unutterable visions" were united with Daisy's "perishable breath," and "she blossomed for him like a flower and the incarnation was complete" (107). All his extravagant dreams were incarnated in this delicate Daisy.

We would do well to remember that this description is wholly in the language of Nick's character. Gatsby tells him of these events after the accident (141, cf. 97) but Nick interprets them for us. Gatsby cannot adequately explain why he is "unutterably" devoted to Daisy. For example, Gatsby describes Daisy's beautiful voice as "full of money" (115). From another man this might be a vulgar or cynical remark. But Nick understands this as Gatsby's way of envisioning Daisy as "High in a white palace, the king's daughter, the golden girl . . ." (115). All the passages treating Gatsby's self-creation, ambitious desires, and extravagant imagination represent Nick's attempt to understand him, not Gatsby's report on himself. When Nick records Gatsby's own language on these subjects, it sounds flat and casual. Gatsby cannot speak fully of his love, even though he lives it to the end.

The evaluative question follows naturally: "Is such an ultimate love a good thing, or a bad thing, and why?" Here is the source of Gatsby's greatness, yet the novel leaves it for us to decide whether we admire this devotion and aspire to it, or whether we think it foolish and self-destructive, or some of both. Is it a moral, or an immoral, love, and why? Similar ambiguities shadow related themes like self-creation and the power of the imagination. In attempting to understand and evaluate Gatsby's falling in love with Daisy, we are at the heart of *The Great Gatsby*. We are also exploring our own hearts, and the heart of the American experience as Fitzgerald treats it in this great American novel.

Provocation #10

Reading Journals

Why are we so happy during the last week of the semester and final exams? Our students are tense, strained, nervous, anxious. We are relaxed, smiling, genial, even jovial. Why? Is what our students suspect about us true, that every teacher's benevolence masks a face of cruelty?

No. We are happy because the burden of education is finally where it should be, on the students. Throughout much of the semester, the classes have been our burden, the teacher's job. We are supposed to organize them, direct them, and provide the energy to make them go. "Make us learn," the faces from Missouri say to us. "Make us want to learn." But during exam week, at long last, we can say, "Your grade, your problem." We listen to the silence and hear the hum of intense and directed intellectual activity. Such a lovely silence! It deserves another cup of coffee.

You might want to start using Reading Journals if you have ever said to yourself in the middle of a course, "Why am I working so hard, while they are taking it so easy?" Teachers have been using these to good effect for more than two decades, and several books describe their use. (See, for example, Nancie Atwell's *In the Middle: New Understandings about Writing, Reading, and Learning, Second Edition*, especially Chapter 8, "Responding to Readers and Reading," and her Bibliography.) Reading Journals mean more work for students, less work for you. More writing and thinking for them, less unrewarded effort for you. Put the burden of their learning on them, every day. But do not think that more writing for them means more reading for you. Just because they write it does not mean that you must read it.

To confront the Great Fear—"If I assign all that writing, then I am obliged to read and grade it"—here are my policies for Reading Journals. What kinds of assignments you might give for them will be addressed later. These policies compel students to create well-organized Journals, and you simply count entries, perhaps reading one. You can grade thirty-five Reading Journals in less than an hour. Consider the following rules:

1. Each entry must begin on the top of a new page.

2. Each entry must be dated, with the Reading Assignment given at the top. The Journal must keep assignments in sequence.

3. Each entry must be two full pages, written in full sentences. Write the entry immediately after you do the reading. Anyone writing an entry in class will be given a zero for that day's work.

4. The whole Reading Journal for a unit must be brought to class every day.

5. The whole Journal must always be up to date. It can be collected without prior notice. Any day's entry can be collected without prior notice.

6. Every missing entry receives a heavy penalty.

These rules emphasize the daily discipline of writing an entry and of keeping the whole well organized. The format creates an easy-to-grade Journal—you count entries, making sure that all meet a minimum length. A complete entry in decent order assures full credit: Students are not penalized for being wrong, only for being lazy. When I collect the entries for a particular day, a missing entry receives a zero, an incomplete one, partial credit. I collect the whole Journal at or near (to be crafty) the end of a unit, and every missing entry means one full grade deducted (from A to B). I weight this daily work heavily—at least 20 percent and sometimes 30 percent—in a final grade for the unit. With this goes my favorite speech about my course:

> *School Is the Real World.* You miss work, you don't get paid. You miss too often, you get fired. You miss an assignment, you are penalized. You miss too many, you fail. I have reasons for everything I ask you to do. Everything you do well is rewarded; everything you do poorly or fail to do involves a penalty. Everything has consequences.

Instituting Reading Journals proves a front-end–loaded operation, for you have to teach students to write the kind of entries you want them to write. Here is one way to go about it; with ninth graders reading a novel at a chapter a night, I ask for a "free-writing response":

> Put down your impressions of whatever you think is important about plot, characters, setting, imagery. I do not want a detailed summary. I want to know *what you think*, and saying what you think will involve some summary. Your thoughts, your reactions, your responses, anything you do not understand, anything that troubles you, any questions you may have—these are the main things. The book may lead you to

think autobiographically about yourself or people you know. That is fine and good. This is not formal writing. This is you thinking out loud to yourself. Write about what you think is important.

Students unfamiliar with this kind of work tend to summarize plot, and stop. To teach them differently, they need plenty of different examples. I have students trade Reading Journals in class and read one or two entries by other students. Often I ask, or assign ahead of time, a few students to read their entries out loud. Commenting on these enables me to lead students to write the kind of entries I want. After a few days of this, when the students think they have a feel for this work, I collect one entry and grade or comment on it, perhaps singling out one or two for reading in class as models, explaining what makes them good. In other words, I work to make explicit what I want at the beginning and help students learn how to produce it. Once this has been accomplished, I use the Journal entries to initiate discussion and occasionally "police" the exercise to make sure that students are doing it.

Students often write about themselves quite personally, especially when a character or situation strikes home. Hence, they always have the option of refusing to read an entry in class. Nevertheless, they can be asked to show you that it was done and to comment on the reading without reference to what they wrote. If they write an entry that they do not want you to read, they can put "Please Do Not Read This" at the top, or clip a blank paper to it. When grading a whole Journal, I sometimes tell them that I will read one entry and that they can choose which one, to be marked "Read This." Excellence here can make up for incompleteness in one other place.

Students who write responses to their reading are ready for a discussion. Having committed themselves in writing, they have something to say and are often eager to say it. Moreover, writing immediately after reading leads them to note their questions and confusions, which they never seem to remember otherwise, when you ask on the next day, "Do you have any questions about the reading?" With Reading Journals, they remember their questions, and these often initiate a good discussion because the class is led to the heart of the reading assignment.

In the class before the discussion, I tell two students that they will be making the opening remarks in the next class, summarizing their Reading Journal responses. In that way, they are prepared to speak—one gives the opening remarks, and the other gets the first reply. Differences of understanding or evaluation quickly come to light, and the discussion is well underway. In general, students who write Journals locate the crucial issues in a book, because they know what issues are crucial for them. Discussion begins from their insights, questions, perspectives, judgments. Because their views are valued in class, they engage themselves more readily in reading, reflecting, and discussing. Instead of being a stand-up, one-teacher show for the congenitally bored, you become a theater manager for their performances. On good days, you may feel more like a ringmaster in a circus, or even a lion-tamer, if a debate heats up.

Another useful strategy, mentioned in the previous chapter, involves having each student pick out a significant passage from the reading to comment on in one paragraph of his or her Journal. Students should explain why this passage is significant to them—perhaps it reveals something new about a character or his relationships, or clues us into the narrator's vision or values, or strikes the student as beautiful writing. Students cannot be wrong, because they select a passage significant *for them*; they need only explain what makes it meaningful. You might ask a student what passage she chose, and why, as a way to begin discussing parts of a work in detail. Usually several students are drawn to the same passage, and the discussion is off and running.

Freewriting responses are the least directive assignments for Reading Journals. In my view, they are the best assignment for younger students, certainly through the ninth and perhaps the tenth grade. They encourage the most autobiographical responses and so foster a deeper, more personal engagement with literature. Hence, they make for the liveliest whole-class discussions. But for older students who have experienced this engagement in reading, especially for those in Honors courses, you might also want to use more directive assignments.

You can always pose Study Questions, of course. Specific questions have the advantage of giving focus to students' thinking. They prove most useful to me when teaching older works, as in a British literature survey in which unfamiliar forms often baffle students. Our students are little accustomed to poetry, and not at all to the poetry of wit, satire, or allegory. Here they can use guidance. But when they are reading novels from the past two centuries, they are on familiar enough ground. Study Questions have the disadvantage of giving focus to thinking, of narrowing its range; however, they prove the best way to prepare for small-group discussions in a class, as freewriting responses do for whole-class work. Moreover, Study Questions help students attend to aspects of narrative they would otherwise not notice: imagery of dress, rooms, or landscape, for example; or the tone of a passage, or its narrative voice. Certainly any single passage you will want to explore in class can be given special attention by assigning a Study Question.

The problem with Study Questions is students' familiarity with them as tools to prove they have done the reading. Students tend to give a minimal answer and stop. You can counter this by insisting that a Study Question is designed to start their thinking, not to finish it. You might assign a minimal length for an answer and tell them to use the question to begin thinking more deeply about the work. But you will meet with resistance, and only your perseverance will lead them to enter the spirit of this kind of thinking.

In general, beware the Study Questions in a textbook. Even if they are good questions in themselves, they may not be good questions for your students or for what you want to accomplish. If you write your own Study Questions, making them interpretive or interpretive and evaluative, you can tailor them to your students' reading experience and abilities. In any case, I suggest you not give too many Study Questions. I recommend that a student never write in response to more than two. If you ask good questions and insist on two pages of writing, then the students will have to force themselves to write more and think more in order to meet the minimum. When teaching old books to college freshmen, I give two or three questions, and they must choose one to write about. This stretches them, I will admit, but to come up with those two pages they do learn to read more attentively and think more deeply or more extensively.

What makes a question "good"? No single or simple answer can be given except the operational result—it leads to two pages of writing that explores the text in an interesting way. An answer will not be narrowly factual, but interpretive or evaluative, or both. A central aim of this book is to show you some ways of formulating good questions, partly by giving many examples. Here are a few more, for parts of *The Great Gatsby* not treated in Chapter 4, and for parts of "The Prodigal Son" not explored in Chapter 1:

> At the end of Chapter 2, why does Myrtle say Daisy's name over and over again? Why does this make Tom so angry? What do you think of his response?

> In Chapter 3, when Gatsby first appears, what are Nick's impressions of him? What kind of person is he? Is he a good person, or not, and why?

> At the end of Chapter 3, what does Nick think of Jordan Baker, and what do his views of her tell us about him? In your view, is she a good person, or not, and why?

> In Chapter 4, what does Nick think of Gatsby? What does he think of Meyer Wolfsheim? What does Gatsby's friendship with Meyer Wolfsheim tell us about Gatsby?

> In "The Prodigal Son," why does the father give his younger son his inheritance, knowing the kind of boy he is? Is this act good, or bad, and why?

> Why does the boy return home when he does, and not earlier? Has he changed and, if so, why, in what ways, and how much?

> Why does the elder son refuse to join the feast? Is this refusal good, or bad, and why? After his father speaks with him, will he go in, or not, and why?

In my experience, students reading *The Great Gatsby* explore the preceding issues on their own because they are used to thinking about characters in novels. But when I lead a discussion of "The Prodigal Son," even well-educated adults accustomed to Bible-study have not thought about these questions before. Hence, in teaching *The Great Gatsby*, I use Reading Journals, with no Study Questions, while I give Study Questions for every class when teaching "The Literature of the Bible."

Reading Journals are not a popular exercise with students. They require daily reading and daily writing; they cut no slack for slackers. But I continue to use them because they generate the best discussions, and for another reason. Once I taught an Honors Colloquium at LSU on the *Divine Comedy*. All the students had already read some Dante in the Medieval Core Course, and they had gone to the dean requesting a course for advanced Honors students on the *Divine Comedy*. So I created one for them. They were well-prepared, bright, ambitious, and hardworking students. In my evaluations at the end, several commented that they hated the Reading Journals but that the exercise made them prepare for class, when otherwise they might have slacked off. When the best and most ambitious students confess that, what must the ordinary ones feel?

Provocation #11

Free Reading

Free reading is probably used more often in middle school than in high schools, but there are high school classes and schools where it would prove useful. It works best when free reading is embraced by a whole English Department, to be used in every course at any level and perhaps even at every level. But any teacher can adopt it and make it work.

The principle is simple—everyone in class has a book that he or she is reading, and the first ten minutes of every class (full-period tests excepted) are spent in free reading. The students get in the routine: They come into class, pull out their free-reading books, and sit down quietly to read. The teacher, too, has free reading. For the practice to succeed, the teacher must particpate in it according to the rules she has set, although occasionally she may wander around to see just what the students are reading. After ten minutes or so, she tells them to mark their places, and the work planned for the day begins.

Free reading is *not* a study hall—no book required for any other course may be read. In my classroom, magazines are not allowed, not even *Scientific American*. (Other teachers may allow magazines and newspapers to be read.) Most students will choose to read fiction or biography, occasionally drama, sometimes essays, but rarely poetry. You may have to make some ad hoc rulings about what is allowed and not allowed in order to maintain some integrity in the practice—for example, no picture books (it is free reading, not free looking). Hopefully, you will never be faced with having to deem a book "pornography," since the Supreme Court cannot articulate sufficient criteria for it; the prohibition of picture books should save you this embarrassment.

Once you begin the practice, you must maintain it and its freedom. No talking is allowed—it is not a free ten minutes but ten minutes of free reading. Students must come prepared: Anyone who does not have a free-reading book is penalized, or may pick a book from the classroom "library." Poverty is no excuse—the school has a library, and so does the town. You can help by keeping a rack of paperbacks suitable to your students' abilities and tastes, and this need not be expensive. You can canvass your colleagues and library sales for old paperbacks, and ask students who buy books to give them to you after they have read them. Moreover, you may be annoyed that this girl reads only the trashiest romances or that that boy only the trashiest "true crime," but you cannot reasonably forbid what is supposed to be *free* reading. You can and should suggest that they might like to try something else—perhaps Elmore Leonard for the boy or even (dare I say it?) Danielle Steele for the girl. You can ask their classmates to recommend something different. But many adults with advanced degrees read only a single genre, like mysteries or spy stories, and free reading reserves the same right to students.

You may ask your students to keep some record of their free reading, perhaps a page of writing whenever they have finished a book. But this is not an exercise for credit, not even for extra credit.

Periodically in the course of a semester I suggest that you spend perhaps half a period on open discussion of the free reading that students have been doing. Ask individuals what they have been reading, whether and how much they like it, whether they would recommend it and to whom and why, and so on. Ideally, students will begin to take recommendations for their reading from one another. Free reading aims to inculcate the habit of reading for pleasure, and such a discussion induces students to share their reading with friends. Many students have little experience of reading for pleasure or of how friendships can be illuminated and strengthened by talking about books. Free reading and an open discussion about what's read foster these experiences.

One of the goals of our courses should be to introduce students to the pleasures of the mind, which include reading, thinking, and friendship. They share their tastes in music, films, sports, and television because these are readily familiar parts of their world. We can help them learn how to share their tastes in books too. Many of them, perhaps, do not know adults who read books for pleasure or who talk about them with friends. But because schools exist to broaden the intellectual vision of the young and reveal to them possibilities of thinking and living not available in the ready-made world of their daily experience, our courses should work to foster the experiences of intellectual discovery, pleasure, and friendship. The crux here is *pleasure*, for what young people learn to enjoy, they will keep on enjoying. We will not only have added to their knowledge but to their lives.

5

Character and Motives in Oedipus the King

Understanding a character's motives in a play presents a different problem from understanding them in a story or a novel. The narrators of "Eveline" and *The Great Gatsby* give summaries of their characters' personal histories and insights into their thoughts and feelings. This "inside information" helps us understand their Moral Characters and motives. Drama, in contrast, has no narrator governing our perceptions of the action, and we only learn about a character's thoughts and feelings insofar as she expresses them. Although a character sometimes expresses her private thoughts in soliloquy, far more often she expresses them publicly to at least one other character. As we all know, public speech is not the same as private understanding, for we are willing to admit some things to ourselves that we would not acknowledge before others. For this reason, interpreting Moral Character and motives in drama proves more complex than in narrative. In fact, understanding character and motives in a drama is much like interpreting them in real life. We know only what other people tell us about themselves, and sometimes what third parties tell us about them, and we are left to make what inferences we can from their deeds, as well as their words. If we want to understand others, we must construe their Moral Characters in just this way.

Nevertheless, real-life interactions have an advantage over reading a play because we can hear the tones in a person's speech. We respond not only to what others say but to how they say it, and the *how* often means more to us than the *what*. As every director knows, the same play can be performed in many different ways. Does Oedipus' sense of his own heroic stature, in his opening speech, illustrate his "arrogance," or should we see it simply as a matter-of-fact Self-Understanding, the truth of which is supported by other characters? Different performances interpret Oedipus' Moral Character in different ways. Also, we have many more gradations of tone than we have words to describe them. Two actors can agree about Oedipus' arrogance, say, yet utter his lines very differently. A

125

drama can be interpreted in many different ways, and performances interpret it with a greater range of effects than can be described in a script.

For these and similar reasons, teaching a play raises many interesting questions about characters and their motives. These questions, interpretive and evaluative, can be discussed without being resolved. They are what I call "real questions" because they have no single right answer, even though some answers are better than others because their interpretations account for more of the relevant details. In the following pages, I want to raise many such questions about Sophocles' *Oedipus the King* while recommending a way to teach the play.

In the course of this chapter, all the Basic Questions will be used to suggest how you might lead your students to understand its characters, action, and plot structure. The chapter includes one in-depth exploration of Oedipus' motives for an Act: *Why does he decide to conduct the murder investigation himself and in public?* There are also detailed analyses of Oedipus and Creon as character foils (*What goes with what?* and *What versus what?*) and of the plot structure of the drama (*What follows what?*). These do not pretend to be indisputable interpretations, for nothing interpretive is beyond dispute. They simply aim to show what a full analysis of these issues looks like. Two sections that follow do not use the Basic Questions, for they are "background discussions" for those who might teach the play: "The Story of Oedipus' Life" and "Removing Misunderstandings." Knowing their purpose, and knowing your own purposes, you can read or skip these, accordingly.

The Story of Oedipus' Life

Some literary theorists distinguish "the story" from "the plot." The *plot* is the unfolding sequence of the work itself as we read it, while the *story* is the "real-world" temporal sequence of events as they would be if told in historical order. To illustrate, imagine a flashback in a film to events that occurred in a character's life before the time of the film proper. That flashback is in the middle of the film's *plot*, while it stands at the beginning of its *story*. This distinction is irrelevant to a work like "The Prodigal Son," where plot and story—the sequence of the narrative and the temporal sequence of its events—are the same. But the distinction is useful in thinking about *Oedipus the King*: In the course of its *plot*, Oedipus discovers the true *story* of his whole life. Getting clear about the details of this story enables us to attend to Sophocles' artistry in constructing his plot.

Most of the story is presented in two flashback speeches, by Jocasta (784–793) and by Oedipus (847–898), in the middle of the play.* Others are scattered throughout the drama or are part of the tradition (for example, the riddle of the

---

* All my references to the play are taken from Sophocles, *The Theban Plays,* translated by Robert Fagles, Introduction and Notes by Bernard Knox (New York: Penguin, 1986).

Sphinx) that Sophocles' audience knew. I will enumerate the sequence in this story, using brackets and NB for comments on details easily overlooked.

1. Laius, king of Thebes, impregnates his young wife, Jocasta. An oracle tells him that the child will be a son who will kill his father. Laius is terrified. [NB: This oracle makes no mention of the son marrying his mother. Hence, Jocasta seems not frightened by it. Tiresias' remark (496–497) reveals that he made the prophecy.] When the baby is born, Laius has its heels pierced and bound together with a thong and the baby is given to a Shepherd (a palace slave) to be exposed on Mount Cithaeron outside of Thebes. [NB: (1) Infanticide was not uncommon in ancient Greece, but it usually happened in families too poor to support more children. Laius, however, possesses wealth, and this infant is his son and heir. This unusual infanticide is motivated solely by his fear arising from the oracle. (2) This Shepherd appears in the play, for he turns out to be the sole surviving witness of the killing of King Laius. (3) You will discover minor discrepancies between Jocasta's and the Shepherd's versions of the heel-piercing and handing over of the baby. I suggest that these discrepancies are rooted in our natural desire to present ourselves to others, even to our own minds, in the best possible light.]

2. The Shepherd takes the baby but, taking pity on it, he does not expose it on the mountainside. Instead, he gives it to a another shepherd from the city of Corinth. [NB: This shepherd appears in the play as the Messenger from Corinth, so I will call him the Messenger from Corinth.] The Messenger from Corinth takes the baby and gives him to the king of Corinth, Polybus, and his wife, Merope, who are childless. They name the baby Oedipus ("swollen-foot"), injured by the piercing of his heels, and they raise him as their own child.

3. Oedipus grows up thinking of himself as the natural son of Polybus and Merope, the prince of Corinth. When Oedipus is a young man attending a banquet, a man who has drunk too much shouts that he is not his father's son. Oedipus barely restrains his anger at this insult, and he later questions "his parents" about it. They, too, are outraged at the accusation, and Oedipus is (temporarily) satisfied that he is their son.

4. But the thought that he might not be their son gnaws at him, so he goes to the oracle of Delphi to ask. [NB: Every Greek knew that the temple of Apollo at Delphi had two inscriptions ironically pertinent to Oedipus: "Know thyself" and "Nothing in excess."] But the oracle does not tell him who his parents are. Rather, she prophesies a terrible fate for him: that he is fated to kill his father, couple with his mother, and breed children by her. [NB: (1) This is the first mention of "marrying his mother" to anyone in the story. (2) The oracle does tell Oedipus that he is fated to do these things,

but she does *not tell him that he is fated to know that he has done them*. This is crucial to the play—fate demands that Oedipus do these terrible things, but he finds out that he has done them by his own efforts.]

5. Oedipus, horrified at the oracle, determines never to return to Corinth, lest by some weird accidents he kill Polybus and couple with Merope. This courageous determination makes him, at a stroke, no longer a wealthy prince but a relatively impoverished vagabond without a home. He has nowhere to go, only a place he is fleeing. In the course of his uncertainty, he arrives at the crossroads of Phocis and sees coming toward him a herald, followed by a wagon—clearly, an important man journeying somewhere with some servants. The servants try to push Oedipus off the road, and the old man in the wagon tries to strike him on the head with the sharpened prod he uses on the horses. Oedipus answers this physical insult and attack with violence, killing them all, or so he believes. [NB: As noted here, one of the servants survives the attack, the same Shepherd who saved Oedipus' life as a baby.]

The old man in the wagon is King Laius, on his way to the oracle of Delphi to seek divine assistance in dealing with the Sphinx. This monster has been lurking near one of the main roads into Thebes: She poses a riddle to passers-by and, when they fail to answer it correctly, she devours them. [NB: Thebes boasts the famous oracle Tiresias as one of its citizens. Evidently, he has been no help against the Sphinx, and so Laius journeys to Delphi.] When Oedipus kills the old man in the wagon, he unwittingly kills his father.

6. Some time afterward, Oedipus approaches the city of Thebes. The Sphinx confronts him with her riddle. The riddle was probably "Four legs, two legs, three legs"—something much harder than "What goes on four legs in the morning, two legs at noon, and three legs in the evening." But the answer is the same, *Anthropos* in Greek—"Man," that is "Human being." Oedipus answers correctly and the Sphinx, with mythically monstrous chagrin, obligingly hurls herself off a cliff to her death. [NB: Oedipus is proud of his quick-thinking acumen in destroying the Sphinx. He is not a professional seer or oracle but, as we might say, a highly talented amateur who succeeds where all others have failed.]

7. Oedipus is a hero, the savior of Thebes. Because the king of the city has been mysteriously killed, he marries the childless queen Jocasta and rules as king. They have two sons and then two daughters, and they seem to live happily for almost twenty years until Thebes is afflicted by a plague, which occurs shortly before the beginning of the play. [NB: Sophocles entitled his play *Oedipous Turannos*, and the second word is the root of our "tyrant." But *turannos* did not necessarily have a negative meaning in ancient Greece. A *turannos* could be a good ruler, even though he was a "usurper." Oedipus

thinks of himself as a *turannos* because he thinks he is really an outsider from Corinth, the son of Polybus and Merope. But actually he is a Theban, and the rightful king, the *basileus* of Thebes—the son of Laius and Jocasta.] Hence, Oedipus is living in profound ignorance of his personal history and his present state. He is living an illusion.

When we ask "What is different at the end of the play than at the beginning?" a summary answer might be: Oedipus begins the play in happiness and illusion, and his own energetic inquiry brings him to misery and truth. He begins as a king, at the top of the social pyramid, and he ends up a blind beggar, at its bottom. He begins as the happy father of a royal family, but as he discovers his own father-murder and mother-incest, he destroys the happiness of them all, for his wife commits suicide, he blinds himself, and he prophesies that his daughters (who are his sisters) will never have husbands.

These inversions do not tell the whole story, however, for Oedipus is not destroyed by his realization of the truth. As the play ends, he is a blind, but not a broken, man. He learns horrible truths about his life that would shatter almost anyone, yet he recovers from the shock rather quickly. His great speech in the final scene (lines 1499–1549) marks the change from the disoriented blind man to the hero-beggar. In it, Oedipus reviews the terrible events of his life, holding up in public speech truths no one else can bear to think of, much less proclaim. His forthrightness in facing the terrifying realities of his father-murder and mother-incest reveals his heroic stature in a new way. The great seeker after knowledge proves able, after all, to bear up under the terrible self-knowledge that he finds. Does that mean that he is better off at the end of the play than he was at the beginning? This evaluative question deserves a discussion in class. I once thought the answer to be "obviously not," but my students have taught me how complex the issue is.

Removing Misunderstandings

Oedipus the King is often taught in a way that undermines the tragic experience of the drama: Oedipus (it is said) suffers from "a tragic flaw," which is "pride," and this leads to his downfall. This line of thinking is drawn from Aristotle's *Poetics*, and it thereby enjoys the authority of a great philosopher, writing a seminal work of literary theory less than a century after Sophocles. But these Aristotelian notions are applied in an un-Aristotelian way: They are not wrong, as far as they go, but they are applied in a way that undercuts Aristotle's whole notion of Greek tragedy. On this understanding, Oedipus' "pride" ruins his whole Moral Character, and this "tragic flaw" causes his downfall. A Christian moral lesson is thereby drawn out of a drama composed long before Christ—as long as we can avoid "pride," we can avoid tragedy.

Although I disagree with this line of thinking, I sympathize with its underlying motivation, to draw a comforting moral lesson from a terrifying tragedy. Oedipus' downfall terrifies me because it comes largely, not from pride, but *from his finest moral qualities*. He loves the people of Thebes; to remove the plague afflicting them, he acts with energy, intelligence, and resolution. He thinks quickly, acts forthrightly, and possesses an intense desire for knowledge. He is a hero, and *his most admirable qualities, his very heroism, lead to his self-destruction*. This result is frightening, morally frightening, and it does not surprise me that we find a way to avoid this tragic terror. To be sure, Oedipus' heroic qualities "go wrong" in the play, and his "pride,"—his *hybris* (or "excessiveness" in Greek)—helps them do so. But the risk is implied in heroism itself, for a hero, by definition, exceeds the measure of ordinary human beings. An ancient Greek hero necessarily risks *hybris* or "pride." It is only in Christianity that pride is considered "the root of sin," and humility becomes a virtue. These notions should not be associated with Sophocles' tragedy or Aristotle's *Poetics*.

The phrase *tragic flaw* translates Aristotle's *hamartia*—the word comes from an archery metaphor and means "missing the target," therefore "an error." The word does not necessarily imply "morally culpable error," though it may. In the Greek of the New Testament, written four hundred years later, *hamartia* means "sin." Even though Renaissance interpreters of Aristotle knew that he could not have meant "sin," their translations gave it the Christian coloring of "tragic flaw." This notion proved fruitful for Renaissance tragedy: It makes some sense to say that Macbeth has a tragic flaw. But, as generally used, finding "a tragic flaw" in Oedipus drastically reduces the character and the play.

To be sure, Oedipus' Moral Character is flawed. Aristotle argues that the downfall of a perfectly good human being would not give rise to the tragic emotions of pity and fear but would simply shock and horrify us. According to the *Poetics*, the tragic hero must be "above the ordinary" but not perfect, for he must bring about his own downfall through his own agency. The tragic emotions of pity and fear are roused because the hero's downfall comes directly from his flawed goodness in action. Nevertheless, a flawed tragic hero does not have "*a* tragic flaw"— a single moral fault radically undermining his entire life. When we look for "*a* tragic flaw" in Oedipus, we do not fully notice how his good qualities grow excessive under the crisis-pressures of his situation. We thereby explain away the tragedy rather than observe it closely.

Teaching *Oedipus the King*

It will come as no surprise that I have my students read the play twice: first, a get-acquainted reading and general discussion, followed by a scene-by-scene rereading over several days. I recommend this way of teaching for several reasons. First, *Oedipus the King* is a masterpiece and repays a rereading. Almost everything you want your students to know about how to understand a play can be taught by reading this one carefully. It is one of the supreme instances of the dramatic art, and so it displays that art fully. Second, because it is translated into a modern idiom, it proves easy to read. Though students may feel awkward at first with its Greek names, its language is much easier than Shakespeare's. Third, it is short, and therefore it can easily be read and reread. A production of the play runs under ninety minutes. It proves much shorter than even a short play by Shakespeare, like *Macbeth*, and so students can hold all of it in their minds more easily. In sum, *Oedipus the King* is dramatically perfect and linguistically easy: a perfect play for reading and rereading, and thereby for teaching students how drama works.

First Reading

Let me suggest two different ways for managing a first reading. The first is to give students an in-class reading day, with a homework assignment on both sides. After two evenings and one class period for reading, they should have finished the play and be prepared to discuss it as a whole. Good students can manage this without undue difficulty, partly because the excitement of the play carries them along. You might ask them to write a Reading Journal entry on one or all of the following questions, and then begin a general discussion of the play with them:

1. What is different at the end of the play than at the beginning? What has Oedipus learned in the course of the play? Is he better for having learned this, or worse, and why? [*What becomes what?*]

2. Considering the play as a whole, is Oedipus a good king, or not, and why? Is he a hero, or not, and why? Is he a good person, or not, and why? [*What is Oedipus' Moral Character?*]

3. For what actions, if any, is Oedipus free and therefore responsible, and why? For what actions, if any, is he not free and responsible, and why?

In a general discussion like this, a class might also assess the Moral Characters of Creon and Jocasta, if time allows.

The second way of managing a first reading may be used with less able readers: It involves pausing after Scene 3, the halfway point in the drama. This is a good time for a general discussion of Oedipus' Moral Character and for reviewing his life story, as it emerges in Scene 3 (see "The Story of Oedipus' Life" above). If the students are having problems following the action, they will let you know and you can give them whatever help they need. You might give them a class period and a homework assignment to get this far, perhaps asking for a Reading Journal entry on Oedipus' Moral Character (see question #2). After discussing that in class, you might help them get clear on the details of Oedipus' life, as revealed in two speeches in Scene 3 (778–800, 847–923). This will prepare them to understand the rest of the play. Then you might give them the time to finish their first reading, aiming toward a general discussion using the questions suggested before. You know your students best, and so you know how much they can assimilate.

You might also prepare them for the play by telling them what Sophocles expected his audience to know about Oedipus, that he unwittingly killed his father and married his mother. Oedipus was a legendary figure who lived a few generations before the Trojan War (c. 1250 B.C.), itself a legendary time even in Sophocles' day (496–406). Like all the Greek tragedians, Sophocles used well-known stories as the basis for his plots, thereby creating dramatic ironies that his audience would recognize. The audience already knew the story, in a general way, though they did not know how the playwright might modify it. Hence, from the beginning of the play they understood Oedipus' ignorance of his true parents and his true condition. When students understand that much before they read, they are in a better position to find the play compelling on their first reading of it. Whatever else you think your students need help with—the many gods of the Greeks, what oracles were, and so on—you might tell them before they begin.

Second Reading

Oedipus the King has six scenes, divided by Choral Odes. Scenes 1 to 3 and 6 break down into two parts—only the two discovery scenes (4–5) do not, the shortest and most intense in the play. Hence, although I present discussion questions for each scene here, you might use them over more than six classes, especially if you wish to use Comparative Performances or Charting Recurring Images (both described in sections later in this chapter). With this significant investment of time for a short work, you might also want students to write a formal essay about the play, and if you give them some paper topics before they reread it, they can prepare themselves better for the essay. The following are possible topics:

1. Considering the whole play, is Oedipus a good king, or not, and why?
2. Considering the whole play, is Oedipus a hero, or not, and why?
3. Is Jocasta a good person and a good wife, or not, and why?
4. Is Oedipus better for knowing the truth, or worse, and why?
5. Who is the better person, Oedipus or Creon, and why?

Each of these is a real question, with good arguments on both sides. Hence, a good paper can be written on either side of each question, and so can a bad one. Moreover, each topic leads students to understand not only the play better but also themselves, their own criteria for evaluating the characters. The first three stand at the same level of difficulty, in my view, and the fourth proves a bit more sophisticated. I would reserve the fifth for only an advanced class—although all classes can discuss the issue, writing an essay on it involves juggling several balls at once. The scene-by-scene study questions suggested next feed into these topics and help students prepare to write a paper.

I suggest giving the students study questions to assist their with rereading, because they have less experience with drama than with narrative. Too much happens too quickly in a scene, and they need help just noticing which Acts are significant before they can begin to think about them. On the other hand, if your students have some skill in interpreting plays, you might simply have them keep open-ended Reading Journals for each scene, where they reflect on what they notice about the characters and the action. Because Greek tragedies have relatively few main characters, every character serves as a foil to the protagonist. Different aspects of Oedipus' Moral Character are highlighted by contrast with Creon, Tiresias, and Jocasta, and the study questions here ask students to explore these contrasts. But if your students explore these and other issues without your directing them, then you have no need for these study questions. And you are a fortunate teacher too.

Scene 1 (1–244)

1. What is Oedipus' Moral Character in this opening scene? What abilities, attitudes, values, and feelings do you see in him? Is he a good king, or not, and why? Is he heroic, or not, and why? Is he a good person, or not, and why?

2. What is Creon's Moral Character in this scene? How do he and Oedipus treat each other? In what ways, if any, are they similar? In what ways, if any, are they different?

3. Why does Oedipus decide to conduct the murder investigation himself rather than delegate it to others? Why does he decide to do it in public rather than inside the palace, as Creon suggests? Is this a good decision, or a bad one, and why?

Scene 2 (245–572)

1. Oedipus begins the murder investigation with a long speech (245–314). What is he trying to accomplish in this speech, and why does he grow more emotional as it unfolds? What does this speech tell us about him as a king and as a human being? What ironies do you find striking, and why?

2. How does Oedipus treat Tiresias in the beginning, and why? How does Tiresias treat Oedipus in the beginning, and why? Where do their relations turn bad, and why? Why does Oedipus think that Creon is plotting against him?

3. Oedipus and Tiresias are character foils: contrast them. Which man is greater, or more heroic, and why? Which is the better human being, and why?

Scene 3 (573–997)

1. What is Creon's Moral Character in this scene, as he responds to Oedipus' accusations? What is Oedipus' Moral Character, as he pursues Creon? The two men are character foils: contrast them. In what respects do you find Oedipus a better man than Creon? In what respects do you find Creon a better man than Oedipus?

2. What is Jocasta's Moral Character in the second part of this scene? Is she a good person, or not, and why? Is she a good wife, or not, and why? Jocasta and Oedipus are character foils: contrast them. Which is the better human being, and why?

3. What is the Chorus thinking and feeling (954–997), and why? Reread the previous Chorus (527–572), where they support Oedipus against Tiresias' accusations. What has happened in Scene 3 to change their attitudes toward their rulers?

Scene 4 (998–1214): Jocasta's Self-Discovery

1. How do Jocasta and Oedipus relate to one another—or, interact with one another—early in this scene? How do they relate to one another near the end of it? What has happened to them?

2. Jocasta discovers the truth about her incestuous marriage at line 1144, per-haps earlier, but she does not pass out or go crazy. Why? What does this tell us about her? What does she try to accomplish over the next thirty lines or so, and what does that tell us about her? The revelation of her incest does not defeat her, but she is defeated at the end of the scene. What defeats her, and what does that tell us about her Moral Character?

3. In this scene, what do we learn about Oedipus that we did not know before? What does he think Jocasta is trying to do near the end of this scene, and why does he think that? In this scene, who is the better person, and why?

Scene 5 (1215–1350): Oedipus' Self-Discovery

1. What are Oedipus' expectations at the beginning of this scene? What are the Messenger from Corinth's hopes? What are the Shepherd's expectations?

2. At what point in the scene does Oedipus learn the horrible truth about his life, and how does he respond to this knowledge? In what ways does his response differ from Jocasta's in the previous scene? What do these differ-ences tell us about the differences in their Moral Characters? In your view, which is the better human being, and why?

3. Oedipus began by investigating Laius' murder, and that is why the Shepherd is originally summoned (950–953). What has happened to that investigation since then, and why? Do you blame Oedipus for dropping the murder investigation, or not, and why? In this respect, is he a good king, or not, and why?

Scene 6 (1351–1684): *What becomes what?*

1. How does Jocasta respond to her terrible discovery, and why? How does Oedipus respond, and why? What do these differences tell us about the differences in their Moral Characters? Why does Oedipus blind himself?

2. In the final scene, what does Oedipus do to come to terms with the new truths of his life? How successful is he in coming to terms with them? In what ways is Oedipus changed by his new self-knowledge? In what ways is he still the same?

3. Compare and contrast Oedipus at the end of the play to how he was at the beginning. Is he better off now, or not, and why? Is he a better person now, or not, and why? Is he more heroic now, or not, and why? Is he better for his new self-knowledge, or not, and why?

4. What do you think of Creon in the final scene? Will Creon be a good king, or not, and why? In the end, who is the better man, Oedipus or Creon, and why?

Applying the Basic Questions

In the following sections you will find an example of the Basic Questions applied to *Oedipus the King*. I have chosen to use them here to explore Oedipus' first significant Act in the play, his decision to conduct the investigation of Laius' murder himself, in public, and later, to consider Oedipus and Creon as character foils.

Why does Oedipus decide to investigate Laius' murder himself, in public?

This is Oedipus' first significant Act in the play, and it comes at the end of the first scene (149–164). The play opens with Oedipus coming forth from the palace to speak to a delegation from the people of Thebes. In a brief speech, he acknowledges the suffering of his city and asks a Priest to speak for the group. In a long appeal, the Priest describes the devastating effects of the plague, praises Oedipus for saving them all from the Sphinx years before, and begs him to save them once again. But Oedipus has already acted: He has sent his trusted brother-in-law Creon to the oracle of Delphi to ask for advice, and his return is expected. Creon enters, and Oedipus has him report his news publicly—the city is suffering because it still harbors the murderer of its former king, Laius. Discover and expel the murderer, Creon reports, and the plague will be removed. At the end of the first scene, Oedipus decides to investigate the murder himself and to do so publicly.

The analysis here gives a detailed answer to questions #1 and #3 for the rereading of Scene 1. It illustrates how the questions posed there for each scene build on one another. Question #2 for Scene 1 has students begin to think about Oedipus and Creon as foils, an analysis pursued in the next major section of this chapter. Please consider these sections, not as *the* answers to their respective questions, but as illustrations of how one might pursue a full answer to the questions. If they help you to think further about the play, agreeing or disagreeing or both, they serve their purpose.

Situation. What is Oedipus' Situation, as he understands it?

Obviously, Thebes is a city in crisis: The plague is killing its herds and its people. Oedipus is the ruler of the city and he is responsible for deciding how to act so as to end its suffering. The office of king carries this responsibility. This responsibility is underscored by Oedipus' portraying himself as "the father of his people," for he addresses them as "my children." To be sure, the metaphor is traditional—a king is like a father, the city is like his family. Oedipus, however, presents himself as taking this idea seriously, for he insists that while each citizen has his own woes, Oedipus is suffering the pain of the whole city (74–76). Oedipus presents himself to his people as a compassionate father who suffers in sympathy more intensely than those who are suffering actually. He understands this situation as a crisis demanding action, and he is responsible for undertaking it. In Oedipus' view, a crisis demands bold and courageous action, and he is just the man for that.

After Creon returns from Delphi, Oedipus knows that a murder committed two decades earlier must be investigated and the murderer expelled from the city. As ruler of Thebes, he is responsible for justice in the city. His office as king lays on him the burden of finding and expelling the murderer. He need not do so himself, for he could delegate the task. But Oedipus prefers to act himself. In his view and, it would seem, in his people's, he is the best man for the job.

Moral Character: Self-Understanding. How does Oedipus understand himself in this situation?

As we have seen in earlier chapters, Situation and Moral Character, especially Self-Understanding, correlate with one another because we explore the character's situation from his point of view. Oedipus, as king of Thebes and like a father to its people, stands in a different relation to the plague than do the citizens, as they acknowledge in coming to him for help. What I said before about Oedipus as king under "Situation" applies equally here to his "Self-Understanding." The categories cannot be rigidly separated: Their questions are intended to bring to light the materials we need to understand a character's motives.

Ruler of Thebes though he is, Oedipus understands himself to be more than a royal officeholder—he is also a hero. He was the savior of Thebes from the Sphinx, and he intends to save it from the plague, and in public. He will display once again his heroic qualities of quick intelligence and courage. Hence, he will conduct the investigation himself and do so *in public*. We may contrast Oedipus with Creon, in this regard, for Creon prefers to deliver the advice from Delphi in private. Creon is not a hero, and he understands a crisis to be fraught with danger, a time for caution. Oedipus, in contrast, sees himself as heroic and thinks a crisis demands bold action.

Oedipus also takes up the investigation of Laius' murder because he is sure of his own innocence. Creon remembers one piece of evidence from the lone surviving witness of Laius' death: A whole band of thieves attacked the group and killed the king (138–139). Oedipus assumes that such a heinous act could only have been planned by conspirators in Thebes (140–141); they planned to seize power for themselves but were thwarted when Oedipus destroyed the Sphinx and married Jocasta. Oedipus understands himself as a Corinthian and knows that he had no part in any plot to kill the king of Thebes. He believes he has never even seen Laius (119). In short, as ruler of Thebes, he is responsible for justice in the city, and as a "non-Theban" he believes himself innocent. Hence, he will investigate the murder himself and in public—he has nothing to hide.

Moral Character. What is Oedipus' Moral Character?

Now the question of his "pride" comes to the fore, especially when he tells the people to take up the votive branches that they have laid at the altars of the gods (160–161). Normally, these would have been taken up only *after* the gods had answered their prayers by removing the plague. Oedipus is so confident of success that he sees his decision to act as the answer to their prayers. In his mind, his future success is so sure that it is already as though the gods have removed the plague. Oedipus thereby presents his action as the godlike answer to his people's prayers to the gods.

When a mortal sees himself as like a god, he is possessed by *hybris*, and everyone in Sophocles' audience knows that Oedipus' self-confidence bodes ill. At the same time, *hybris* is the risk that every ancient hero runs, for a hero stands above ordinary mortals even though he is less than the immortal gods. His very greatness as a man—and the Priest acknowledges Oedipus' superiority to other men—gives him a status somehow "above the human." Some human beings, like Hercules and Theseus, were believed to have been granted the immortality of the gods, and the Greeks called them *heroes* and prayed at their shrines. Hence, Oedipus has some reason to believe himself "above" the ordinary human and, therefore, "close to" the gods. Nevertheless, insofar as he sees himself as the divine answer to his people's prayers, he succumbs to *hybris*, or "pride," in his self-confidence.

At the same time, the people of Thebes need a confident leader, and Oedipus desires to do his best for them. The plague has not touched his own household, yet he sympathizes deeply with the sufferings of his city. He devotes himself to the welfare of his people with great energy and intelligence. In addition, he conducts the investigation in public not only because he is sure of his own innocence and aims to display his greatness, but also because the people deserve to witness the end of the crisis. The plague is a public catastrophe, and its resolution therefore is a public concern. Oedipus' compassion for his people moves him to a public investigation. Although Oedipus' sense of his own greatness may display his pride, it also engenders his great compassion for his people. In other words, Oedipus is not an egotist merely "full of himself," but a hero conscious of his greatness and full of concern for others.

Oedipus' other character traits have already been mentioned. His keen intelligence, displayed in solving the Sphinx's riddle, is manifested here as foresight, for he has already acted on behalf of his people, days before they asked him to. His daring and determination, also evident in his confronting the Sphinx, are displayed in his eagerly undertaking investigatation of a murder that occurred twenty years earlier, publicly confident of his success. Add to these his acknowledged responsibilities as ruler of Thebes, his sense of his own heroic stature, his great compassion, his openness to his people in conducting the investigation in public and Oedipus emerges as an attractive character at this point in the play.

Purpose, Attitude. What is Oedipus' Purpose? What is his Attitude?

His primary Purpose is to save Thebes by discovering and expelling Laius' murderer, in obedience to the command of Apollo through the oracle at Delphi. Secondarily, he intends his public investigation to manifest his heroic qualities and earn anew the praises of his people. His Attitude in undertaking the investigation may be described as eager, confident of success, bold, and determined. Some may prefer to describe him as overconfident and overbold in his *hybris*; but, as we have seen before, every character trait is ambiguous or double-sided. The bold have a tendency to be overbold, and the determined are often stubborn, just as the humble often underrate themselves, and the innocent are easily gulled. Sophocles has a profound sense of the double-sidedness of moral characteristics, as we shall see in exploring the foil-relation between Oedipus and Creon.

Evaluation: Truth. In what ways is Oedipus' understanding of his Situation and of himself true?

Obviously, he correctly understands that Thebes is in crisis, and that it is his responsibility as ruler to do something about it. His people acknowledge him not only as king but as a hero, and he may justly see himself as heroic too. But he is wrong on several points. Laius' was not killed through a conspiracy of Thebans, and Oedipus is not innocent of the murder. Oedipus is not a Corinthian, as he thinks, but a Theban. The Greek audience knows all this, and Oedipus' words resound with dramatic irony—he speaks sincerely when he says that he never even saw Laius (119)—but the audience knows that he both saw and killed him, and that Laius was his father. We know Oedipus' fate before the play begins, and its drama lies in watching him discover it.

Evaluation: Goodness. Is Oedipus' Act good in its intentions?

In my view, Oedipus acts as a good king should, primarily for the benefit of his people. He aims to remove the plague, and the praises he hopes to gain can be earned only by success. His desire to manifest his own heroic qualities does not mar but even energizes his benificent Purpose. However ominous his *hybris* is, he intends well and acts forthrightly.

Nevertheless, Oedipus overlooks the obvious first move in his investigation, perhaps because he is so concerned about displaying his heroism publicly. Creon tells him that a witness of Laius' killing survived (133–139); all Oedipus needs to do is have that witness brought to him for questioning. With one surviving witness to an unsolved murder, the obvious first step in solving the crime would be to question him, but Oedipus does not think to do this. Granted, Creon reports the evidence given by the witness—that a band of thieves killed the king—and Oedipus assumes that the real murderers are the Theban conspirators, presumably wealthy aristocrats, who paid them (140–142). Naturally, the witness, a slave in the palace, did not want to admit that a lone traveler vanquished so many escorts of a king, and Jocasta later mentions that when he saw Oedipus on the throne, he asked for employment far away from Thebes (834–846). Eventually, this witness is summoned to Oedipus (950–953). He turns out to be the Shepherd who saved Oedipus as a baby (1153–1175), and when he is finally brought for questioning (1215–1224), Oedipus is no longer seeking information of Laius' murderer but of the secret of his own origins.

Consequences. In what ways are the consequences of Oedipus' act good, and bad?

Oedipus' decision to undertake the investigation himself and in public proves disastrous in the next scene when Tiresias accuses him of the murder. Oedipus answers this public action with public outrage, and he thinks that Creon is using Tiresias in a plot to depose himself. If Oedipus had questioned Tiresias privately, he could have dismissed the seer's accusations as worthless. But he cannot dismiss a public accusation, and he accuses Creon of conspiracy and would have him executed, except that Jocasta intervenes. These public quarrels increase the suffering of the city and bring to a halt the investigation Oedipus is supposed to be conducting: The plague is forgotten while Oedipus acts to preserve his rule. Shortly afterward, Oedipus is more concerned about investigating the mystery of his birth and his parents, quite forgetting the plague and Laius' murderer. It just so happens that these seemingly unrelated concerns are tied in a single "knot of fate." In short, making the investigation public leads Oedipus into entanglements that he could have avoided had he conducted it behind closed doors.

What would have happened had Oedipus called the one surviving witness and questioned him privately? He would have learned that he was Laius' killer and he would have been obliged to leave Thebes so that the gods would remove the plague. Unfortunate as this exile would be, it cannot compare with what happens when Jocasta and Oedipus discover the full truth and horror about their lives. Oedipus' desire to act in public, admirable in its intentions, proves disastrous in its consequences for him and for all those he loves. But these consequences spring from Oedipus' character, especially from his insatiable desire to know the truth.

Oedipus and Creon as Foils: What goes with what? *and* What versus what?

In this play, as in most, every major character serves as a foil for the tragic protagonist. Tiresias, Creon, and Jocasta each serve to highlight different aspects of Oedipus' moral character. Oedipus' interaction with each of them reveals a certain greatness, and a certain blindness, in his moral character. For example, Creon makes a long speech explaining why he would never want to be king, for he prefers to have the honor of royal influence without the burdens of power (651–690). Yet Oedipus, his close friend for twenty years, knows so little about him as to think that a man of such admitted mediocrity would aspire to royal power. When Jocasta enters in the middle of their quarrel (709–724), she knows immediately that Oedipus' accusation is wrong. She knows that Creon's moral character contains no desire for kingship, with all its burdens. Oedipus, for all his intelligence, is blind to Creon's true moral character. Oedipus loves being king so much that he assumes Creon wants to be king himself, and so he regards Creon's professed distaste for the burdens of rule as a lie.

The contrast between Oedipus and Creon reveals Sophocles' profound sense of the double-sidedness of character traits. I will explore this contrast between Oedipus as "the heroic man" and Creon as "the mediocre man." The hero has the vices that come with the greatness of his virtues, and the mediocre man has the virtues that come with his mediocrity. When I teach the play, I assign the contrast for homework as the students reread Scene 3. (See question #1 for Scene 3, in the previous section "Teaching *Oedipus the King*.") I usually put two pairs of columns on the board—Oedipus (+) versus Creon (–) and Oedipus (–) versus Creon (+)—and then record and work with the students' responses. These contrasts need lots of board space because they cannot be rendered easily in a word or a phrase. Hence, I simply set forth my sense of these contrasts, first to Oedipus' advantage, and then to Creon's.

First, Oedipus is a hero and a king and he loves being both. He enjoys being prominent, and the burden of power seems no burden to him, for exercising it brings him notice. Thus, we see him as a public man with an open character—he has "nothing to hide." Creon, in contrast, is neither a hero nor a king, and he cannot understand why anyone would want to be either. A hero is exposed to danger, and a king to hard work. Creon presents himself as a kind of accountant of pleasure and pain (651–675). As Oedipus' friend and brother-in-law, he enjoys prominence and influence in comfort, without the many duties of a king. Creon prefers less prominence and an easy life to Oedipus' high position and onerous duties. At the same time, Creon does not have an open character. He prefers to report the advice from Delphi in private, while Oedipus insists that he speak it publicly (102–106), and at the end of the play, he hurries the blinded Oedipus out of public view.

Second, we have already seen Oedipus' quick intelligence, courage, and resolution; this heroic self-confidence gives him an open character. Creon, in contrast, tends to be cautious—he would prefer a private to a public meeting with Oedipus—and even uncertain; in the final scene, he contradicts himself about what he will do with Oedipus. While a crisis for Oedipus demands quick action, a crisis leads Creon to act cautiously, even to defer acting. He lacks self-confidence and he does not want to make a mistake. At the same time, when he is sure he is right, as in defending himself from Oedipus' accusation, he speaks ably and even rises to some indignation.

Third, Oedipus feels deeply and powerfully, while Creon's emotions are comparatively shallow. When Oedipus first thinks that Creon has plotted against him, he bursts into a lament for friendship betrayed, and his words are filled with feeling (432–442). When Creon enters at the beginning of Scene 3, he worries to the Chorus about his reputation and the damage to it from Oedipus' accustion (573–583). He intends to express deep resentment at Oedipus' "terrible charges," but his language is as flat as his accounting of damage to his reputation. Similarly, in the final scene, we see Oedipus pouring forth his love for his daughters from a full heart, while Creon seems cool and a little embarrassed.

Nevertheless—now to Creon's advantage—Creon is innocent and he knows it. When he accuses Oedipus of being hasty, irrational, and jumping to conclusions, he is right. Oedipus is being unjust, as Jocasta and the Chorus so clearly see. Creon will never be hasty or unjust, for his lack of powerful feelings makes him cautious and lucid. (The Creon of Sophocles' *Antigone* is a different figure in a play written some fifteen years earlier.) He will never be a hero, like Oedipus, but neither will he accuse a friend of betrayal without first gathering the evidence.

Second, Oedipus is blind to Creon's moral character, while Creon possesses a good understanding of Oedipus. The king insists that he must act quickly against anyone he sees plotting against him (693–697); this would be true against an enemy as bold as himself, but false against someone as cautious as Creon. Oedipus' projects his own moral character onto Creon, quite misunderstanding a man he has known for years. Creon's lucidity and rationality, in contrast, enable him to understand Oedipus and to sympathize with him in his misfortune. Where the heroic king is blind to Creon, the mediocre accountant understands Oedipus' moral character.

Finally, students invariably (and rightly) recall Creon's compassion for Oedipus in the final scene, bringing his daughters out to him, knowing the blind father would want to embrace them. Even though Oedipus raged unjustly against him and wanted to have him killed, Creon's resentment has its measure and he does not exploit Oedipus' vulnerability to achieve some revenge. Creon is king now, by necessity, but he does not gloat. He does not have great or powerful feelings, and so he has them under control. Not being a great man, it proves easier for him to be a decent one.

In short, Creon's lucidity and rationality make him a relatively cool and cautious man, decent but hardly heroic, while Oedipus' quick intelligence and self-confident resolution make him heroic at the play's beginning and tragic by its end. Creon's rational balance goes hand-in-hand with his mediocrity, while Oedipus' powerful feelings and energies make him great. The extraordinary man suffers an extraordinarily tragic fate, while the ordinary Creon is incapable either of greatness or of tragedy.

Further Ideas for Teaching *Oedipus the King*

The sections that follow contain some teaching ideas that have proved useful for my students as we explore *Oedipus the King*. First, you will find some activities that aid students in their understanding of the plot structure: *What follows what?*; second, I describe a favorite assignment I call "Comparative Performances," which helps lead students into the intimacies of the action of the play while developing their understanding of drama and technique. Finally, you will find a discussion of recurrent images in the play and some ways to help students think about them.

Plot Structure. What follows what?

In the previous chapter, I described a way of teaching students how to think about the structure of a plot. In this case, the teacher (or the class as a whole) makes an outline of *Oedipus the King*, scene by scene, while rereading it. The outline need not be detailed, for it is simply a way to jog students' memories of what went on in each scene. When I put it on the board, I use abbreviations for names, and the merest sketch of the action—for example, "1–168: O. and people re plague, Creon comes with oracle." Once students have the whole play before them in a single vision, they can begin to look for how Sophocles intensifies the action and builds to the climax.

We can appeal to their experience of films as a way of helping think about a playwright's fundamental problem: holding the attention of an audience. Think of an action film, such as *The Terminator*, and how the writer or director works to keep the audience involved in it (see Provocation #12, "Educational Videos and *The Terminator*"). The film must progress climactically, and climax means progressively intensifying the action. Later chase scenes or scenes of violence need to be longer and more exciting than earlier ones. If the later ones grow shorter and less exciting, the film proves anticlimactic, only suitable as the parody of an action film. At the same time, one chase scene after another is a bore, no matter how extravagant the special effects, so the action needs to be varied. The tension, heightened by chase scenes, needs to be relaxed. In *The Terminator*, a love story between the two human characters punctuates the Terminator's attempts to kill them. This love story gives the film its heart, its human interest. It makes us want to see the indestructible robot defeated. A battle between two invulnerable robots would make for more violent effects, but who cares about a robot? The action scenes would be better, the film would be worse. In *The Terminator*, the love story seems secondary, but it binds the action sequences into a compelling film.

Like any dramatist, Sophocles faces problems similar to those of an action-film writer: He must intensify the action from scene to scene, yet vary it to lighten the dark forward movement of the plot. The convention of Choral Odes in Greek drama helps to alleviate the tension, as do moments of hope in Scenes 4 and 5, before disaster strikes. Here is one way of presenting the activity for homework:

> How does Sophocles structure his plot so as to build effectively to the climax? Examine your outline of the play and make five observations on how Sophocles intensifies or varies the action. Begin by focusing only on two adjacent scenes at a time. For example, how does Scene 2 build on and intensify Scene 1? This may happen in several ways, and each way you find counts as one observation.

❋

Naturally, you may want to give your class an example or two to help them get started, and you may prefer simply to use this analysis as an in-class exercise. It proves one useful way of reviewing the whole play, albeit with new questions in mind.

Let me present my analysis of the plot structure to illustrate how you might think about these issues. The outline given here is somewhat detailed so that you might use it to understand the analysis. Because my students undertake this exercise after reading the play just twice, the outline they use is much sketchier:

1–168, Scene 1

1–96, Oedipus comes from the palace to meet the people of Thebes, who ask for his help against the plague. He has already sent Creon to Delphi for Apollo's advice.

97–168, Creon returns: "Discover and expel King Laius' murderer." Oedipus will undertake the task himself.

169–244, First Choral Ode

245–526, Scene 2

245–314, Oedipus condemns and curses Laius' murderer and whoever conceals him.

315–526, Oedipus quarrels with Tiresias, suspects Creon of plotting against him.

527–572, Second Choral Ode

573–952, Scene 3

573–708, Creon speaks to the Chorus, expressing his anger at Oedipus' accusation; he and Oedipus quarrel.

709–952, Jocasta tries to soothe Oedipus, and in referring to Laius' death "where three roads meet" terrifies him with the thought that he may have killed Laius. He tells the story of his life, sends for the Shepherd (sole witness of Laius' murder), then exits in fear.

953–997, Third Choral Ode

998–1194, Scene 4

The Messenger from Corinth brings the news that Polybus and Merope are dead; Jocasta and Oedipus are elated: The prophecy about Oedipus cannot be true. They then learn that the Messenger was given the infant Oedipus by the Shepherd. Jocasta realizes the horrible truth about their lives and tries to keep Oedipus from questioning the Shepherd, but he refuses, and she rushes wildly into the palace.

1195–1214, Fourth Choral Ode

1215–1310, Scene 5

Oedipus, eager to discover the secret of his birth, forces the Shepherd into answering his questions and learns the horrible truth that he has fulfilled all the prophecies. He rushes wildly into the palace.

1311–1350, Fifth Choral Ode

1351–1684, Scene 6

1351–1421, Messenger from the palace reveals what happened inside the palace—Jocasta hanged herself; and Oedipus, who appeared about to slay her and then himself with a sword, blinds himself with her brooch.

1422–1534, Oedipus emerges, disoriented and speaking incoherently, but recovers by reviewing publicly his whole life.

1560–1676, Creon brings Oedipus' daughters to him, and the two men speak, before Creon leads him back inside.

✳

In what ways does Sophocles intensify the dramatic action? First, the play moves from harmony to discord and conflict. In Scene 1, even though the plague has thrown Thebes into crisis, Oedipus and his people and Creon are united in their desire to solve it. In Scene 2, however, Oedipus quarrels with Tiresias, a respected Theban, and then in Scene 3 he quarrels with Creon. The quarrel between two extraordinary men, Oedipus and Tiresias, is followed by the quarrel between the extraordinary and the ordinary—the heroic and the mediocre—man. Jocasta tries to smooth over this conflict, yet succeeds only by making Oedipus fear that he may have killed Laius himself. Jocasta never quarrels with Oedipus, as do the two male characters, yet her attempt to comfort him causes much greater anguish than do the earlier quarrels.

Second, therefore, we can see a gradual intensification and interior movement of violent disorder with respect to Oedipus. In Scene 1, the plague is an external problem that Oedipus intends to solve. In Scene 2, Tiresias' public accusation makes Oedipus think that Creon is plotting against him. Here the threat is "closer to home," for Creon has been a trusted member of his household, but still an external problem that Oedipus can solve by executing his enemy. But when Jocasta's speech leads him to think he may have killed Laius, the problem is no longer external and cannot be solved. He cannot undo a past Act. The threat to Oedipus now proves so interior, so irrevocably a part of him, that it cannot be met by any action, and this "man of action" exits the stage in dread. This "interiorization" will intensify as Oedipus' search for truth turns from discovering the killer of Laius to the secret of his birth. At the end of Scene 3, he is terrified at being exiled from Thebes at his own orders for a deed he may have done. What Jocasta and Oedipus learn about their life in Scenes 4 and 5 proves far more horrifying.

Third, every attempt to make things better in the play only makes things worse. In this way, Sophocles relieves and varies the tensions in his plot, in the short term, even as he intensifies them in the long term. The play opens with the audience being told about the plague, but Oedipus has already sent Creon to Delphi to discover what to do, and he then takes action to follow the oracle's advice, confident of success. But Oedipus' public investigation does not make things better, but only embroils him in further difficulties: He quarrels with Tiresias and then with Creon, sure that they are plotting to depose him. In the midst of his quarrel with Creon in Scene 3, Jocasta attempts to make things better with her "Don't believe in oracles" speech (778–800), but she only leads Oedipus into deeper terror, fearing that he himself may have killed Laius. In Scene 4, the Messenger from Corinth brings the news that Polybus and Merope are dead, and Jocasta and Oedipus greet this as saving relief: This makes things better, because the oracle about Oedipus killing his father and coupling with his mother cannot possibly have been true. But further questioning of the Messenger leads Jocasta to know that it is all true, and when she knows that she cannot stop Oedipus from knowing the truth, she rushes into the palace to kill herself. When the Shepherd comes in Scene 5, Oedipus rejoices that he will soon learn who his true parents are. When he learns that truth, all joy is ended for him forever.

Fourth is a related point—everything that distracts Oedipus from the murder investigation leads him closer to the truth about it. Every "irrelevant" interruption of that investigation turns out to be perfectly relevant. The first instance comes in Oedipus' quarrel with Tiresias. We know that Tiresias is speaking the truth, but Oedipus thinks that the seer's public accusations are part of a conspiracy with Creon. Hence, Oedipus turns away from the murder investigation to protect himself from "Creon's conspiracy," and the two men quarrel in Scene 3. Jocasta intervenes with her "Don't believe in oracles" speech. On the one hand, her speech is irrelevant to the quarrel with Creon, for Oedipus does not believe what Tiresias said, and also to the murder investigation, for everyone believes that Jocasta's baby is long dead. On the other hand, we know that the "false oracle" about her child is true, and Oedipus realizes, from her chance phrase about "where three roads meet," that he may have killed Laius. Her "irrelevant" speech on an "unrelated" topic leads Oedipus closer to solving the murder.

Again, in the Scene 4, the Messenger from Corinth brings the news that Polybus and Merope are dead. Jocasta and Oedipus greet this with joy, as life-saving news: They take it as proof that the oracle was wrong in the prophecies given to the young Oedipus, and it seems to lift the doom that haunts him. On the one hand, this news is irrelevant to Oedipus' most recent fear—whether the man he killed was King Laius, or not, has nothing to do with the natural deaths of Polybus and Merope. On the other hand, learning that Polypus and Merope are not his real parents drives Oedipus to learn the secret of his birth, and this leads him to discover himself as the killer of Laius. Yet this discovery, in Scene 5, proves rather indirect. Oedipus questions the Shepherd, originally summoned as the only surviving witness of Laius' killing (832–845, 925–952), not to ask him about Laius' death but about who his own parents were. At the beginning of the scene, Oedipus assumes that these two issues have nothing to do with each other. At its climax, he realizes that they have everything to do with each other. Oedipus has quite forgotten to investigate Laius' murder, so eager is he to discover the secret of his birth. But discovering that secret, he discovers himself as Laius' murderer. No one else on stage realizes the whole truth, except for the Shepherd. The Chorus, as the following ode makes clear (1311–1350), understands only about the incest. Oedipus' quick intelligence has once again leaped far beyond what others understand, this time to his own cost.

Finally, let us not overlook the comparative length of the scenes. Note that the first three scenes are progressively longer, while the following two "discovery scenes" grow progressively shorter. After the social harmony in Scene 1 sets up the action of the play, the quarrels with Tiresias and with Creon in Scenes 2 and 3 stretch out the action with verbal violence. Scene 3, in addition, reveals the whole story of Oedipus' life, as he understands it, with the oracle he heard at Delphi and with Jocasta's story of the oracle at her baby's birth. The audience understands the full truth about these two oracles, which seem unrelated to Oedipus and Jocasta, and so we are prepared for the discoveries in Scenes 4 and 5. In these two scenes, there are no quarrels and no verbal violence, as in Scenes 2 and 3, only some wild words by Jocasta, in Scene 4, and by Oedipus, in Scene 5, before each rushes off stage. Yet, though verbally quiet, Scenes 4 and 5 are filled with dramatic tension as Jocasta and Oedipus realize the terrible truth about their lives. This dramatic tension is matched by the compression of these scenes: So much is revealed to Jocasta and Oedipus in so short and quiet a space, and it overturns their lives utterly.

The play features radically different understandings of the truth of things both between different characters and between them and the audience. We know the secret truths upon which the whole plot turns, so we can see clearly what the other characters do not see. In this way, Oedipus' cursing the killer of Laius resounds with dramatic ironies, as does his scorn for Jocasta's desperate attempts to keep him from learning the truth about his birth (1155–1178). Oedipus' whole life is based on illusions, and the play shows us how, by his passionate desire to discover the truth, he moves simultaneously from illusion to truth and from happiness to misery. Oedipus destroys his life and Jocasta's by exercising his most admirable qualities. He employs all his intelligence and initiative in his passionate desire to save the city he loves and to learn the truth about himself. And he succeeds in both.

Comparative Performances

There is another way of leading students into the intimacies of the action, and it lends drama and variety to class periods—assigning "Comparative Performances" for each scene. With Scene 1, for example, you might assign Oedipus' opening speech to at least two different students. Each student must prepare to read the speech dramatically—that is, in the way each thinks it should be delivered so as to reveal Oedipus' moral character at the beginning of the play. Before they read aloud, tell the class to listen carefully and make notes to *describe the differences* between the two performances as interpretations of Oedipus. You are not looking for evaluations of the students' reading or acting. (In fact, each reading must be followed by decent applause; sooner or later, every student must stand up to read performatively.) Rather, you want students to begin to hear and define for themselves the differences, often subtle, between two performative interpretations. I suggest that you also tell two students *before the readings* that they must make the opening remarks. That way, you will have at least two responses, and these encourage others to agree and disagree.

You will find, I think, that this assignment won't go well at first. Students are not used to defining their impressions of a performance-as-interpretation, and they flounder. But I urge you to persevere, for two reasons. First, student responses help student performances. Your readers–actors will perform more dramatically as they learn to feel that their audience appreciates their efforts. This is one reason for demanding decent applause after each performance and also for insisting that every student perform sooner or later. Second, by insisting that students define their impressions in an interpretive performance, you are helping them to become a more alert audience and more self-observant human beings. You are encouraging them to be aware of and to understand their experience by insisting that they find words to describe their otherwise inarticulate impressions of an actor's tones and attitudes. Although I have often found a student's articulated impressions to be the opposite of my own, I never say so. Because I am encouraging them to develop an unfamiliar skill, I tell them, "Your impressions cannot be wrong, you can only lie about them." With practice they improve, and considerably.

The passages you select for "Comparative Performances" should not be longer than, say, forty lines, so that students can actually compare the two performances. The quarrels between Oedipus and Tiresias and between Oedipus and Creon make for lively action, but you need to select a stretch of lines in the middle of the scenes, as the quarrels heat up, or the passages grow too long for comparing. (Let me suggest lines 373 to 413 and lines 610 to 650 as examples.) You should insist that students rehearse their performances fully before class so that the quarrel between Oedipus and Tiresias (say) proves no mere shouting match: It needs to make dramatic sense as a public conflict between two men of heroic stature. In the discovery scenes, three actors play roles, and intelligent preparation before class is all the more important in order to perform them successfully.

You can even create an "Academy Awards" for the end of the unit, with certificates for things like "Best Oedipus," "Best Jocasta," "Best Supporting Actor," "Best Quarrel," and "Best Group Performance." The students form the Academy and their votes (by secret ballot) decide the winners. Naturally, an awards ceremony takes place. If you are lucky, your award-winners from different classes will want to prove that they are the best and will freely perform in a competition outside of class.

Charting Recurring Images

In every literary work, certain images (keywords, ideas, themes) recur, and these recurrences lend coherence to the whole. We saw, for example, how eating imagery functioned in "The Prodigal Son" and how images of "dust" and "music" worked in "Eveline." Moreover, some images are clearly related and thereby form a kind of "family" or cluster. In *Macbeth*, for example, "crown," "gold," and "nobility" images recur often and are clearly related, so they form a cluster, as do the various images associated with "life" and "death" in "Eveline." Because the audience for a play cannot stop to reread or linger to reflect, a dramatist uses certain images, which must be emphasized in every way possible with great frequency in a play to underscore central themes. The dramatist uses not only the ideas that the characters express and the acts they perform but also the repetition of keywords.

In *Oedipus the King*, I focus on two main clusters of imagery, related to themes of knowledge and of power, respectively:

1. Knowledge/ignorance; light (fire)/darkness; sight/blindness; revelation/ concealment; truth/illusion

2. Power: medicine, hunting, navigation, agriculture

The first is dramatized most effectively in Oedipus' confrontation with Tiresias: The king's physical sight and spiritual blindness to his true condition contrast with the seer's physical blindness and spiritual insight. The sighted Oedipus experiences knowledge as something humans acquire through investigation; he was a clever problem solver of the Sphinx's riddle and he understands Laius' murder as a similarly external problem to be solved with human intelligence. The blind Tiresias, in contrast, sees only what Apollo permits him to see. His knowledge is not under his control; it comes to him unbidden, at the god's will. He cannot acquire knowledge, but can only receive it. It does not give him power to rule or to act heroically, like

Oedipus; yet his knowledge is deeper, more riddling, and more powerful in its way than Oedipus' cleverness. The play turns on the difference in kind between the knowledge possessed by the gods and their oracles, on the one hand, and that of mere humans, on the other, even if one is a hero.

Although this theme is superbly dramatized in the scene with Tiresias, it functions throughout the play: Oedipus is ignorant of his true condition, of himself, of who his parents are, and he gains this knowledge by his own efforts and to his own cost. The keywords echo in the name of Oedipus—it means "swollen foot" but it chimes with the Greek verb *oida*, which means "I know" and is related to "I have seen." The vision–imagery comes to have new meanings as the play unfolds, especially "eye contact" as a sign of personal relationships with others. The plot enacts a progressive revelation of what is concealed, culminating in the final scene when the palace doors are opened and Oedipus appears, self-blinded, so that he will not have to see how other people look at him.

The images of power point to human control over nature and are given a similar ironic twist in the final scene. Oedipus acts as physician, intending to cure Thebes of the plague, but he is himself the cause of the disease. As an investigator, he is a hunter, following in the tracks of a murderer, but the hunter is really the hunted—he is hunting himself. As ruler of Thebes, Oedipus is likened to the pilot of a ship, steering "the ship of state" in the "storm" of the plague, trying to bring them home to safe harbor. Ironically, Oedipus discovers that in his incest he already "sailed into his home harbor" years ago (1450–1455), thereby causing the storm. Similarly, the farmer works "mother earth" to bring forth the food that sustains life—an image of human beings governing nature in harmony—while Oedipus ploughed his mother earth (1380–1385) incestuously. In sum, all these images of human knowledge and power are transformed with the revelation of Oedipus' father–murder and mother–incest. Oedipus' transformation brings about a transformation in the play's central images.

It is Oedipus' fate to have done these terrible deeds, for the murder was prophesied before his birth, the murder and incest told him at Delphi. Before the play, as it were, he does all he can to avoid this fate, while during the play, he does all he can to discover the truth. Oedipus is not free to avoid these fated deeds, but he is free to discover them, or not. Even though he is warned by Jocasta to seek no further, he refuses to heed her and discovers the horrible truth. Oedipus' passionate desire for knowledge is deeply rooted in his Moral Character, itself a kind of fate, but not one governed by the gods. The knowledge and power of divine fate, in this play, dictates Oedipus' terrible deeds but not his discovery of them; Oedipus' own knowledge and power do that.

Let me suggest a way of teaching students to think about recurrent images in this play. You might give every student an image to track as each one rereads the play; tell them to note precisely its occurrence (line number, who speaks it, in what situation, giving it certain meanings). After the class has reread the play, each student needs to prepare *a chart that visibly displays every use of the assigned image, with all its various meanings, over the course of the play.* The chart thereby functions as a graph of the whole play as seen through this particular image. It should appear on a large piece of heavy paper or cardboard, and each student must present the findings to the class in a brief presentation (one to two minutes). Because the presentation is so brief, the chart must be readily intelligible to everyone in the class. Encourage students to exercise their imaginations—to color code the charts, annotate and even illuminate them (as in manuscript illuminations)—so as to reveal "the whole play" through the window of their image. In my experience, the best charts tend to be made by visual learners—students who often struggle with the linear thinking demanded by essays. This exercise enables them to display their insights into literature and their talents to advantage.

✸

Because *Oedipus the King* has such dramatic power, and because it is not linguistically difficult, students find it exciting. With a little encouragement, they are willing to reread it, to think more deeply about it, and to dramatize parts of it in Comparative Performances; and they often enjoy debating their evaluations of the characters and their acts. If your students "catch fire" as performers, you may want to spend two days on some scenes in order to discuss and to perform them fully. With perhaps two days on the ending of the play, a discussion of its plot and structure, and another in which the students present their Charts of Recurring Images—not to mention an "Academy Awards Ceremony" maybe with a "Great Performances" rerun—you can spend a full three weeks on *Oedipus the King*, not counting a major paper or a test, or both. This drama repays all the time you spend on it. The characters are so compelling and the action so intense that they rouse class discussion. The students' performances will "tune their ears" to poetry and give them new poise and self-assurance. Best of all, they will achieve a deep and detailed knowledge of a literary masterpiece, and have a good time doing it.

Provocation #12

Educational Videos and The Terminator

Video technology makes available to teachers of English an embarrassment of riches, old and new films of classic novels and plays. What was produced for the screen, even half a century ago, can be obtained for the classroom television: Laurence Olivier's *Henry V*, Max Reinhardt's *A Midsummer Night's Dream*, *Pride and Prejudice* with Greer Garson. More recent works are even more readily available. Before the advent of video, films were expensive and projectors capricious, often possessed by demons delighting to reveal a teacher's clumsy fingers and mechanical obtuseness. But videos are easy to show, easy to stop, easy to rewind, and easy to view over and over. Now the demons cannot so easily ruin a class or rend the film. Videos of first-rate productions are widely available and not prohibitively expensive. Period costumes and language, the complex interactions of characters, the tensions in the unfolding plot, are all rendered vivid, immediate, vital, accessible. Students affirm that they "get so much" and "learn a lot" from watching them.

Unfortunately, this embarrassment of riches has impoverished the teaching of English. Whatever students learn from a video about a play or novel is overborne by the tacit lesson: The video is better than the book. Students are too shrewd to say it, but they know it: "Why should I read *Pride and Prejudice* when I can watch the video?" The immediacy of the film condemns the book. Nothing fails like success.

Good teachers often counter this tendency by showing the film only after the class has worked through a classic novel or a Shakespeare play, after students have labored at understanding it. Maybe the teacher has assigned them parts in certain scenes to rehearse, and so the class has not only studied the work but read much of it aloud, read it dramatically, perhaps even acted it. The film comes as a reward at the end of all this interpretive labor, a well-earned reward.

Unfortunately, the reward only reveals the poverty of the students' work. They are not professional readers or actors; they do not have the financial or the imaginative resources of a mature director. The film sparkles with the artless ease of art. It makes so easy what for students is so hard. The lesson is clear and they will never forget it. After they leave school, should they ever want to experience a classic work, they will rent the video.

Preaching against this inclination merely wastes your time; students may listen politely, but they will not hear. Like some parents, they think "Literature is for enjoyment," and they believe, deeply, that enjoyment must be easy. In fact, for them enjoyment means entertainment, and what entertainment means continues, surprisingly, to be debased by television. Even though they have considerable experience to the contrary—they actually do enjoy hard exercise, demanding sports, and working on music or dance or art—they do not easily recognize these activities as enjoyable. For them, enjoyment means "play" and play means "no effort."

So save your breath. True, reading exercises the imagination, as watching films does not. True, anyone lacking imagination lacks compassion in the same measure, and a lack of the capacity for compassion cripples a human being by crippling human relationships. Reading literature nourishes one's understanding of others— of their values, feelings, decisions, and acts—because it nourishes the imagination. Reading also fosters the ability to communicate because it increases our range and flexibility with words. Films, in contrast, are already imagined and need only to be watched. They present the feeling-full acts of others so as to evoke our participation. They do not demand an imaginative response from us; they do not explore, as do novels, the troubling ground of evaluation and decision in important acts. Because films stimulate feelings so immediately, they do not readily move us to deeper consideration of ourselves and others. Because films present action, they evoke immediate responses. Because literature represents action, it demands imagination and provokes reflection.

All this may be true, but so what? It is just another "Shut up and eat your spinach" speech before the video dessert. To be sure, every English teacher needs to have convictions about why "Reading is good for us" as thoroughly worked out and as explicit as possible. Students need to hear these reasons, not all at once, but in coherent bits, and often. If young people are ever going to acquire positive convictions about reading, they can only do so from adults who have them, live them, and speak them. "Reading is good for us" is betrayed, however, by videos. To them, the video is always so much better. If it were not, it would not be worth showing.

Hence, I have this rule: *Never show a video.* Students already know how to watch television; our task is to help them learn to read and to reflect. That task compels us to struggle against the powers and principalities of this world, among whom "television is Prince." Granted, there may be days when your exhaustion excuses it, though better "free reading" than the tube. Television, with its banal and smarmy immediacy, is always your enemy. Never allow one to enter your classroom.

If this be excessive, then consider an addendum: *Never show a video unless you show two, and never show all of either.* In other words, if you use videos, use them to teach students how to reflect interpretively on films and on the relations between a film and a book. Never show *a* film of a Shakespeare play—always show corresponding *parts* of *two*—and then help the class discuss their similarities and differences.

For example, say the class has read and discussed *Henry V*, and you obtain videos of Laurence Olivier's and of Kenneth Branagh's films. After some preliminary remarks about when they were made, you can show the opening scene of both and start a discussion. Which do you like better, and why? Which is closer to your sense of the play? How does each portray Henry? If you had a large budget to film this play, what would you do? . . . and so on. Branagh has Olivier's version continuously in mind—he is both director and star in his first film. Throughout the film he works with and against Olivier's famous original so as to distinguish himself. Nowhere is this effort more evident than in the opening scene. Rightly cued, students will see how Branagh tries to accomplish it. Does he succeed?

You should never show all of both films, that would take too much time. In addition, you want to leave something for the enterprising or extra-credit-hungry students to do on their own. But openings and endings always have special importance, and close comparison of different versions can reveal much; for middle scenes, be selective. In this instance, you might show both "St. Crispin's Day" speeches and the ensuing battles; or, perhaps, show how Branagh includes some negative scenes about Henry that Olivier simply cut. Olivier's film was made during World War II for a British audience beleaguered by Hitler, and it adapts Shakespeare's play to war-time propaganda. Branagh's version has a different tone for a different time.

Similar procedures could be followed for, say, *The Great Gatsby*. We have the film starring Mia Farrow as Daisy and a recent A&E video with Mira Sorvino. Compare and contrast the openings and the endings, and a few crucial scenes in the middle. The more different the versions are, the more useful they will be. A recent film and a miniseries create two different kinds of productions because of the time elements involved. Students can think about these differences, and what differences the productions have. Or take a recent film and an older one—differences in characterization will abound, even if the period settings are close. The sharper the differences, the quicker a discussion gets moving.

One aim of this exercise is to make young people more thoughtful viewers. When I wrote that they already knew how to watch television, I meant that they were accustomed to opening their eyes in front of the screen. They think that films are realistic, that plots are one thing after another, and that camera movements, like eye movements, are natural. Many know nothing about plot structure, shot composition, montage, or about all the artifice required to make people "look real" in a film. Seeing how differently two films interpret a play or a novel helps liberate the students from a brutish naïveté. They begin to see what is involved in imagining a literary work and translating it into film. They begin to acquire a sense for the artfulness of film.

This brings me to *The Terminator*, the best B-movie ever made. I am told there are other candidates for that honor, but I will defend mine against them all. Should you ever want to teach students to look intelligently and analytically at a film—perhaps second-semester seniors grown feckless at the assurance of graduating—you could not do better than *The Terminator*. They think it is an action film, but it is a love story, which is beautifully structured. Because they think they understand it, you can use the film to show them how limited their understanding is, and how their pleasure can grow into appreciation with their increased knowledge.

A film is a work of art designed to hold an audience's attention. So are a novel and a play; only the artistic means differ. The opening of *The Terminator* thrusts us into mystery: What is happening here? What is going on? Little by little the mystery unfolds, but a satisfying explanation does not come until the first car chase, which ends Act 1. Not until then do we know why the Terminator (Arnold Schwarzenegger) wants to kill Sarah Connor (Linda Hamilton), and why Kyle Reese (Michael Biehn) has come back in time to save her.

The film opens with *doublets*—scenes showing us that the Terminator and Kyle Reese are foils. The Terminator appears first, mysteriously, naked, from nowhere: posed, poised, still. He moves slowly and deliberately to obtain clothing, and though one of the punks whose clothing he demands knifes him, he stands invulnerable and stolid even as he rips the punk's guts out. Then cut to another setting, and Kyle Reese appears: he, too, is naked but hurls along the ground, groaning, and then he is up and sprinting. He obtains clothing with stealth and speed, but without violence. He is evidently vulnerable, but tough and resourceful, and a man in a hurry. Why, we do not know. The Terminator seems invulnerable as he moves at a slow, steady, but unrelenting pace. Why, we do not know. We only know that he will kill coldly and brutally, while Kyle avoids violence even though pursued.

This contrast is the *axis* of the film, present in every action sequence, implied in every scene: Invulnerable Death hunts vulnerable mortals. It appears, in a minor key, in the recurring images of machinery, or technology—the garbage truck of the opening scene, vehicles and weapons of many kinds, the Techno-Bar discotheque, even a plastic toy truck crushed by the Terminator as he steps out of a car. Overtly and subtly, the film portrays technology as the enemy. Whether so highly technological a medium as film can do so in good faith proves a question external to the film itself.

155

The Terminator is not merely an action film, for a mere action film fails miserably. Once, on a memorable afternoon a long time ago, I was watching a mere action film at a matinee—a graduate student in a crowded theater of students, all shirking their work. The action sequences were excellent, but the film, abysmal. The plot was spit without the chewing gum, trying to hold the chase scenes together. The film had no core, no heart, and so the dialogue was meaningless. In the middle of yet another tedious lull, a voice from the back of the hall shrieked, "SHUDDUP AND KILL SOMEBODY!" It was the only good line of the day.

The Terminator tells two intertwined love stories. It tells the story of a man who loves a woman he has never met; he loves her so much that he leaves everything he has ever known in order to save her life. Even though he has never met her, he loves her so much that he is willing to die for her, and eventually he does. It takes considerable time in the film before we understand the full range of Kyle's motives in coming back from the future to save Sarah Connor, but once we do, we know why he literally hit the ground running.

This love story is the core, the living heart, of *The Terminator*. The action sequences, splendid as they are, make no sense apart from it. Kyle's love for Sarah makes the plot go, holds the story together. Although his love, as I have described it, seems out of this world, the film makes it convincing and we suspend our disbelief. Surely this premise for a plot is no more outlandish than those governing *Oedipus Rex* and *Othello*.

Kyle's love for her, confessed only late in the film, evokes Sarah's love for him, and this leads to her transformation. Sarah begins the film as a sweet incompetent, late for work as a waitress where she gets everything wrong. By the final scene she has grown unbelievably tough—mastering the pain of a leg wound, she literally crawls her way to victory over the invincible machine. She does not acquire this toughness through force of necessity or through the influence of the hostile "environment" into which she has been thrust, for it does not come gradually. It happens all of a sudden because it happens through her love for Kyle. It is manifested in the final action sequence, after they have confessed their love. Kyle, wounded and exhausted, cannot go on, and he tells Sarah to run and save herself. She cannot leave, but she must. She endures a moment of despair. And then a voice from her abdomen growls—"On your feet, soldier!"—and she pulls him up with her. She will not abandon him, and she will run, and so they must run, hobbling, together. For the first time, she takes the lead in their struggle. The sweet incompetent has become a tigress. Although Kyle perishes as he tries to save her, she avenges his death and vindicates her love, crushing their indestructible enemy.

Like teaching any novel or play, teaching *The Terminator*, or any film, means attending to its large structures of imagery and plot. But the small structures deserve attention too, perhaps not throughout the whole, but in several parts. If you are going to teach a film you should give the students a critical vocabulary to describe the artfulness of the art. They should come to see the film as a thing made, and well-made, not as something that happens. Students should learn how to describe, analyze, and appreciate camera angles and movements, cutting, the pace of the cuts—how and why these sometimes change quickly and sometimes slowly.

They should come to understand a film from the filmmaker's perspective. A scene is shot from a variety of angles and then composed by editors into a sequence designed to involve the audience continuously, never over- or understimulating them to fatigue or boredom. Each scene or sequence has its characteristic pace and tone; action sequences are set off by passages that give meaning to the story and get progressively longer and more violent as the film goes on. (If they get shorter or less violent, the film proves anticlimactic rather than climactic.) If you can obtain a stopwatch, you can have students record the pace of each shot in a sequence. You can walk them through the kinds of decisions the filmmaker faced: "What are they doing here, and why? Does it succeed? Why, or why not" Video-cassette players are wonderful for such close and attentive work—a scene can be stopped and reviewed over and over.

If you regularly have a class of second-semester seniors, feckless and arrogant in the pride of their hormones, you might try teaching *The Terminator*, or another equally great film, in this way. You will know that you are succeeding when students complain that you have ruined their pleasure in movies, because now they cannot stop themselves from thinking whenever they go to see one.

Provocation #13

The Minidrama

Young people think that literature, like film, should be "realistic." They think that they emphasize the *real*, but they much prefer the *istic*. You can perhaps bring them to glimpse this truth about themselves by describing two films by Yoko Ono. One shows a man taking a shower; it lasts about fifteen minutes: a short-subject, a long shower. The other shows a person sleeping and runs about eight hours.

Art films, of course, are boring. If they were not boring, they would not be art. But Yoko Ono's realistic films make a telling point about both realism and art. We expect artistic forms to intensify ordinary experience by eliminating the irrelevant and highlighting the essential. Generally, intensification involves abbreviation—the shower is mentioned but not narrated. It takes place off-page or off-screen because it does not concern the main action. Occasionally, as in *Psycho* or *Carrie*, a shower becomes part of the action, though not for fifteen minutes. Only literary experimenters like Proust dare spend fifty pages on a person's waking up. But that, too, intensifies and illuminates ordinary experience. Yoko One's two films also illuminate art and ordinary experience by being deliberately and realistically boring.

What students mean by their preference for *the realistic* is a film conforming to their expectations of the genre. In fact, they prefer the fantastic: baroque action sequences and extravagant romances, shown in the ways they have come to expect. Hitchcock's films are "not realistic enough" because the students are used to Brian de Palma and James Cameron, and Truffaut's romances fail the test of "realism" because they are ironic and French.

But if you ask students to write their own dramatic scenes, they will begin with realistic and boring small talk. Unless you have drawn their attention to how dramatists actually begin their scenes—fast, with no wasted motion—students

158

assume that a play should be "like real life," where two people will meet with *Hellos* and *I'm-fines*. They have never noticed that their favorite films waste no time on small talk. Every shot, every exchange, is designed to do something to the audience. If a film fails to move the action along in one scene, everyone yawns; if it fails two scenes in a row, people start leaving. Students experience this failure as *not* realistic. They have not noticed that the realism they prefer in films has in it very little of real life.

As a first exercise to help them understand drama, try assigning students to write a miniplay: two characters, two exchanges, no stage directions. Students must bring in two copies of their plays, for these will be given to students to act in class. The curtain opens (as it were) on a scene, and the playwrights' mindramas have to create some kind of dramatic interest or tension with only two exchanges. The drama must lie in the words spoken; the actors will have to render the scene after only a few minutes of rehearsal. The dramatist can specify the genders of the speakers, but no more.

Here is a miniplay written by a high school junior:

> MALE: Pass the sugar.
> FEMALE: What?
> MALE: Pass the sugar.
> FEMALE: Please!

This little masterpiece presents an unspoken tension. The characters can be acted as son and mother, man and wife, even brother and sister, and the lines so spoken and paused so as to evoke any number of qualities of tension. You might prepare students for writing their miniplays by distributing this one to several pairs of actors to rehearse separately and then present in class. The various performances make for a good discussion.

Students' first plays are rarely this good, but the exercise can be repeated and extended. It aims to teach students how a dramatist employs an economy of means to make meaning. Shakespeare often begins his scenes in the middle of a conversation, as the characters walk on stage; Oedipus addresses the people of Thebes in a crisis; Ibsen wastes no time insinuating the tensions barely below the surface of his bourgeois families. Television wastes time with cars leaving and planes arriving because writers cannot accurately predict how long a scene will take on film and, since television is ruled by the advertiser's clock, they save room for filler. Viewers are used to it. But on the stage, mere filler stands out. Audiences expect more from a play than from television, and the playwright dawdles at his peril.

Students can also be assigned to write miniplays based on poems or stories they have read. This at least provides them with a subject, characters, and possible tensions to evoke. In this case, they must define the situation and setting where the drama occurs. Consider these possible miniplays—five exchanges, maximum—for "The Prodigal Son" and for "Eveline":

1. The younger son asks his father for his inheritance.

2. The father gives both boys their inheritance.

3. The prodigal son meets his brother for the first time after his return.

4. Frank, walking Eveline home, first suggests that she run away with him: his "proposal of marriage."

5. Frank, walking Eveline home, wants to know her decision.

6. Eveline tries to get money from her father to buy the week's groceries.

7. Eveline, Father, and the two children left to her care are all at breakfast, the morning after #6.

These situations are filled with tensions and, thus, with dramatic possibilities. Even a seemingly casual exchange—like "Pass the sugar" and "Please!"—can be used to evoke feeling and reveal character.

Writing miniplays helps students understand several things. First, it reveals to them the difficulties in the dramatist's art—beauty is difficult. In a good play, even the slightest exchanges evoke feeling, reveal character, and move the action forward. Students will notice these effects in their reading more easily after struggling with them in writing. Second, miniplays can be used to deepen their imaginative engagement with other literary works, especially short stories. Different students will imagine Frank's proposal to Eveline, or the prodigal's seeking his inheritance, in quite different ways, yet all of them are valid and relevant to the story. The life of literature will appear in the liveliness of their literary responses.

Finally, they may begin to hear daily conversations with a new ear, a playwright's ear. Ordinary exchanges have their undertones, and these will take on a new resonance. As students acquire a playwright's ear, they will hear more in what other people say. Daily life will appear less ordinary, and literature will have revealed the complexity, the richness, and even the oddity of the ordinary. The truly *realistic* opens up the real.

Provocation #14

The Reader-Response Game

Reader-response criticism, sometimes called *affective stylistics*, enjoyed a scholarly vogue in the early 1980s. It emerges from an important principle: Literary works are designed to work on readers. A plot, for example, sets up certain expectations and then fulfills or frustrates them in the end, after frustrating or fulfilling them in the middle. "Boy meets girl; boy loses girl; boy gets girl": *Pride and Prejudice* from Mr. Darcy's perspective. Or a character is introduced favorably—Mr. Wickham's manners charm everyone, for he has no pride—but the truth about him is gradually revealed: He has no scruples, either. Or a keyword is loaded with negative connotations, only to partake of the pattern of reversals fulfilling the plot: Although Elizabeth Bennett condemns Darcy's "pride" early in the book, she is eventually filled with "pride" (in a good sense) at his conduct in rescuing her family from disgrace. Reader-response criticism attends to the expectations a work generates in readers and to how these are strengthened, amplified, complicated, countered, undermined, or reversed as the work unfolds.

The Reader-Response Game applies this method to the lines of a poem. Every poem has its own little *plot*—it generates expectations and fulfills or frustrates them, just like the plot of a story or play. In my Reader-Response Game, the whole class reads an easy poem *one line at a time*. In this way, they are led step by step into the "dramatic plot" of the lyric. To play it, each student needs a four-by-six card or a piece of heavy paper, preferably colored. They use this to cover the parts of the poem still to be read. The exercise begins with a bit of mystery, at least the first time: You pass out the cards and then copies of the poem *upside down* because the whole class will turn the poem over at the same time and immediately cover the whole text with the cards. (This gives the whole exercise its atmosphere of being a game.) No cheating by reading ahead! Of course, you could use an overhead projector to control the line-by-line discovery of the poem but I prefer to give students hard copies to annotate as the discussion unfolds. For this purpose, the poem should be double or even triple spaced.

Once again, the game involves reading a poem progressively, commenting on one line at a time. Students read without knowing what comes next, but being able to see all they have read so far. Not knowing the whole poem, they can hazard guesses without fear of being wrong. You can discuss words and images in their fullness of possibility, raise odd and digressive questions, and then see, as successive lines are read, which ones finally work for the poem. You can have students guess "What comes next?" If they are right, huzzah! If wrong, no fault; the Reader-Response Game is a no-lose proposition for students.

The first line to comment on is the title, with nothing more:

A White Rose

Comment on any word in the title. What does "white" suggest?—cleanness, innocence, goodness, purity. What does "rose" suggest?—women, girls, perfume, the Blessed Virgin Mary. What does a "white rose" symbolize? (a red rose? a pink rose? a yellow rose?) Students give answers, and you work with them until you are ready to move on to the next line:

A White Rose

The red rose whispers of passion,

Comment on any word or phrase here. Why is "red" connected with "passion"?—blood, heat, hot flashes, fire in the belly, fire in the loins. What passion is the poem talking about?—anger, envy, love, lust. How do you know? Why "whispers of" for "passion"? How would "pants of," or "heaves with," or "seethes with" be different? When a poem is titled "A White Rose" and the first line concerns "the red rose," what do you think? What do you think the next line will say? (Notice the punctuation at the end of this one.) When the line is exhausted, or the class, or you have spent enough time on it, the students uncover the next line:

A White Rose

The red rose whispers of passion,
And the white rose breathes of love;

Students can comment on anything here. What does "love" mean in the second line? Why is it associated with "the white rose"? Why does it use "breathes of"? What contrasts are set up in these two lines, and what do you think they mean, or suggest? How can a rose "whisper" and "breathe"?—symbolism, suggestion, odor. Are the odors of a red rose and a white rose different? Is that difference represented in these two different verbs? Is there a connection between the different odors of red and white roses and the different things they symbolize? Or does the different symbolism lie only in the colors? Primarily in the colors? Okay, we have a poem called "A White Rose," with a first line about "the red rose" and the second line about "the white"; what do you think comes next?

A White Rose

The red rose whispers of passion,
  And the white rose breathes of love;
Oh, the red rose is a falcon,

What is this new line telling us? What do you know about falcons? A falcon is a kind of hawk. What do you know about hawks? What connection can there be between "the red rose," "passion," and "a falcon"? In what ways is a falcon, or a hawk, passionate? Why did the poet write "the red rose is a falcon," not "the red rose is like a falcon"? With this shift to bird imagery in line 3, what do you think will happen in line 4? (Students usually see "dove" coming next.)

I need not spin out the assignment further. You get the drill, and you know how to read poetry. Here is the whole poem:

A White Rose

The red rose whispers of passion,
  And the white rose breathes of love;
Oh, the red rose is a falcon,
  And the white rose is a dove.
But I send you a cream-white rosebud,
  With a flush on its petal tips,
For the love that is purest and sweetest
  Has a kiss of desire on its lips.

—*John Boyle O'Reilly*
(1844–1890)

This poem is easy enough to "get" on a first reading, yet it has its subtleties. The contrasts between the roses and the birds prove rich with implications. Your students might not know that falcons will hunt and kill doves for food. But do not tell them this straight off: They might surprise you. Rather, ask them what do they know about falcons? About doves? High school students have some experience about "passion" and "love," and so they might infer that falcons kill doves simply from that experience. The traditional symbolism of the Holy Spirit as a dove is not directly relevant to this little love poem, but it does pertain to the contrasts developed here. Why bird images for love, not fish or animal images? What does the bird imagery add to the flower imagery?

Unless you have a florist in the class, your students are not likely to know much about the rosebud sent with the poem. The rose is called "Fire and Ice"; when it opens, it remains cream-white on the very outside but is all red within. What does this knowledge add to the meaning of the poem?

These specialized bits of knowledge complicate the poem interestingly. Yet it remains an easy work, for it uses familiar symbols for a familiar situation. Its contrasts can be elaborated and their implications clarified. It employs the resources of poetry—metaphor, rhyme, meter, indirect suggestion—to make meaning. The poem conveys a social situation, the parameters of which can be discussed. How old, do you think, is the boy or man sending the flower and the poem? How old the girl or woman? What might their relationship be? What is their relationship clearly *not*?—father and daughter, husband and wife. How do we know?

The second stanza nicely fuses and complicates the contrasting images from the first. Although our students are not familiar with the traditional "language of flowers," they possess enough cultural knowledge to make sense of the poem. It raises related questions: Why are flowers associated with females? Why especially with girls? Jane, if you received an anonymous bouquet here at school, how would you feel? If it happened to you, Peter, how would you feel? Why the difference? Is there an equivalent gift for boys or men? And so on, if you like, to the differences in social relations between unmarried males and females, then and now.

Finally, if you are the girl, how are you going to feel as you watch the rose open and reveal the passionate red interior? If you know that the name of the rose is "Fire and Ice," does that change the meaning of the gift? Ice is traditionally associated with a virgin's chastity; we know the associations of fire. Is the rose of the poem about his desire only? Or is it also a statement about the way *she* has kissed *him*?

A poem implies a context, and it opens onto a world. The world of this poem is distant from ours in time and social mores, but not entirely unfamiliar. It is just unfamiliar enough to emerge clearly and distinctly, and so enables students to reflect on their own mores. It stretches their imaginative sympathies without straining or breaking them. Moreover, the playful aspect of the Reader-Response Game encourages them to see and appreciate the playful yet serious wit of the poem. Their own cross-sexual banter evinces similar qualities daily. Distant though the world of this poem may be from our students, it is a human thing and not alien to them.

Provocation # 15

The Diction Game

In the Diction Game, you create a document analogous to a poet's drafts or working papers for a poem. You take an easy poem and offer students two choices for certain words or phrases, mirroring the kinds of choices the poet made, consciously or unconsciously, while writing. Here is an instance, using the same poem as in Provocation #14:

A White Rose

The red rose ⟨murmurs of / whispers of⟩ passion,

And the white rose ⟨breathes of / seethes with⟩ love;

Oh, the red rose is a ⟨lion, / falcon,⟩

And the white rose is a dove.

⟨But / So⟩ I send you a ⟨cream- / bright-⟩ white rosebud

With ⟨a flush / some rouge⟩ on its petal tips,

165

For the love that is purest and ^{clearest} / sweetest

Has ^{the fire} / a kiss of desire on its lips.

—*John Boyle O'Reilly*
(1844–1890)

Some of these choices are easy, and some rather subtle. In my experience, few students will opt for "lion" in line 3 with "dove" in line 4 clueing them into the bird imagery; in line 6, "some rouge" is ludicrous, and girls who know about make-up and roses will not opt for it. At the other end of the scale, the choice between "whispers" and "murmurs" in line 2 proves delicate, and that between "But" and "So" in line 5, subtler still.

You can make the choices as easy or as hard as you like. You do not even need to preserve meter and rhyme, if you do not mind giveaway answers, or you want to test for tin ears. You can use this as an in-class exercise or for homework; you can require a written explanation for every choice or simply discuss their choices in class. It also makes for an interesting examination because you can give credit for a "wrong" answer if the reasons given are cogent. The Diction Game helps students think like writers and engenders more thoughtful reading as well.

Provocation # 16

Imitation and Parody

When we were in high school and college, we noticed the mannerisms of our teachers. Some had more than others; a few had distinctive styles as teachers; but all had mannerisms of clothing, voice, and gesture. In high school, some teachers were much imitated—in their absence, of course, though sometimes the imitators were caught in the act. When I was young and so foolish as to be a first-year high school teacher—for the existence of second-year high school teachers ranks among the greater miracles—I was so foolish as to believe myself inimitable, without mannerisms. But one day, I was late to class and arrived to look through the doorway at a ninth grader, my best student, imitating me. That minute was worth a semester of education courses. It did not compel me to abandon my mannerisms, for I needed them too badly, but at least it stripped me of a delusion.

The young have an acute sense for style. They will remember your sweaters longer than your jokes, and much longer than whatever it was you taught them. Parody may be the last refuge of a noble talent, but it proves a favorite genre for the young. They enjoy parody in films, on *Saturday Night Live*, in political cartoons, and at your expense.

English teachers can harness this delight in stylistic imitation. It makes for writing exercises that the whole class will enjoy listening to and even doing. It only demands some steady acquaintance with a writer whose style has enough characteristic features to be imitable. Nor do these need to be analyzed—they need only to be experienced long enough. The more extravagant the style, whether baroque or minimalist, the better. Middle styles seem too natural to be easily imitated or parodied.

Unfortunately, we English teachers and our textbooks rarely sow the seeds of imitation and parody. Textbooks tend to be anthologies—they do not present enough of a writer to stimulate imitation. The seeds of imitation are two: sufficient time spent with a writer and considerable reading aloud. Textbooks hardly allow the first, though we could do more to encourage the second. Textbooks can be supplemented, and English teachers are often ready to try something new. Consider this exercise.

Take a poet like Whitman or like e e cummings—a poet with a distinctive style attracted toward characteristic subjects. (Avoid poets writing in meter and rhyme: You need a poet whom your students can imitate.) Create an anthology of this poet's work, perhaps in conjunction with your textbook. Tell the students at the beginning of the unit that they will be asked to write imitations or parodies of this poet at the end. Spend at least two weeks on the poet, reading many poems on a characteristic subject, and reading them aloud in class, over and over again. You might require students to memorize a poem (cummings) or a passage (Whitman). In order to imitate a writer, they must absorb the style, and the more reading aloud and reciting they do, the more thorough the absorption.

The climax of the exercise comes on Performance Day. The students have written either imitations, honoring the poetry, or parodies, making fun of it. The students commit themselves to one or the other on the pages they will hand in, but they perform their poems for the class *without saying which one theirs is*. The class then votes: Is it imitation, or parody? A good imitation is clearly not a parody, but a good parody sounds at first like an imitation. Performance Day is always fun. You can even offer a prize for the best imitation and the best parody.

At the end of each performance, the whole class must applaud. I make this an invariable rule. The students may not like the performance and it may, in truth, be poor. The applause may be no more than token appreciation for the courage it takes to stand up before the class and perform. But applaud we all must. Most often the applause will prove vigorous and well-deserved. A student may not care much for what you think of him, but his classmates' opinion he values.

At the end of it all, you might even bring out a professional parody of your poet from an anthology of parodies. You could present it as a parody, or as a problem: Did Whitman write this, or someone else? The best English teacher I know uses this exercise as the final examination in her advanced seniors' course, "Yeats, Eliot, and Auden"; she gives them a parody of one of these, and the students must explain which poet is being parodied and how.

One benefit of this exercise lies in its revealing of the relations between style and content in poetry. Whitman's free-flowing and rambunctious style fits the energy of the young Republic, whose poet he declares himself to be. But although Whitman's expansive manner would include everything ("I contain multitudes"), it is hardly suited to express the tensions, hesitations, and complexities of the feeling of love as evoked in an Elizabethan sonnet. Nor can a sonnet readily convey the Whitmaniac energy that bursts all restrictive, metered forms. Students will understand this difference more surely after absorbing a writer's style. Should you care to use the exercise on both Whitman and cummings, students will hold it in their mind's ear and know it in their bones.

Provocation # 17

Derived Poems

Students who read poems should write them. It does not matter that they may have little talent for poetry. They may have small talent for exposition and argument, too, yet we compel them to write essays. Most people have little talent for most things, for talents are not distributed with Mardi Gras largesse, and we learn to be happy with our one or two. Writing poetry is a time-honored school exercise: All the great poets in our language, up to this century, wrote poetry in grammar school in Latin and sometimes in Greek. Presumably they did not write great poetry in antique languages in grammar school, but they learned something about putting the best words in the best order. Writing poetry or, if you are a purist, writing verse, is simply another exercise in composition.

By *derived poems*, I do not mean "creative writing." You can no more assign creativity than you can give genius. Assigning students to write "something creative" is akin to asking an interviewee to "Tell us something about yourself." Rather, derived poems imply a specific assignment emerging from a poem or a kind of poetry the class has been studying.

Consider a poem you might assign after studying "The White Rose":

Write "The Lady's Reply" to "The White Rose." Use the same meter (seven to nine syllables per line) and form (four line stanzas, with at least one pair of rhymes). Choose one of the following possibilities, unless you imagine another one that you prefer:

1. She accepts the rose and encourages his courtship.

2. She accepts the rose, suggesting that he better propose marriage soon.

3. She returns the rose gracefully, telling him she is not interested in his attentions.

4. She returns the rose ungracefully, saying she could never be interested in him.

5. She kept the rosebud, flattered, but when she noticed the red interior as it bloomed, she was outraged at the suggestion. She returns the blooming rose (perhaps faded, by now) with her outraged reply.

This would be an overnight or over-the-weekend assignment; strike while the poem is fresh in their ears. The next class is Performance Day. After a student stands up and reads her poem aloud and the class applauds, others must define the character of her "Lady's Reply." You will be pleasantly surprised, I think, at the wit some students will bring to this exercise. The formal restrictions of meter and rhyme usually inspire, rather than hamper, ingenuity.

How does one grade an assigned poem? You can give full credit for completing it with honest effort, with extra credit possible for extraordinary achievement. Or you can not grade it at all. These options presume that writing poetry stands in a different category from writing prose, that everyone should be able to write prose but not necessarily verse. On the other hand, you could assume that writing is writing and that talent for prose, like talent for poetry, is unequally distributed. Hence, you can grade poetic compositions as you do essays—the best get high marks, and the worst get low. It is easy to tell the difference.

Not all poems imply social situations inviting a reply as readily as "The White Rose," but all poems imply social contexts. Perhaps you are not inclined to assign "The Horse-Poet's Reply to Robert Frost" or "Frostbite in Woods on a Snowy Evening" or "Mrs. Frost's Irritation at a Late Supper." Nevertheless, you might ask for a derived poem in a different sense:

> Write a meditative poem in the manner of Frost's "Stopping by Woods on a Snowy Evening." Imagine a situation where you pause to observe or to think or to relish a precious moment: turn it into a poem. (Stanzas of four lines; a regular meter, though not necessarily Frost's; at least one pair of rhymes per stanza.)

> If you insist, you can write a poem about a situation where you refuse to stop and think, for some reason which you name or suggest. But the poem must be in meter and rhyme, as above.

An exercise like this accomplishes several things. First, it removes some of the weirdness from poetry. I have had college students insist that Frost's horse really talks to him in the third stanza, and they have a positive penchant for dead men speaking in poems (Shakespeare's "When in Disgrace with Fortune and Men's Eyes," among others). They leap to such views not only because they are inexperienced and inattentive readers but because they think poets talk about weird things like that. Assignments like this one put students in contact with their own equivalent experiences. They may not have "stopped by woods on a snowy evening" to converse with a horse, but they have paused at a sunset, or mused while fishing, or felt keen loneliness at a dance. Writing poems about equivalent experiences helps students feel that poetry is not all that weird—its concerns are our concerns. A poem can emerge from and illuminate common experience.

Second, poetry writing helps students appreciate the beauties of poetry. Beauty is difficult. After they grapple with the difficulties of meter and rhyme, they can more easily feel the artistry of good verse, how it resolves meaning and feeling with the turn of a phrase or echoing rhyme. To understand a poem as "the best words in the best order," they must feel its union of form and content. They will feel this more forcefully after having faced the struggle of poetic composition.

Third, verse composition helps them with their writing of prose. It teaches economy of syntax, grace of style, and the force of implication. As Alexander Pope put it: "True Ease in Writing comes from Art, not Chance, / As those move easiest who have learn'd to dance." The dancing art of verse composition makes prose movement easier, more graceful, more effective.

Finally, poetic composition exercises different talents than expository and argumentative prose. Even though your best essayists will usually be among your best poets, simply because of their verbal gifts, some students who are dim in essays will shine in poetry. Perhaps they have an "ear" for rhythm—a sense for rhyme—or minds that delight at the leaping connection that falls flat in prose but soars in poetry. Students with nonlinear minds often thrive in verse composition, and then they enjoy literature and succeed in English as they never have before. They deserve their lark in the sun.

Provocation # 18

A Good Word for Rote Memorizing

Let's face it: For all the decades-long ballyhoo about teaching students inquiry and fostering their curiosity and leading them to the joy of discovery and, hence, about the evils of "rote memorizing," most examinations in English and social studies are regurgitation tests. Even the essay questions are often designed to be regurgitation essays. If an algebra teacher should give a test of the same problems covered in class, or a Latin teacher composed one full of sentences the class had already translated, he or she would be suspect. Teachers are expected to use different problems and sentences to test students' understanding. But how many of us give tests on which students are asked to work on a poem not covered in class? And if their number is high, they can manage this only with poetry. Tests on a novel, or play or short-story unit, demand regurgitation—adroit, perhaps, and not without understanding, but still regurgitation.

Still, learning does involve memory, and in my view there is nothing wrong with tests that require some regurgitation. Life in that common fantasy known as the real world is full of them. People work up material for sales presentations, do homework for job interviews, bone up for important meetings, put together cases for court, prepare sermons, and forget the details soon after. They hold what they need in their heads for as long as they need it, then let it go. A good memory is invaluable. Antimemory educational theory does not serve students, and it induces teachers to deceive themselves about what they actually ask students to do.

The memory is a muscle. Just as some people have natural strength, some have naturally good memories. But every memory can be developed with exercise, and schools should provide for it from the earliest years. Memorizing has its pleasures. Children love learning the alphabet, and learning a new language is like waxing a floor—your progress is evident every time you look. Whereas learning to write well takes years and progress is often halting or invisible, learning French means acquiring new words and constructions every week. The gratification is almost immediate.

We can help our students in many ways simply by implementing a neglected exercise: require students to memorize poetry and prose. Let the watchword be: "Not mere memory-learning, but Rote Memorizing." Make it a policy that the work be cumulative—what has been memorized must stay memorized. Let it be a rule that students can be tested, in writing or by recitation, without prior notice. After all, if they have really memorized something, it should always be available to them. You need not test every student every time, nor does the whole of anything need to be written or recited. Once students are used to the drill, you can say: "Cheryl, Joseph, and William, recite 'The Road Not Taken,' one stanza each, in that order; Sarah, you prompt them if they get stuck." The wailing and gnashing of teeth will subside once students find that you are consistent in your demands. If the whole department adopts the practice, you will hear nary a groan.

Rote memorizing "strengthens" the muscles of students' memories. As they come to memorize larger pieces, their stronger memories will help them do well on tests in all their classes, not least of all by fostering their self-confidence. You will need to help them discover to what extent they are auditory or visual learners, and that will add to students' self-knowledge. Perhaps best of all, it will help their reading and their writing. They will hold instances of good writing in their minds—all of it vivid, some of it rather complex. If you lead them to memorize passages of fine prose, they will be familiar, intimately, with syntactic structures far more complex than anything they hear in the media or from one another. Thus, they will prove more able to understand a long, complex sentence when they read one and more inclined to write one on their own. No other exercise, aside from writing itself, so fosters the ability to understand and to generate complex meaning in a sentence than does rote memorizing.

This is not an exercise for dabbling. If you decide to implement it, for however long a period, I suggest selecting your passages in advance, beginning small but steadily extending their length. Prose will be harder for students than poetry because, after all, their memories already hold the words to scores of popular songs. I have found that starting with one prose sentence works best, before gradually building up a passage from a famous speech. Encouragement is essential, but so are consistent, disciplining expectations. Have them memorize something new every week, or every other week. When they have completed the program, they will be as amazed at their memorative stamina as freshmen long-distance runners are when comparing their preseason and end-of-season times.

As teachers, I believe we are obliged to do all this memorizing too. That is not hard, especially with all the recitations you hear in class. To be sure, our memories are older and lack the resilience of the young. But, I think you will find, as I did, that the labor quickens your feel for language, renews your pleasure in well-turned phrases, and increases your powers of expression.

Appendix A

"The Prodigal Son"
(Luke 15:11–32, King James Version)

11 A certain man had two sons:

12 And the younger of them said to his father, Father, give me the portion of goods that falleth unto me. And he divided unto them his living.

13 And not many days after the younger son gathered all together, and took his journey into a far country, and there wasted his substance with riotous living.

14 And when he had spent all, there arose a mighty famine in that land, and he began to be in want.

15 And he went and joined himself to a citizen of that country; and he sent him into his fields to feed swine.

16 And he would fain have filled his belly with the husks that the swine did eat; and no man gave unto him.

17 And when he came to himself, he said, How many hired servants of my father's have bread enough and to spare, and I perish with hunger!

18 I will arise and go to my father, and will say unto him, Father, I have sinned against heaven, and before thee,

19 And am no more worthy to be called thy son: make me as one of thy hired servants.

20 And he arose, and came to his father. But when he was yet a great way off, his father saw him, and had compassion, and ran, and fell on his neck, and kissed him.

21 And the son said unto him, Father, I have sinned against heaven, and in thy sight, and am no more worthy to be called thy son.

22 But the father said to his servants, Bring forth the best robe, and put it on him; and put a ring on his hand, and shoes on his feet:

23 And bring hither the fatted calf, and kill it; and let us eat, and be merry:

24 For this my son was dead, and is alive again; he was lost, and is found. And they began to be merry.

25 Now his elder brother was in the field; and as he came and drew nigh to the house, he heard music and dancing.

26 And he called one of the servants, and asked what these things meant.

27 And he said unto him, Thy brother is come; and thy father hath killed the fatted calf, because he hath received him safe and sound.

28 And he was angry, and would not go in; therefore came his father out, and entreated him.

29 And he answering said to his father, Lo, these many years do I serve thee, neither transgressed I at any time thy commandment: and yet thou never gavest me a kid, that I might make merry with my friends;

30 But as soon as this thy son was come, which hath devoured thy living with harlots, thou hast killed for him the fatted calf.

31 And he said unto him, Son, thou art ever with me, and all that I have is thine.

32 It was meet that we should make merry, and be glad: for this thy brother was dead, and is alive again; and was lost, and is found.

Appendix B

"Eveline," James Joyce

She sat at the window watching the evening invade the avenue. Her head was leaned against the window curtains and in her nostrils was the odor of dusty cretonne. She was tired.

Few people passed. The man out of the last house passed on his way home; she heard his footsteps clacking along the concrete pavement and afterwards crunching on the cinder path before the new red houses. One time there used to be a field in which they used to play every evening with other people's children. Then a man from Belfast bought the field and built houses in it—not like their little brown houses, but bright brick houses with shining roofs. The children of the avenue used to play together in that field—the Devines, the Waters, the Dunns, little Keogh the cripple, she and her brothers and sisters. Ernest, however, never played: he was too grown up. Her father used often to hunt them in out of the field with his blackthorn stick; but usually little Keogh used to keep *nix* and call out when he saw their father coming. Still they seemed to have been rather happy then. Her father was not so bad then; and besides, her mother was alive. That was a long time ago; she and her brothers and sisters were all grown up; her mother was dead. Tizzie Dunn was dead, too, and the Waters had gone back to England. Everything changes. Now she was going away like the others, to leave her home.

Home! She looked round the room, reviewing all its familiar objects which she had dusted once a week for so many years, wondering where on earth all the dust had come from. Perhaps she would never see again those familiar objects from which she had never dreamed of being divided. And yet during all those years she had never found out the name of the priest whose yellowing photograph hung on the wall above the broken harmonium beside the coloured print of the promises made to Blessed Margaret Mary Alacoque. He had been a school friend of her father. Whenever she showed the photograph to a visitor her father used to pass it with a casual word:

"He is in Melbourne now."

She had consented to go away, to leave her home. Was that wise? She tried to weigh each side of the question. In her home anyway she had shelter and food; she had those whom she had known all her life about her. Of course she had to work hard, both in the house and at business. What would they say of her in the Stores when they found out that she had run away with a fellow? Say she was a fool, perhaps; and her place would be filled up by advertisement. Miss Gavan would be glad. She always had an edge on her, especially whenever there were people listening.

"Miss Hill, don't you see these ladies are waiting?"

"Look lively, Miss Hill, please."

She would not cry many tears at leaving the Stores.

But in her new home, in a distant unknown country, it would not be like that. Then she would be married—she, Eveline. People would treat her with respect then. She would not be treated as her mother had been. Even now, though she was over nineteen, she sometimes felt herself in danger of her father's violence. She knew it was that that had given her the palpitations. When they were growing up he had never gone for her, like he used to go for Harry and Ernest, because she was a girl; but latterly he had begun to threaten her and say what he would do to her only for her dead mother's sake. And now she had nobody to protect her. Ernest was dead and Harry, who was in the church decorating business, was nearly always down somewhere in the country. Besides, the invariable squabble for money on Saturday nights had begun to weary her unspeakably. She always gave her entire wages—seven shillings—and Harry always sent up what he could but the trouble was to get any money from her father. He said she used to squander the money, that she had no head, that he wasn't going to give her his hard-earned money to throw about the streets, and much more, for he was usually fairly bad of a Saturday night. In the end he would give her the money and ask her had she any intention of buying Sunday's dinner. Then she had to rush out as quickly as she could and do her marketing, holding her black leather purse tightly in her hand as she elbowed her way through the crowds and returning home late under her load of provisions. She had hard work to keep the house together and to see that the two young children who had been left to her charge went to school regularly and got their meals regularly. It was hard work—a hard life—but now that she was about to leave it she did not find it a wholly undesirable life.

She was about to explore another life with Frank. Frank was very kind, manly, open-hearted. She was to go away with him by the night-boat to be his wife and to live with him in Buenos Aires where he had a home waiting for her. How well she remembered the first time she had seen him; he was lodging in a house on the main road where she used to visit. It seemed a few weeks ago. He was standing at the gate, his peaked cap pushed back on his head and his hair tumbled forward over a face of bronze. Then they had come to know each other. He used to meet her outside the Stores every evening and see her home. He took her to see *The Bohemian Girl* and she felt elated as she sat in an unaccustomed part of the theatre with him. He was awfully fond of music and sang a little. People knew that they were courting and, when he sang about the lass that loves a sailor, she always felt pleasantly confused. He used to call her Poppens out of fun. First of all it had been an excitement for her to have a fellow and then she had begun to like him. He had tales of distant countries. He had started as a deck boy at a pound a month on a ship of the Allan Line going out to Canada. He told her the names of the ships he had been on and the names of the different services. He had sailed through the Straits of Magellan and he told her stories of the terrible Patagonians. He had fallen on his feet in Buenos Aires, he said, and had come over to the old country just for a holiday. Of course, her father had found out the affair and had forbidden her to have anything to say to him.

"I know these sailor chaps," he said.

One day he had quarreled with Frank and after that she had to meet her lover secretly.

The evening deepened in the avenue. The white of two letters in her lap grew indistinct. One was to Harry; the other was to her father. Ernest had been her favourite but she liked Harry too. Her father was becoming old lately, she noticed; he would miss her. Sometimes he could be very nice. Not long before, when she had been laid up for a day, he had read her out a ghost story and made toast for her at the fire. Another day, when their mother was alive, they had all gone for a picnic to the Hill of Howth. She remembered her father putting on her mother's bonnet to make the children laugh.

Her time was running out but she continued to sit by the window, leaning her head against the window curtain, inhaling the odor of dusty cretonne. Down far in the avenue she could hear a street organ playing. She knew the air. Strange that it should come that very night to remind her of the promise to her mother, her promise to keep the home together as long as she could. She remembered the last night of her mother's illness; she was again in the close dark room at the other side of the hall and outside she heard a melancholy air of Italy. The organ-grinder had been ordered to go away and given sixpence. She remembered her father strutting back into the sickroom saying: "Damned Italians! coming over here!"

As she mused the pitiful vision of her mother's life laid its spell on the very quick of her being—that life of commonplace sacrifices closing in final craziness. She trembled as she heard again her mother's voice saying constantly with foolish insistence: "Derevaun Seraun! Derevaun Seraun!"

She stood up in a sudden impulse of terror. Escape! She must escape! Frank would save her. He would give her life, perhaps love, too. But she wanted to live. Why should she be unhappy? She had a right to happiness. Frank would take her in his arms, fold her in his arms. He would save her.

❋

She stood among the swaying crowd in the station at the North Wall. He held her hand and she knew that he was speaking to her, saying something about the passage over and over again. The station was full of soldiers with brown baggages. Through the wide doors of the sheds she caught a glimpse of the black mass of the boat, lying in beside the quay wall, with illumined portholes. She answered nothing. She felt her cheek pale and cold and, out of a maze of distress, she prayed to God to direct her, to show her what was her duty. The boat blew a long mournful whistle into the mist. If she went, tomorrow she would be on the sea with Frank, steaming toward Buenos Aires. Their passage had been booked. Could she still draw back after all he had done for her? The distress awoke a nausea in her body and she kept moving her lips in silent fervent prayer.

A bell clanged upon her heart. She felt him seize her hand:

"Come!"

All the seas of the world tumbled about her heart. He was drawing her into them. He would drown her. She gripped with both hands at the iron railing.

"Come!"

No! No! No! It was impossible. Her hands clutched the iron in frenzy. Amid the seas she sent a cry of anguish!

"Eveline! Evvy!"

He rushed to go beyond the barrier and called to her to follow. He was shouted at to go on but he still called to her. She set her white face to him, passive, like a helpless animal. Her eyes gave him no sign of love or farewell or recognition.

Bibliography and Recommended Reading

The list of topics below follows roughly the sequence of the chapters and Provocations. I have attempted to recommend books you are not so likely to know already, so if this list seems eccentric, it is.

Kenneth Burke

My model of human action is drawn from Kenneth Burke's "Dramatistic pentad" in *A Grammar of Motives* (Berkeley: University of California Press, 1969), and Michael Oakeshott's *On Human Conduct* (Oxford: Clarendon Press, 1975, pp. 31–107). The four questions about literary structure ("What goes with what?" and so on) are taken from Kenneth Burke, *The Philosophy of Literary Form*, Third Edition (Berkeley: University of California Press, 1973).

The best introduction to Burke, especially for a teacher of literature, remains William H. Rueckert, *Kenneth Burke and the Drama of Human Relations*, Second Edition (Berkeley: University of California Press, 1982); Greig E. Henderson's *Kenneth Burke: Literature and Language as Symbolic Action* (Athens, GA: University of Georgia Press, 1988), is also clear and useful. Burke's own best introduction to his thought is *Language as Symbolic Action: Essays on Life, Literature, and Method* (Berkeley: University of California Press, 1966).

Asking Questions

R. G. Collingwood, a philosopher and an archaeologist, sets forth and illustrates his "logic of question-and-answer" in his *An Autobiography* (Oxford: Clarendon Press, 1978, pp. 29–146). Although his subject is "historical thinking," what he says clearly applies to thinking about literature. *An Introduction to Shared Inquiry*, Third Edition (Chicago: The Great Books Foundation, 1992), offers practical guidance for learning how to formulate good questions and lead discussions. Jeffrey D. Wilhelm, Tanya N. Baker, and Julie Dube in *Strategic Reading: Guiding Students to Lifelong Literacy, 6–12* (Portsmouth, NH: Heinemann, 2001) develop a heuristic for asking questions in Chapter 5.

In my view, the greatest philosophical work on the role of asking questions in the pursuit of knowledge remains Bernard J. F. Lonergan, *Insight: A Study in Human Understanding* (originally published in 1957; Toronto: University of Toronto Press, 1992). Some useful guides have been written to make Lonergan's insights into insight available to a general audience. One of the best is Terry J. Tekippe, *What Is Lonergan Up to in 'Insight': A Primer* (Collegeville, MN: The Liturgical Press, 1996).

Philosophy of Education

I regularly reread two discourses in John Henry Newman, *The Idea of a University* (many editions)—"Knowledge Viewed in Relation to Learning" and "Knowledge Viewed in Relation to Professional Skill." More often, I reread Michael Oakeshott, *The Voice of Liberal Learning: Michael Oakeshott on Education*, edited by Timothy Fuller (New Haven: Yale University Press, 1989; reprinted by Liberty Fund, Indianapolis, 2001). Oakeshott's chapter, "Teaching and Learning," is the best philosophical treatment of teaching I have ever read. Fuller's Introduction should be read first, for it will help you successfully come to grips with Oakeshott's essays.

James Joyce, "Eveline"

Hugh Kenner's book, *The Pound Era* (Berkeley: University of California Press, 1971, p. 36), has a picture of James Joyce in 1904, looking like Frank when Eveline first sees him (see pp. 34–39 for his discussion of the story). The book by Robert Scholes, *Semiotics and the Interpretation of Literature* (New Haven: Yale University Press, 1982), contains a fine essay on "Eveline," and offers a lucid introduction to using semiotics in interpretation.

Life of the Imagination

Most serious writers of fiction and poetry today also write essays about their craft and their contemporaries, and these essays often touch on what the life of the imagination means for our lives. A few of my favorites are mentioned here, but I suggest that you seek out essays, especially books of essays, by your favorite poets and novelists. My favorites for rereading include: Kathleen Raine, *The Inner Journey of the Poet and Other Papers*, edited by Brian Keeble (London: George Allen and Unwin, 1982); Howard Nemerov, *New and Selected Essays* (Carbondale: Southern Illinois Press, 1985); and Flannery O'Connor, *Mystery and Manners*, edited by Sally and Robert Fitzgerald (New York: Farrar, Straus, and Giroux, 1969).

Robert Coles' book, *The Call of Stories: Teaching and the Moral Imagination* (Boston: Houghton Mifflin, 1989), could be subtitled "How the study of literature will make you a better physician." Coles is on the faculty of Harvard Medical School, and in these personal reflections, he explores the value of literature for understanding ourselves and others.

If you want to know what various thinkers have said about the imagination, consult Eva Brann, *The World of the Imagination: Sum and Substance* (Savage, MD: Rowman and Littlefield, 1991).

Literary Theory Applied to Reading Literature

I find it easiest to grasp what a literary theory *says* by seeing what it *does*. In the past two decades, biblical scholars have been using literary theories to treat various books of the Bible. If you are interested in it and are not offended by its being treated as literature, you can learn a great deal about the Bible and about literary theory at the same time.

Robert Alter, *The Art of Biblical Narrative* (New York: Basic Books, 1981), sets forth the poetics of Hebrew narrative through a series of close readings. You might begin reading it with Chapter 3 because Alter spends his first two chapters defending his project against what was then prevailing academic practice in biblical studies. He followed this book with *The Art of Biblical Poetry* (New York: Basic Books, 1985).

For the New Testament, you might begin with David M. Rhoads, Joanna Dewey, and Donald Michie, *Mark as Story*, Second Edition (Minneapolis: Fortress Press, 1999). Two books draw on several different methods to illuminate the Gospel of John: R. Alan Culpepper, *Anatomy of the Fourth Gospel: A Study in Literary Design* (Philadelphia: Fortress Press, 1983) and Mark W. G. Stibbe, *John's Gospel* (New York: Routledge, 1994).

Northrop Frye has applied his literary theory to the Christian Bible considered as a coherent whole in *The Great Code: The Bible and Literature* (New York: Harcourt Brace, 1982), with a follow-up study entitled *Words with Power: Being a Second Study of "The Bible as Literature"* (New York: Harcourt Brace, 1990). Because Frye repeats his central ideas often, applying them now in one context, now in another, you can find "all of Frye" in almost any of his books. If you are not interested in the Bible, see Frye's collection—*Myth and Metaphor: Selected Essays, 1974–1988*, edited by Robert D. Denham (Charlottesville: University of Virginia Press, 1990), especially "The Koine of Myth."

Kenneth Quinn, in *How Literature Works* (London: Macmillan, 1992), delivers a lucid account of how literature works. It began as a series of radio talks and so it has little theoretical baggage, though Quinn provides a glossary of the critical terms he uses. He writes so well about the passages that he treats as examples that he makes you want to go out and read the books he is writing about.

Against the Reductionist Tendencies of Literary Theory

For two defenses of literature against the reductionist tendencies of theory, see Robert Alter, *The Pleasures of Reading in an Ideological Age* (New York: Simon and Schuster, 1989), and Denis Donoghue, *The Practice of Reading* (New Haven: Yale University Press, 1998).

Narrative

Robert Scholes and Robert Kellogg, *The Nature of Narrative* (New York: Oxford University Press, 1966), treat the fundamentals of narrative clearly and well. Caroline Gordon, *How to Read a Novel* (New York: Viking Press, 1957), gives a novelist's advice about how to read a novel well. Robert Penn Warren's essay, "Why Do We Read Fiction?" gives a lucid, graceful, and concise answer to the question in its title. Originally published in *The Saturday Evening Post* (October 20, 1962), it is reprinted in Warren's *New and Selected Essays* (New York: Random House, 1989).

Reading Aloud

Francois Truffaut's charming film about children, *Small Change*, has a memorable reading aloud in class scene. Roger Shattuck argues beautifully for reading aloud as a way of making it live in "How to Rescue Literature" in his book *The Innocent Eye: On Modern Literature and the Arts* (New York: Farrar Straus and Giroux, 1984, pp. 311–328).

Free Reading

A useful book on sustained silent reading programs is Janice Pilgreen, *The SSR Handbook: How to Organize and Manage a Sustained Silent Reading Program* (Portsmouth, NH: Heinemann, 2000).

Prose Style: Analysis

Richard A. Lanham, *Analyzing Prose* (New York: Scribner, 1983), treats the theoretical elements of the subject and shows how to employ them in analyzing individual works. In a different vein, Francis-Noel Thomas and Mark Turner, *Clear and Simple as the Truth: Writing Classic Prose* (Princeton: Princeton University Press, 1994), argue that classic prose style is founded on a set of attitudes about language and reality. The first half of the book defines the classic style and the second half, "The Museum," examines closely many different specimens of writing.

Shapes of Language

Arthur Quine, *Figures of Speech: 60 Ways to Turn a Phrase* (Salt Lake City: Gibbs M. Smith, 1982), treats a small number of basic schemes and tropes, giving many examples of each. Richard A. Lanham, *A Handlist of Rhetorical Terms: A Guide for Students of English Literature* (Berkeley: University of California Press, 1968), defines some three hundred rhetorical terms but does not give many examples. If you have access to inter-library borrowing and you love Shakespeare, consult Sister Miriam Joseph, *Shakespeare's Use of the Arts of Language* (New York: Columbia University Press, 1947)—a treasure trove of examples.

Sophocles, Oedipus the King

Sophocles, *The Three Theban Plays: Antigone, Oedipus the King, Oedipus at Colonus* (translated by Robert Fagles, Introductions and Notes by Bernard Knox). Fagles' translations are idiomatic and intelligible, and therefore make for good performances. Knox's Notes are informative and helpful, and his Introduction to *Oedipus the King* condenses into a few pages the lines of thought more fully developed in the Bernard M. Knox book, *Oedipus at Thebes: Sophocles' Tragic Hero and His Time* (New Haven: Yale University Press, 1957).

Screenplay Writing

If you want to teach your students about film, especially if you assign "Transpositions" into film, you might consult one of the following: Andrew Horton, *Writing the Character-Centered Screenplay* (Berkeley: University of California Press, 1994); Richard Walters, *The Art, Craft, and Business of Film and Television Writing* (New York: Plume, 1988); Jana Gelfand, *A Practical Guide to Flawless Screenplay Form* (Los Angeles: Screenwriting Inc., 1990); Syd Field, *Screenplay* (New York: Dell, 1982).

Poetry

Mary Kinzie's book, *A Poet's Guide to Poetry* (Chicago: University of Chicago Press, 1999), is a fine handbook with an excellent annotated bibliography. Working through this book will inform your intelligence and attune your sensibilities to poetic artistry in a renewed way. In *How to Read a Poem: And Fall in Love with Poetry* (New York: Harcourt, 1999), the poet Edward Hirsch writes about a wide range of poems, passionately and intelligently. This book is not academic criticism, but a poet writing about poems he loves deeply. If I could recommend only one essay on poetry, it would be Helen Vendler's "Introduction" to her book *The Art of Shakespeare's Sonnets* (Cambridge: Belknap Press of Harvard University Press, 1997).